THEY CALL IT PACIFIC

THEY CALL IT PACIFIC

AN EYE-WITNESS STORY OF OUR WAR AGAINST JAPAN FROM BATAAN TO THE SOLOMONS

BY

CLARK LEE

Ship to Shore Books
2018

Published 2018 by Ship to Shore Books.

FIRST PRINTING, 2018.

ISBN: 9781729466353.

CONTENTS

1

SERGEANT HAJIME MATSUI OF THE IMPERIAL JAPANESE ARMY leaned closer to me across the table and said in a low voice, "I have a message for you from the Colonel."

He glanced cautiously around the windowless, smoke-filled room. In the booth next to us, two husky Japanese privates in weather-beaten khaki were flirting loudly with a moon-faced girl recently imported from Nagasaki to help entertain the Emperor's soldiers in China.*

On the other side, a Japanese captain was sprawled face up across a table, snoring noisily. Beer had spilled down the unbuttoned coat of his uniform; his sword dangled from his belt to the floor.

"It was at the Colonel's suggestion," Matsui continued, "that I asked you to meet me here. The Colonel says he believes that you appreciate Japan's national problems and are personally friendly to the Japanese people. He says that during your trips to the front with the Japanese Army, on which he served as your escort, he has grown to like you personally; even though your newspaper stories have been highly critical of Japan's conduct in China."

Matsui's English was perfect, for he was a native of Southern California. In other ways, too, he was not an ordinary Japanese sergeant. His family was one of the most prominent in Japan: one uncle was a general; another uncle an important official of the foreign office. Talking to Sergeant Matsui wasn't exactly the same as talking to Premier Tojo or Foreign Minister Togo, but from my point of view it was better. The sergeant knew what was going on in Japan, and would talk about it.

"The Colonel has been informed," he continued, "that at the Japanese army press conferences you have recently made inquiries as to whether the Japanese barracks at Kiangwan, outside of Shanghai, would be used as an internment camp for Americans in the unfortunate event of war between Japan and America."

I began to get the picture: a friendly tip regarding internment camps and how to stay out of them.

Matsui went on, "It has also been called to the Colonel's attention that you plan to go to the United States on home leave in about two months. You have been quoted as saying you, "... hoped to get home and back before the shooting started."

"That's right," I said. "It's been five years, six months and sixteen days since I left San Francisco. I've been two years in Hawaii and the rest of the time in China and Japan. I want to get home just long enough to visit my family, and maybe see a football or baseball game again. Then I'll be glad to come back to the Orient for the duration."

"The Colonel takes the liberty of reminding you," Matsui continued, "that there have been no regular transpacific ship schedules from Shanghai for some months. He wishes to point out that except for two Dutch vessels and one French, no departures are scheduled from Shanghai. There is a possibility that after the next ten days there may not be any way to get out."

The pieces of the puzzle fell into place. The shooting might start any time after the next ten days.

"Then the powder keg ..." I began.

"Is almost certain to explode shortly and blow up the Orient with it," the sergeant concluded. "Mr. Kurusu, who is now on his way to Washington, will tell Mr. Hull that Japan is anxious for peace on Japan's terms, terms that cannot involve surrender of any of the territory which Japan has taken in the past four years at the cost of so much blood and treasure. Mr. Kurusu ..."

This time I interrupted. "Mr. Kurusu will be told that Japan's terms are impossible. And then we will go to war!"

Matsui had said as much as he could. I asked him, "And what about yourself?"

He took a sip of tea, sucking it in noisily in Japanese fashion. "I'm here for the duration, or until I get killed. As a youngster, I thought of myself as an American. I was born there and went to college there. I failed to find a place in my native country compatible with my education and background. People would not accept me as an American, because I look Japanese. I went back to Japan and they put me in uniform. Here I am."

I shook hands with him. "Goodbye, Jimmy. I won't see you until after the war, unless we happen to come face to face in a trench. But I won't forget what you have told me. And thank the Colonel for me."

I WALKED OUT INTO THE SPARKLING AFTERNOON SUNSHINE and crisp fall air of Shanghai. The date was November 14, 1941.

My rickshaw boy started weaving through the traffic, dodging speeding Japanese army trucks, a camouflaged light tank, swarms of rickshaws and slow-moving coolies tugging heavily loaded carts by long ropes. Japanese soldiers, sailors, and marines crowded the sidewalks, jostling Japanese girls in bright-colored kimonos. This part of Shanghai was part of Japan's New Order now.

I directed the rickshaw puller, "Garden Bridge. Chop-chop." I intended to act quickly on the advice that Matsui had given me. What he had said merely re-emphasized my own conviction that war had to come. For months, in stories and letters, I had been writing that it was inevitable.

Several other Japanese officers and civilians had given me "friendly" warnings that I would be wise to leave Shanghai as soon as possible, but none had been as specific as Matsui.

8

The Japanese made it perfectly clear that unless the United States surrendered completely and discontinued its moral aid to Generalissimo Chiang Kai-shek—aid backed by a few planes and other war materials being sent into Free China—there could be no settlement of Japanese-American difficulties. They said Japan had no intention of getting out of Manchukuo, China, Indo-China, and Hainan Island and going back to Japan itself. Those were the American terms, and they were not much less stringent than the terms that would be imposed on a defeated Japan.

The Japanese were playing for much bigger stakes than the areas they had already conquered. To go on playing power politics, they had to gain free access to certain raw materials they had been purchasing from the United States and from European colonies in the western Pacific. They needed oil, aluminum, iron, nickel, tin, tungsten, chrome, manganese, and rubber. All these, except iron, were ready to hand in Malaya, the Netherlands East Indies, and the Philippines. The iron was, and is, in Shansi province in North China. To get those things meant fighting the United States, Britain, and the Dutch, and taking away our Asiatic possessions.

Once having those sources of raw materials, Japan would become potentially the strongest power in the world. The next step, then, would be to unite the races of Asia under Japanese leadership and domination, and to embark on the program of world conquest that Japan's militarists and statesmen had outlined long before.

As for the United States, we could not afford to let Japan seize the wealth of the Orient without fighting. So war had to come, and for a long time nearly every American and every Japanese in the Far East had seen it coming...

My rickshaw man pulled up at Garden Bridge, which led across Soochow Creek to the heart of the International Settlement. Rickshaws were not allowed to pass the Japanese sentries on the bridge. I walked across, dropping my cigarette before reaching the sentries. They considered themselves representatives of Emperor Hirohito, and many foreigners had been slapped or clubbed for "disrespectfully" smoking in front of Imperial Representatives. The Chinese walking ahead of me suddenly stumbled to the pavement. He had forgotten to remove his hat and the sentry struck him a slashing blow across the face with the butt of his rifle. I kept my hat on and walked past rapidly. There was nothing I could do about it—yet.

Across the bridge I took another rickshaw. "Take me corner Szechuan Road, Foochow Road," I directed the puller. "One dollar for go chop-chop." The grinning Chinese youngster sprinted up the Bund in his bare feet, passing the tall, solid buildings from which flew the national flags and house flags of American, British, Japanese, French, Italian, and German banks, steamship companies, and business firms. He darted into a side street and halted outside of the Java-China-Japan-Lijn office.

I had been keeping in close touch with the steamship offices, both for news stories and because of my plans for home leave, which The Associated Press had approved for "late December or early January." There had been no ships, until the Tjibadak came in.

Since the American freezing of Japanese credits in July, transpacific shipping had been nearly at a standstill. American ships were going directly from Honolulu to Manila and then back to the United States. Most of Japan's big liners had been diverted from their regular runs and sent to bring Japanese nationals home from the United States, the Philippines, Singapore, Batavia, and Australia. Early in November the Japanese announced that the Tatsuta Maru would sail for California on a similar trip on December 2. A grim-faced naval attaché in Shanghai told me, "That is a trap and we know it very well. They are trying to get us to send our ships out here for them to grab. They'd certainly like to get the Coolidge and four or five other big ones on the first day of war."

In the Java-China-Japan-Lijn offices, the Dutch agent recognized me and called to me over the heads of a group of foreigners and Chinese crowded anxiously against the counter. "If you want to leave," he said, "you are just in time. There has just been a cancellation. One cabin is available on the Tjibadak tomorrow morning. It is going to Manila and you may be able to connect with the President Coolidge for the United States."

The agent beckoned a man standing nearby. "This will be your roommate."

I found myself shaking hands with an old friend, Senor Roberto Mujica Lainez of the Argentine Embassy in Tokyo. Roberto had been trying for weeks to get passage from Shanghai to his new post in San Francisco.

I paid for my ticket and went over to The AP office to tell the Chief of Bureau, Morris Harris, that I was jumping the gun on my home leave. Jimmy White of our Peiping Bureau was on his way to Shanghai so our office would be well staffed.

"If I can get even as far as Manila, I can help cover the war from there," I said to Harris. "Or if I make the Coolidge and reach Honolulu, I can be assigned to the Pacific Fleet. There is no use of all three of us getting interned in Shanghai."

Weeks before, I had planned ways and means for escaping from Shanghai when the Japanese should take over the entire city, as they were certain to do on the first day of war. With a group of other Americans I established contact with headquarters of the Chinese New Fourth (former Chinese Communist) Army, just outside the city. They sent an emissary who slipped through the Jap lines and met us in a back room of the King Kong restaurant. We ate spicy Szechuan duck, and, as is the custom in China, said nothing whatever about the purpose of our meeting. He was looking us over.

As a result of the dinner, a young American-born Chinese came quietly into our office one day. He introduced himself as Washington Woo. He told us, "Buy Chinese gowns, caps and dark glasses, and Bibles." We never did find out what the Bibles were for.

We mapped a half-dozen possible routes through the mazes of the International Settlement, across the French Concession and the Badlands, and finally over the barbed wire guarding the Shanghai-Hangchow Railway and thus to Free China and a 1,400-mile hike to Chungking. We knew it would be touch and go getting out, for Shanghai was already a huge concentration camp. Its streets were crisscrossed with barricades and patrolled by sentries, and the entire city was surrounded by double lines of barbed wire. In September we burned most of our AP office files, after some Nazi friends warned us that the Japanese Army was getting impatient and might take over the entire settlement at any time. There were a lot of data in the files that the local Japanese had never seen, and we knew it would go hard with us if they ever discovered the source of some of the stories that had been printed in American newspapers concerning the Japanese Army and Navy in China. Those stories had gone out under Manila or Hong Kong datelines, having been smuggled from Shanghai, where the Japanese operated an illegal and surreptitious mail censorship.

In some of the smuggled stories I had reported Japan's war plans and preparations. During the summer and fall Japan had carried out a gigantic military mobilization and had called home from the Seven Seas her vast merchant fleet totaling more than 5,000,000 tons of shipping. The ships were turned over to the Army and Navy.

Major Frank Merrill, American military attaché in Tokyo, came over to Shanghai en route to his new post in Chungking, and gave me details of the mobilization.

"The Japanese have got every able-bodied man, and some who aren't so able-bodied, in uniform. They have 2,670,000 men under arms. Of these 1,667,000 are combat troops. Their reserves number 3,300,000. They have a total of 10,500,000 men to draw from, but some of those are undoubtedly essential to their industry.

"They now have only sixteen divisions in Manchukuo. Since October, the first of the others have been moving southward, probably to Hainan Island and Saigon. They are getting set to jump."

I kept in close touch with the Japanese military and the information they had given me coincided with Major Merrill's.

One Japanese officer, Captain M. Takada, graduate of Columbia University and army spokesman in Peiping, came down to Shanghai for a visit. We had christened him "Baroness Takada," because of the mock elegance of his manners—manners which he had so far forgotten one night in our home in Peiping as to chase our comely Chinese amah [maid] around and around the garden in the middle of a snowstorm—(she won the race!). Takada was good-humored and informative, although indirectly so.

He told me, by indirection, that although the Japanese mobilization had taken place in Manchukuo, it would be "quite easy" for Japan to move her troops to other areas, as necessity might dictate. He said what happened in Manchukuo would depend on the fighting on the Moscow front. "War with Russia is inevitable someday, of course."

Lieutenant Colonel Kunio Akiyama, the Japanese spokesman in Shanghai who looked exactly like a caricature of Japanese militarism but who was a friendly and even a timid person underneath his military trappings, made a hurried trip to Tokyo to report. He told us on his return that he had found all Japan hopeful that an agreement would be reached in the Washington talks between Japanese Ambassador Kichisaburo Nomura and Secretary of State Cordell Hull, but, alas, "agreement would be possible, ah, only if United States recognize Japan's true position as leading nation of Orient." With appropriate gestures, he told us the American embargo was "strangling Japan," and Japan could not put up with it much longer.

The Japanese Army and Navy liaison men entertained the American correspondents more frequently than formerly, but in smaller groups. There were fewer geisha girls, less sake and more serious conversation than at previous similar dinners in the Japanese restaurants of Hongkew. At those dinners we discussed war plans and possibilities and invariably they asked the question, "Will America fight?" Our answer was always, "We certainly will."

One night a Japanese naval captain asked an American Marine officer and me to dinner. He said, "The Japanese Navy is invincible in the western and southwestern Pacific. We will capture your bases. If you send your ships out to try to retake them, our dive-bomber and torpedo-plane pilots will crash their planes on your decks and sink your ships."

The Marine officer answered, "Nobody doubts the suicidal courage of your pilots, my dear Muriyama-san. But when your ships come into our waters our pilots will go just as low and just as close as necessary to get home their bombs and torpedoes. And if it is necessary to crash-dive on your ships, they will do that too."

Underlying the conversation of many of our Japanese friends we sensed their fear that Japan in the long run could not win, and a hope that the United States would back down at the last moment. There was never any suggestion that Japan could recede from a position which it considered to be honorable and just.

Those Japanese who hoped that war would be averted were mostly businessmen and a sprinkling of Army and Navy officers who had traveled in the United States and knew our potential strength. The only reason that they did not want to fight was that they thought Japan would lose. They did not abhor war, nor did they lack sympathy with Japan's desire to rule the Orient. They were just afraid of the ultimate outcome.

Reports from Chungking said the Japanese had, in recent raids, ceased their aimless "area" bombing of the Chinese capital and had suddenly begun to hit their targets on the nose. They hinted at a new bombsight.

Late in September, I had a close-up of the Japanese Air Force. Together with a few other correspondents I flew with the Japanese Army over the Changsha battlefield. Changsha, seven hundred miles from the seacoast, was one of the gateways to Chungking, and the Japanese advance was of great importance because of the possibility that they might at last be attempting a knockout blow against China. Twice, since 1937, the Japanese had been turned back outside Changsha, but this time they took the city in a lightning drive which covered more than ninety miles over plains and mountains in ten days. They plunged on southward for fifteen miles past Changsha—and then withdrew. When the Japanese quit Changsha we reported the withdrawal as voluntary and surmised that the Japanese drive was primarily combat training of troops. We didn't guess, of course, that within less than three months those same troops would be using those same tactics in the Philippines and Burma and Malaya.

We saw Army "97" dive-bombers and fast Navy fighters in action that may have been Zeros, although we had never heard of Zeros at the time. We took movies and still pictures of the Japanese planes on the ground and in flight, and by devious methods succeeded in getting our pictures past the Japanese military censorship and turning them over to quarters where they should have done the most good.

We were surprised at the extensive and extremely effective use the Japanese made of dive-bombers.

The Nazi correspondent said, "These Japanese monkey men haf learned well dere lesson from der Fuehrer, ja!"

He elaborated. Since the Chinese invented gunpowder every weapon had served the same purpose: to shoot lead or steel and explosives from one place to another and kill your enemy and destroy his own guns and his fortifications, cities, and ships. The airplane was the greatest artillery piece ever invented. It had its own eyes and unbeatable mobility. Would anyone deny that a sufficient number of 18-inch guns firing into New York City or any other city could devastate the city and force its occupants to surrender? Would anyone deny that enough airplanes could accomplish the same end? To do so was to deny that steel and TNT could win wars.

"If der Fuehrer had only had enough airplanes to continue to blitz England for three more weeks..." the Nazi correspondent continued. And so on.

Our sympathy with the Chinese redoubled on that trip, because we saw what an army was up against without artillery, and most of all without airplanes. We saw how the Japanese Air Force co-operated perfectly with the

ground troops. When the ground forces ran into a strong point they would radio back for a plane. The dive-bombers would come over, locate the Chinese
machine-gun nest or pillbox, and swarm down on it. Then the Chinese would
be dead and the Japanese ground forces would march on past or drive on in
their trucks and tanks.

It was about this time that Japan's future enemies missed a chance to
learn all about the Mitsubishi Zero fighter plane that was to astound and con-
found them a few months later. A report came into Chungking, the capital of
Generalissimo Chiang Kai-shek's Free China, that a new, fast Japanese fighter
had made a forced landing on an airfield in Western China and had been
captured intact by the Chinese Army. A special plane was put at the disposal
of the American and British air attaché in Chungking to fly over and inspect
the Japanese aircraft. But when they arrived they found the pursuit plane a
messed-up wreck on the airfield. Only the wingtips, with their bright-red "Rising Sun" insignia, were undamaged. An over-anxious Chinese army pilot had
taken the Zero up for a test flight and had found it too hot to handle.

Chiang Kai-shek (1887-1975).

When I returned to Shanghai from the Changsha trip I found further signs that Japan was on the march. The youthful Japanese soldiers who had been on guard duty around Shanghai had disappeared. They had been a tough, cruel lot, whose officers had taught them to cultivate what we called the "China Face" with outthrust jaw and sneering, down-turned mouth.

They were replaced by thin, undernourished reservists—office workers and older men who looked ill at ease in their uniforms. The Chinese were greatly pleased at the change, because the newcomers kicked and beat them less often at the barriers and barricades around Shanghai.

Through the Chinese secret service I learned that the younger Japanese troops had been put in transports and sent, not to Manchukuo, but to the south. That could mean only one thing: the Japanese had abandoned their plans for attacking Siberia.

The Kwantung army generals, the rulers of Manchukuo, had wanted to fight Russia first, while the Japanese Navy had always argued that its "historic destiny" lay to the south. If Moscow had fallen the Kwantung Army would probably have had its way and Japs would have attacked Vladivostok and surged across the Amur River into Siberia.

But when Moscow held and the Siberian winter came on, and simultaneously the United States began to tighten its pressure on Japan, the Kwantung army generals agreed with the admirals, finally, that the blows must be struck to the south and must be all out.

One by one the Japanese commanders in China went home to confer with the new premier, General Tojo, with the general staff, and with the admirals. Prince Chichibu, brother of the Emperor, flew down to Indo-China to tie up the loose strings there. Shortly after his visit, Japan took over all of southern Indo-China, including the excellent harbor of Camranh and the southern capital of Saigon, which was the obvious jumping-off place for an attack on Malaya and the Dutch East Indies.

In a series of stories written for the AP in February of 1941, I had said, "When the Japanese mass troops and ships and planes at Saigon in large numbers, the danger of war between the United States and Japan must be reckoned from day to day or even from hour to hour, since the practice of the Japanese has always been to strike first, and explain afterward." Now, on the evening of November 14, they were quickly massing troops, ships, and planes at Saigon "in large numbers."

I was glad that I was leaving Shanghai—getting out of Japanese territory—the next morning. I wanted to see the war, but not from an internment camp.

*The anonymous 'moon-faced girl' was one of tens of thousands of Chinese (and non-Chinese) women captured by the Japanese and forced into sexual bondage for troops on the move. World War 2 'Comfort brides' as these women came to be known, is the subject of a continuing controversy between China and Japan.

Following image: Asian comfort brides kidnapped from Penang. The Japanese Army seized Australian and European women for the same purposes as the war progressed.

2

I TOOK A RICKSHAW BACK TO MY ROOMS AT THE METROPOLE HOTEL and told the *amah* to start packing my clothes: "Everything this time."

I had moved to the hotel after my wife had gone home in August, following a very polite suggestion from Japanese Army and Navy officers that "perhaps, in view of growing tension in Orient, it would be more better if Mrs. Ree returning Honoruru." We got the point, even if the Japanese always pronounced the letter "l" as "r."

Most of the Americans had left Shanghai months before, heeding our State Department's thrice-repeated advice that all American women, children, and "non-essential" men return to the United States from the Orient. The American businessmen, whose import and export trade had collapsed as a result of Washington's embargo on shipments of strategic materials to the Far East and as a result of Japan's bayonet-enforced monopolies of trade in the Yangtze River hinterland, had little to do except roll dice for drinks at the American club. As many of them as could get space on ships left for Manila or for home. We expected every ship to be the last one.

Carroll Alcott, the Far East's favorite radio commentator, had gotten out just in time. He boarded a ship for home under the escort of a Marine bodyguard. The Japanese hated Alcott and had tried to kill him three times. Of the five American newsmen on the original Japanese "blacklist," only J. B. Powell remained in Shanghai to continue in his China Weekly Review a courageous and dangerous expose of Japan's murderous outrages in China and of the warlord's preparations to fight America. Powell stayed too long, and when he finally returned to the United States both his feet had been amputated as a result of an infection contracted during six months in a Japanese jail.

Colonel Samuel Howard, Major "Duke" Hamilton, and the other officers of the Fourth U.S. Marines entertained the American community on the occasion of the Marine Corps' 166th birthday party on November 10. It seemed more like a funeral wake than a celebration. The sole topic of discussion was war, and the only questions talked about were: "How soon will the Japanese attack?" and "What will become of us?"

There were only a handful of American women present. The women and their husbands were keeping their eyes on the Marines, who had come to China sixteen years before to protect American interests and who had always been the trouble barometer for Americans. The husbands said, "When the Marines go, we'll send our families." But when the Marines left on the President Harrison late in November, it was too late for others. There were no more ships. On its return trip to pick up additional Marines and a few

American men, women, and children from North China, the Harrison was captured off Chinwangtao by Japanese destroyers.

That last night in Shanghai, I went out on the balcony for a last look at the city that had been my home for three years, except for assignments in Japan, Manchukuo, and North China, and trips to the front with the Japanese Army.

In the twilight, Shanghai sprawled vast and uneasy from the massive buildings of the Bund through the jumbled tangle of slums where four million Chinese lived in space built for half that many; and then on out to the residential areas where Americans, Britons, Frenchmen, and the people of a score of nations had tried to reproduce the atmosphere of their own home countries on the mud flats of the Yangtze delta.

Shanghai and the other great cities of the eastern coast were all in the grip of Japanese military rule; a regime characterized by corruption, graft, violence, poverty, and narcotics. Beyond and between the Japanese lines was the real China of four hundred million people, free and unconquerable, but sadly under armed. They had been unable to fight against a Japanese war machine which American airplanes, gasoline, steel, scrap iron, and automobiles had made great and powerful.

I recalled that if Shanghai could last until 1942 it would be one hundred years old. But the chances seemed slim. Since 1937, Shanghai had been in its death throes as a white man's city. For more than four years Shanghai had been living practically in a state of siege, with bombs, bullets, and barbed wire for its daily diet, with its streets stinking of the death, starvation, misery, and corruption of war. The sound of assassins' pistols and the explosion of terrorists' bombs had become a part of everyday life.

There was too much Champagne in Shanghai, and not enough rice. The price of rice kept going up and up, and so did the number of starved Chinese whose bodies were picked up from streets each morning.

From my hotel balcony, I watched the wretched and tattered Chinese street scavengers follow the rice trucks along Foochow Road. They carried short brooms and dustpans, and fought for the few crumbs of rice that tumbled to the pavement when the trucks passed. Sometimes they chased the trucks and slit the bags with long knives, ignoring the blows rained on their heads by truck guards armed with bamboo poles.

That was one of the last street scenes I saw in Shanghai. Some friends came in during the evening to say farewell, and shortly afterward I was notified that two Japanese army officers were waiting for me in the hotel grill. They were Lieutenant Colonel Akiyama, the army spokesman, and his interpreter, Sublieutenant K. Matsuda, ex-Princeton and graduate of the University of Missouri. At first I thought that perhaps their spies had overheard my conversation with Sergeant Matsui that afternoon. Then I saw Matsuda was carrying a carefully boxed package containing a beautiful gold lacquer vase.

Akiyama made a little presentation speech before handing me the package.

"You have traveled great deal with Japanese Army in past three years. You have ridden in our military planes, seen our bombers operate and our troops fight. This present is in appreciation your effort to report truthfully true intentions of Imperial Japanese Army in bringing peace and order to East Asia." Since I had always tried very diligently to report the "true intentions" of the Japanese Army, I accepted the gift.

Akiyama wiped the remains of his second cocktail from his black mustache and added, "Japanese Army still hoping United States, Japan not going war, but situation now very difficult. Mr. Kurusu-san was ordered by Emperor himself to ask America recognize Japan's honorable intentions. If America refusing—"

"Colonel," I said, "it looks like war."

He replied gravely, "So desu, ne! (That is true!) Very unfortunate."

Matsuda, who had once worked for The AP in Tokyo, said, "Well, if we are both alive after it, maybe we can have some more tennis games."

No flowers to fill the gold vase were forthcoming from the Japanese Navy. They had recently traced to me the authorship of some stories reporting how Japanese officers were making fortunes by selling safe conducts for ships to run their blockade of the China coast and how the Imperial Navy had engaged in wholesale piracy. I was on their blacklist.

I went back up to my room, and an American naval officer from the gunboat out in the Whangpoo called me aside. I told him what Akiyama had said, and asked him if we would have trouble defeating the Japanese Navy. He replied with the estimate of our future enemies then fashionable among our Navy officers, "Their ship handling is superb, their morale and discipline are excellent. Their gunnery is not so good and they lack imagination and daring. They haven't fought since they beat a battered Russian fleet in Tsushima Straits in 1904."

I reminded him, "Well, as a Navy we haven't fought since Dewey sailed into Manila Bay and shot up the outnumbered and demoralized Spanish fleet. The last real knock-down, drag-out fight was between the Monitor and the Merrimac."

Another American officer had joined us. "I don't know exactly how good or how bad the Japs are," he said, "but I am dead sure we are going to fight them. And I'm just as sure that I'll never see the United States again."

A few days later, he was transferred to Manila where he found his new orders awaiting him. He was assigned to the U.S.S. Houston just before she went down with all hands in the Java Sea.

On the morning of November 15, I went aboard the Tjibadak. My Argentine friend, Senor Mujica Lainez, made it by the skin of his teeth. Out of touch with his government, he was without funds. Rear Admiral William C. Glassford, commander of the United States Yangtze patrol and once naval attaché in Buenos Aires, heard of Roberto's plight and put the 'Good Neighbor' policy into practical effect by advancing the necessary money.

Riding down the Whangpoo by launch to the docks where the Tjibadak was moored, I experienced the sensations of a condemned man who is granted a last-minute reprieve. As we passed the last Japanese destroyer anchored in midstream even the air seemed freer. I was leaving behind the gigantic prison camp that was Shanghai.

The 8,000-ton Tjibadak was in war paint, her hull a dark gray and her masts light brown. Her captain wasted no time in casting off and heading down the curving Whangpoo and into the vast, muddy Yangtze delta.

"This is the last trip that we shall make here," he told me nervously. "Maybe we were foolish to make this one. My government in the Netherlands East Indies believes that Japan will attack soon."

We promptly christened the Tjibadak the "S.S. Jitterbug." Our fellow passengers in first and second class included an American authoress who had spent seven years making an "esoteric study of exotic religions." She insisted on instructing the Standard Oil official in Yogi. The grass widow from Batavia wanted Roberto to give her tango lessons on the blacked-out moonlit deck. The Mexican, who was engaged in the dangerous business of carrying forbidden currency from Oriental country to country for a profit, sat in the smoking room for hours at a time, taking potshots at cockroaches with a toy .45 which fired BB shot. He was a crack marksman. The naval commander who had tried to drink Shanghai dry—and like thousands before him had failed—was watched constantly by his two Medical Corps "escorts."

In Amoy, [Xiamen] two days south of Shanghai down the China Coast, we ran into trouble. I snapped a few pictures of Japanese ships and shore installations, and then luckily changed the roll in my camera before taking one more. A Japanese patrol boat spotted me and Marine officers in khaki uniform, with their swords swinging threateningly, hurried aboard and demanded that I be brought to the bridge. They examined the camera. I had not turned the crank on my Rolleiflex* after taking one shot and the shutter would not click and the indicator pointed to "1." I told them that meant no pictures had been taken. The interpreter, anxious to show his knowledge of cameras, confirmed my statement, "Hail Yes! That is so. I myself having Rorreifrex." The senior officer, who had given no sign that he understood English, said, "Okay, you can go."

The officers searched the ship for other cameras, found and confiscated a few, and then went ashore to develop the films. The Tjibadak's captain was sweating blood, fearing his ship would be held up indefinitely, but they let us proceed.

We steamed southwestward down the coast for twenty-four hours and next day sailed into Hong Kong's beautiful harbor. A patrol boat pitched on the sparkling blue waters at the harbor entrance and a bearded English naval officer challenged us through a megaphone. Our captain shouted back, "Her Imperial Netherlands Majesty's ship Tjibadak, sailing under British Admiralty orders." Then the patrol boat guided us through the minefields, while an ancient "Singapore" flying boat, with twin puller and pusher motors, lumbered overhead.

That, and a few other planes of similar vintage, were Hong Kong's air force. Great Britain had neither the men nor airplanes nor guns to spare for the defense of this once mighty bastion of Far Eastern Empire. But the high hills of the Kowloon Peninsula, behind which lurked the Japanese Army, looked formidable, and Victoria Island, on which the city of Hong Kong is located, bristled with guns and machine-gun

Nearly all the foreigners ashore were in uniform, with Canadian and Indian troops predominating. Most of the British families were gone, but a few officials were congratulating themselves on evading the evacuation order and keeping their wives and families with them. There were blockhouses and barbed wire along the waterfront, and across the island at Repulse Bay. The Royal Navy was represented by a few torpedo boats and a destroyer or two in the harbor. The town was as filthy, in the crowded waterfront areas, as ever, and as magnificent from the soaring [Victoria] Peak. People were still dancing in the Hong Kong and Gloucester Hotels, and some of the more beautiful Chinese and Eurasian girls had as many as five handsome, uniformed escorts. Everybody was talking about the recent defense scandal which revealed that part of the funds set aside to build air raid shelters had found its way into the bank account of Mimi Lau, a young Cantonese beauty. At least one official had taken the honorable way out: a single shot through the temple. On our strolls through the city, Roberto would stop aghast, and stare angrily, as he saw for the first time what the British Colonial thought of the Chinese. Time after time we saw amiable-appearing British businessmen push Chinese who got in their way on the sidewalks, or urge on rickshaw men with a few light strokes of a cane. It was all done casually, as something in the normal course of events.

The Canadian troops had just arrived and their transports and a light cruiser were still in the harbor. Their first day ashore some Canadians went into the Gloucester lounge for tea and were told no men in uniform, except officers, would be served. They went out muttering, "So we came here to fight for democracy. Oh yeah, what democracy?" A few days later, the order was changed and the Canadians went wherever they pleased until December 8.

As in Shanghai, business for foreigners was dead in Hong Kong, and nobody thought much about the future except that it was obvious that something had to break soon. With no shipping, it was impossible to plan.

Some of our Hong Kong friends recalled the prophecy of a Chinese historian in 1841, when the British first took Hong Kong, that "British rule will last exactly one hundred years." I told them that the Japanese plan called for the capture of Hong Kong within nine days after the initial attack. That information came from my ex-friend, Major T. Nishihara of the Imperial Japanese Army, who had spent four years in Hong Kong as a "language student," and who at a Shanghai party one night amused us by drawing a map of Victoria Island and sketching in every one of Hong Kong's big gun positions. Actually, Hong Kong held for eighteen days.

During the two-day trip from Hong Kong to Manila we failed to sight a single ship, but the Hong Kong-bound Pan American Clipper flew low over us on the opposite course.

Entering Manila Bay we glanced only casually at the Bataan Peninsula and the impressive saddle of Mt. Mariveles. The channels through the minefields led us close to the shore of Bataan, although we didn't know at the time that it was Bataan. The peninsula looked forbidding and uninhabited. We turned our glasses on the vast bulk of Corregidor, with its huge barracks atop the highest point and the American flag waving over them. Somebody pointed out the radio masts at the Cavite naval base as we passed.

Behind the breakwater in Manila Harbor we saw the Coolidge tied up, with an American cruiser in battle paint beyond it. Tanks and trucks and boxes of ammunition and crated planes were being unloaded from many ships of a convoy just in from the United States.

The harbor seemed to be full of the submarines and destroyers of Admiral Thomas C. Hart's Asiatic Fleet. Navy catapult planes buzzed overhead and an occasional pursuit and four-engined bomber. Those were the first American warplanes I'd seen in more than two years.

I called to Roberto, "Look at those American ships and planes. Don't they make you feel good?" Roberto, who like all Argentines is meticulous about the use of the adjective "American," replied, "You mean those United States of North America ships and planes, my amigo."

I said, "Well, American or United States of North America as you please. They certainly are beautiful. When the Japs come down here, they'll be playing in the Big League for the first time in their lives."

*The Rolleiflex, more commonly referred to as the Rollei, was a popular German-made camera favored by reporters. The Lower Saxony firm of Franke & Heidecke began manufacturing the device in 1920.

3

THOSE WARSHIPS LOOKED WONDERFUL BUT, IN A WAY, the Coolidge looked even better. I hadn't known until the Tjibadak reached Manila whether or not the Coolidge had already sailed. Now there was a chance that I could get home for Christmas, see the Rose Bowl game, and be on my way back to the Orient before war started.

I wanted to walk up Fifth Avenue in the snow on Christmas Eve.

Those were splendid dreams. But two days before the Coolidge departed a telegram came for me. Before opening it I knew what it was. It said: "Remain Manila until further orders stop regards kenper." Kenper is Kent Cooper, general manager of The Associated Press.

The telegram was disappointing; but it was no great surprise. I had felt guilty about planning to leave the Orient at a time when tension was growing so great that something had to snap soon. In a series of stories written on the trip down on the Tjibadak, I had predicted that Japan would "soon go to war" against the United States and Great Britain. I had also reported how three thousand Nazi technical, industrial, naval, and aerial experts had been working in Japan for the past year, co-operating actively with those Japanese admirals and generals who believed that Japan's hour of destiny had struck.

With the Kurusu-Hull talks deadlocked and with the air of suspense so thick in the Far East that you could cut it with a samurai broadsword, the AP needed all its available staff men in the prospective trouble areas.

Besides, I was accustomed to messages like that. Three years before, I had had my suitcases all packed to leave Honolulu for New York en route to an assignment in South America. Just before my ship sailed I received a cable saying, in effect: "So sorry for you but please go to Tokyo to cover the Japanese-Soviet undeclared war at Changkufeng Hill." I had been in the Orient ever since. In nine years, I had spent only thirty-four days in the continental United States.

This was my first visit to the Philippines, and I was anxious to determine how the attitude of Americans toward the Filipinos contrasted with that of the Britons in Hong Kong and Shanghai toward the Chinese. My first experience was not reassuring.

The night before the Coolidge sailed, a small group of us went to the modern chromium, steel, and glass Jai Alai building and afterwards stopped in at the Manila Hotel tap room for a nightcap. The only other customer was an American woman who had taken about fourteen whiskies beyond her limit.

After 2 A.M., the legal closing time, she demanded another drink. A sergeant of the Philippine Constabulary, who was assigned to the bar to see that the law was obeyed, told her politely that the boys were not allowed to serve her.

She turned on him in blazing fury and poured forth insult after insult. The words were unprintable, but the general tenor was: "We Americans are the ruling race here. You Filipinos are dirt." She struck the sergeant in the face with her clenched fist, and tried to tear the badge from his uniform blouse. We could see him fighting to control himself, and he did. Finally, the waiters took the woman to her room.

Roberto Mujica Lainez shook his head sadly. "And you have been telling me, my amigo, that the Chinese in Hong Kong and the natives in Malaya and Burma will not fight for the British when war comes, because the British have mistreated them and have offered them nothing. Now you are aware why Argentina says 'No' when the United States asks for naval bases."

I didn't answer, except to walk over and ask the constabularyman his name. He told me he was Sergeant Hilario Francisco, I shook hands with him and congratulated him on the way he had conducted himself.

When I walked back, Roberto said, "Well, maybe that was an isolated incident and most Americans feel the way you do. I know your country has given the Filipinos schools and hospitals and improved their economic status. Maybe they will be loyal to you and fight for you after all."

Next day I went down to the Coolidge before sailing time. To read on the trip, I gave Roberto a copy of the [1937] book, Japan Must Fight Britain by Lt. Commander Tota Ishimaru of the Japanese Navy, in which he told why, how, and when Japan would attack Singapore; and also a translation of Ishimaru's recent magazine article stating that the "encirclement" of Japan by the United States, Britain, and the Netherlands East Indies could easily be broken.

I assured Roberto that Ishimaru's writings were required reading in the United States Navy, and that our officers had taken careful note of Japan's plans—as openly set forth by many retired admirals—of striking "smashing" blows at our Pacific naval bases before the actual declaration of hostilities.

"They won't catch us napping as they did the Russian Fleet at Port Arthur back in 1904," I told Roberto. "Even a year ago last spring, when I visited Honolulu, Admiral Richardson was so concerned over the possibility of a Japanese sneak attack that he wouldn't allow more than two or three of our capital ships in Pearl Harbor at one time. The Navy was maintaining aerial patrols far out to sea. The Japs will be the ones to be surprised this time."

I went back to my room in the Manila Hotel and watched the Coolidge sail out of the harbor with the tropical afternoon sun shining brightly on the red, white, and blue insignia painted on the sides and funnel of the ship. While the Coolidge grew smaller and smaller in the distances of the bay and finally passed out of sight around Corregidor, I read the headlines in the evening newspapers:

TOJO* DECLARES JAPAN "ONE BALL OF FIERY RESOLUTION"
AGAINST DEMOCRACIES

U.S. ADMIRAL SAYS NAVY CAN SINK JAP FLEET IN THREE WEEKS

HULL-KURUSU NEGOTIATIONS STILL DEADLOCKED

If there was any hope of avoiding war between the United States and Japan it wasn't evident in the headlines. The Philippines would obviously be one of Japan's first targets, and I set out to learn how well the islands were defended.

The commanders of our armed forces, General Douglas MacArthur and Admiral Hart, were neighbors of mine in the Manila Hotel but they were too busy to give private interviews. I frequently saw Admiral Hart coming into the hotel, steely-eyed, immaculate in his white tropic uniform, and always looking as if he had a chip on his straight shoulders; but I never saw MacArthur. He was in his office most of the time.

A number of correspondents had been in the Philippines for varying lengths of time, including Ray Cronin and Russell Brines of The AP, Carl and Shelley Mydans of Life, Arch Royal Gunnison of North American Newspaper Alliance, and Jack Percival of the Sydney Morning Herald, and with them I discussed the vulnerability of the islands. The Coolidge had just brought in several thousand American soldiers—its second such trip—and the consensus was that "there are some three divisions of American troops here, about sixty thousand men."

"And what are the Philippine forces?" I asked.

"The Filipino Scouts, who are soldiers of the regular American Army under American officers, probably number ten thousand to fifteen thousand. They are professional soldiers and first-class ones, the best riflemen in the whole U.S. Army, for example. In addition there are some fifty or sixty thousand in the Philippine Army, which consists of youngsters just recently called into service and now being trained."

"How about our air force?"

"There must be five hundred planes, pursuits, and heavy bombers. The Navy has a lot of PBY patrol bombers."

"What else is there in the Navy?"

"Admiral Hart has about thirty-six submarines, of which half are new and the others old 'S' boats. He has about the same number of destroyers and one heavy cruiser, the Houston, and a light cruiser, the Marblehead. And those motor torpedo boats tied up outside the Manila Hotel, those black-hulled babies with four torpedo tubes and .50-caliber machine-guns.

"Manila Bay is mined and no enemy ships can ever get in there under the guns of Corregidor and the other forts guarding the entrance to the bay. Corregidor, itself, of course is impregnable."*

*This had been the prevailing opinion for centuries. Like Alcatraz Island off San Francisco, Corregidor is a rock situated at the entrance of Manila Harbor. Because of the bay's important strategic position, the Isla del Corregidor had always been heavily fortified by occupiers of the Philippines, a defensive measure continued by America from 1902 on. But the Imperial Japanese Army found the fort's Achilles heel and shrewdly avoided the heavy coastal guns of Corregidor by invading from the north, via the Lingayen Gulf and Luzon.

Our war strategy, as we worked it out, was for the heavy bombers to attack Formosa and Hainan Island and mess up the enemy transports before they reached Luzon. Admiral Hart's patrol planes would spot the enemy ships, and the subs and destroyers and cruisers would tear into them. If any survived to reach the islands, American forces would mop them up on the beaches and chase them back into the sea. Then the U.S. Fleet would come out and close in behind the Japs in Indo-China, Malaya, and the Dutch East Indies—if they had dared to go that far. There were plenty of planes in Singapore, we thought, and the Dutch had a strong force of American airplanes and a small but capable navy.

With Ray Cronin and Russell Brines I visited various military establishments around Manila. We saw P-40's landing and taking off at Nichols Field and talked to some of the pilots. They told us it was a red-hot airplane with plenty of guns and plenty of speed, but was a little heavy to handle. Being Americans, we agreed that it was undoubtedly the best pursuit ship in the world, certainly better than anything the Japs could hope to have.

The defense picture in the Philippines appeared reassuring; and bit by bit I began to learn more about the islands themselves and their inhabitants. About all I had known beforehand was that some eighteen dialects were spoken in the more than seven thousand islands that made up the Philippines; that the Moros of Mindanao were such tough and durable little fighters that we had never been able to subdue them after purchasing the Philippines from Spain; and that colorful little Manuel Quezon had recently been re-elected President of the Commonwealth.*

*With the Japanese invasion, the Philippine government would be plagued by upheaval in personnel, ultimately abolishing its current system and adopting a new line of succession from December 1941 on.

The Philippines were scheduled to become independent in 1946, largely owing to Quezon's fight for complete separation from American control, but I considered the president's policy of independence unrealistic as long as Japan was on the march. I rather suspected that Don Manuel himself would be willing to postpone the independence question for a while until the Pacific situation cleared up. Actually, as it turned out, it couldn't have been much worse for the Filipinos even if they had been on their own when Japan attacked. They lost their country, which was all that could have happened anyway.

I read some books on the history and economy of the Philippines and learned enough about them to argue with those Americans who contended that our record was one of unmixed altruism—that we had spent more money in the islands than we had taken out of them. That was true as far as official government funds were concerned, but the amounts taken out by the government failed to include the vast riches in gold, sugar, and copra which individual Americans and American companies had made in the islands.

The Filipinos of Manila spoke an English which was grammatically impeccable but very formal. They had a grave dignity and little gaiety, and their sense of humor was restrained rather than exuberant. They dressed soberly, the men in white suits and dark ties.

At first, their frequent use of the word "sir" annoyed me because I misinterpreted it as a symbol of servility and I thought that spoke badly for the record of the United States in the islands. But later I learned that the "sir" was a hold-over from the polite Spanish "senor," and more than anything else was a mark of the complete trust and confidence that the Filipinos of Manila felt for the Americans. We told them we were big and strong and powerful, and would take care of them, and they believed us.

Russell Brines of The AP, a former coworker in the Honolulu bureau, arranged a sightseeing tour of the city in his ancient Ford. ROTC cadets, with papier-mâché helmets, were going through casual bayonet drills on the green lawns surrounding the ancient walled city. They seemed to be having a lot of fun. We drove forty miles up into the hills, along a smooth cement highway running through rice fields and past nipa shacks built on stilts.

At the mountain resort of Tagaitay [Tagaytay] we said hello to Melville Jacoby of Time Magazine and his wife, who were on their honeymoon. Mel was tall, dark, and slim, alternately boyish and then mature beyond his twenty-five years; and Annalee a pretty, intense girl with a keen sense of humor and a prodigious memory. We offered them some entirely unnecessary and unheeded advice on the care and feeding of two baby pandas which they were tending and photographing. The pandas, a gift from Madame Chiang Kai-shek to the women of America, were awaiting shipment to the United States.

Back in town we cashed checks at a bank owned by Catholic priests, and learned that the Church was almost as big and powerful a landowner and financial factor here as it was in Mexico, pre-revolution. The priests had raised large sums of money in the Philippines for General Francisco Franco.

In the Manila Hotel barber shop I met Admiral Glassford and his chief of staff, Commander Charles Jeffs. They reported a rough trip from Shanghai in their two Yangtze River gunboats, which were never built for seagoing. Washington had ordered them out when the Marines left.

"Jap destroyers shadowed us all the way past Formosa. The Japs are on the move everywhere. Troops are coming down the Yangtze and going south in transports, to Hainan and Indo-China."

The President Harrison arrived from Shanghai, after landing most of the Fourth U.S. Marines at Olangapo [Olongapo], and its few civilian passengers were just too late to get accommodations on the Coolidge. The Harrison turned around and went back to North China to pick up the rest of the Marines. In the first days of December, excitement mounted in the Philippines as the headlines from Washington and Tokyo recorded official pessimism over prospects of a peaceful settlement in the Pacific. Nearly everyone in Manila thought war was coming, and it was just a question of "How soon?" Life in Manila was no longer life as usual. There was an unusual number of marriages of youths called to service in the Army. As in Hong Kong and Shanghai few people could make any arrangements for the future because commercial shipping had stopped and the economy of the Philippines was keyed to its trade with the United States.

There were still a few optimists. My wife's cousin, George Fairchild, called at the hotel. He had just returned by clipper from Washington, where he had tried to arrange for some ships to carry Philippine sugar to the United States instead of the cargos of chrome ore with which most of the vessels were loaded. He had talked to Roosevelt who, he reported, "is very anxious to avoid war with Japan and hopes it can be done." I told him the situation looked hopeless.

The Philippine government called up more recruits and General MacArthur was quoted as saying privately that 120,000 Filipinos would be in uniform within the next few months. The problem was to get equipment for all of them.

Making his first public appearance in months. President Quezon told students gathered on the campus of the University of the Philippines, "Bombs may be falling on this campus soon." Some of the students laughed, and Quezon raised his arms over his head and shouted into the microphone, "It can happen, I tell you."

He paused solemnly and then went on, "I pray God that the Philippines be spared from the horrors of war. But, if we should be participants in the struggle, it will be a good thing for us for two reasons: First, it will give us an opportunity to show the American people we are willing and ready to lay down our fortunes and our lives in defense of the American flag; and second, because it will teach our youth—which, reared in the ease and comfort of an American-protected market, has whiled away its time in luxury and frivolity—how to suffer and how to die. For no nation is worth anything unless it has learned how to suffer and how to die."

On December 4 we got definite news that Japan was on the march. Newspaper dispatches from Shanghai reported several new and huge convoys were moving southward from the mouth of the Yangtze River. Almost simultaneously Australian airmen, flying American-built Hudson reconnaissance bombers out of Singapore, sighted a force of eighty Japanese transports escorted by cruisers and destroyers headed into the Gulf of Siam in the direction of Malaya or Thailand.

At the same time most of the warships of the Asiatic Fleet slipped out of the harbor and we knew they were out scouting for signs of a Japanese invasion force headed toward the Philippines.

The next day, December 5, our New York headquarters advised us to inform our staff correspondents throughout the Far East: "Washington says situation critical." As a result of a similar warning, Allied defense forces throughout the Far East were put on the alert.

The following morning, General MacArthur and Admiral Hart held separate conferences with local reporters and correspondents. The military commanders conveyed to the newsmen the import of messages from Washington indicating that war was imminent. General MacArthur thought the attack would come sometime after January 1. Both the general and admiral said they were prepared, however, and would fight with all the forces at their command. Hart had sent his ships to sea to scout, and he was optimistic about the striking power of his subs.

Sunday night, which was December 7 in Manila but December 6 back in Pearl Harbor, a group of us sat over cool drinks in the spacious, palm-lined lobby of the Manila Hotel. There was one Filipino, who made only one contribution to the conversation. He was Joaquin Miranda, a master draftsman attached to the United States Engineers.

"In the opinion of the Filipinos," he said, "the present situation is becoming intolerable. We find it most difficult to sit and wait while an enemy chooses his own time to bomb our cities and kill our families and seize our country. We would be very happy if the United States found it convenient to force Japan to discontinue her threats against our people."

We took a poll of those around the table and found that all but one of us thought war was very close. The dissenter was C. C. "Chappie" Chapman of Mackay Radio, who had lived in Japan longer than any of us. He was convinced the Japanese people were opposed to war.

I bet Chappie the cost of a message to my wife in Honolulu that we would be at war within a week. I borrowed his pencil and wrote the radiogram: "Take care of yourself okay here." She got it while the bombs were falling on Pearl Harbor. It was the last civilian message received there before censorship was established.

On Monday morning December 8, at 2 A.M., Ray Cronin telephoned. "The Japs have blasted hell out of Pearl Harbor." I was sleepy and didn't hear him, and he repeated it. I scrambled out of bed, pulled on a slack suit and a pair of sandals, and took a taxi to our office in the Manila Bulletin building.

*The infamous radio broadcast by General Hideki Tojo, the 27th Prime Minister of Japan, on December 7 1941, declaring war on America, was followed by a playing of the popular military song *Umi Yukabe* (Across the Sea). That same morning, Tojo ordered the surprise attack on Pearl Harbor, a war-crime for which he was tried, condemned and hanged in 1948.

Following image: Hideki Tojo (1884-1948).

4

Rus [sic] Brines was already in the office with Cronin, and we discussed plans for covering the war. We debated whether we should enlist, but decided we would be more useful in our own jobs.

When Manila bestirred itself and awakened, shortly after sunrise, the people of the city could not believe their eyes when they read the newspaper extras nor their ears when their radios repeated over and over, "Japan attacks America."

They had known how intolerably tense the situation had become, they had known that the United States and Japan were deadlocked with no solution in sight, but it was incredible that the lightning had struck so soon.

I telephoned several friends and advised them to take their families to one of the mountain resort towns. I said, "Pearl Harbor has been bombed." They couldn't grasp it at first. I told them, "The United States and Japan are at war." Then they understood.

From our office we telephoned the cable companies. Up to eight-thirty in the morning they still had contact with Guam. The Guam manager reported: "Many Japanese planes are attacking us. We have been in and out of our shelter since six o'clock. Our small forces are still fighting but the Japanese have landed and are advancing. This can't last long."

I knew that the Japanese were very well acquainted with Guam. Two years before, at a press conference in the Navy office in Tokyo, smiling Rear Admiral Kanazawa had contested the statement by. American correspondents that Guam was of no military value. That was during the controversy in the American Congress over whether Guam should be fortified or not. Congress was afraid of offending Japan, so the project was dropped. Kanazawa had taken his pencil and rapidly sketched the principal harbor of Guam. "It is an ideal harbor," he said. "The depth here is fifteen fathoms, there thirty fathoms. By simply blasting the coral heads here—" he pointed to a place on his map—"there will be ample room for ships of all sizes."

The cable companies got a few brief messages from Hong Kong. The Japanese were attacking overland from Kowloon and bombing the Hong Kong waterfront. The Pan American Clipper, which had arrived in Hong Kong from Manila the previous day and was scheduled to take off on its return trip to Manila at dawn, had been riddled with bullets from strafing planes and sunk at its pier.

A message sent by Jimmy White came in from Shanghai. It ended abruptly in the middle of a sentence. It said, "Japanese seized International Settlement U.S.S. Wake captured in Whangpoo stop heavy machine-gun firing audible from Bund British gunboat went down with guns blazing under—"

I knew that when the Japs took Shanghai they would go first to the Press Wireless and Globe Wireless stations which were both in the International Settlement and were the only uncensored means of communication. I guessed that Jimmy White had gotten his brief message through Globe Wireless at the risk of his life while Japanese troops were advancing up the Bund after shooting down the White Russian police at the Soochow Creek bridges.

An urgent press message came from Davao. Japanese planes were bombing the city, the most important on the southern Philippine island of Mindanao. One Japanese plane had been shot down. An American Navy PBY* had gone down in flames. The ancient aircraft tender Langley had been attacked.

The attack on Davao had been long planned by the Japanese and carefully prepared. No less than twenty-five thousand Japanese had settled there, prior to the prewar immigration restrictions, and some seven thousand of them were said to be of military age and Japanese army reservists. They were rumored to have been armed.

When we learned that the Japs had also bombed Singapore we realized for the first time the magnitude of the attack they had launched on a far-flung front from Hawaii to Malaya.

Then, in midmorning, the war suddenly came closer. Our correspondent telephoned from the mountain resort and summer capital of Baguio, only 125 miles to the north of Manila. Japanese planes had bombed Camp John Hay, which they evidently thought was a big barracks but was actually a recuperation camp. An American woman and her baby were among the nine victims. President Quezon was at Baguio and the bombs fell near enough to bounce him around. Russell Brines had also been at Baguio for the weekend, but we had reached him by telephone and he was speeding back to Manila by automobile when the bombs fell.

He passed Clark Field and Fort Stotsenberg at about 11 A.M. MacArthur's headquarters telephoned. The general issued a message of "serenity and confidence" to the people of the Philippines. His forces were on the alert and prepared to fight off attack.

The spokesman arranged to meet the press at 11 A.M., so I went over to headquarters at Fort Santiago in the Walled City. Intramuros, which means "within walls," was an old Spanish fort. About a mile square, its thick walls rose to thirty-five feet from the ground and were wide enough on top for three tanks—if there had been any tanks—to travel abreast. The wide, ancient moat was overgrown with thick grass and was used by American Army officers as a golf course.

You drove into Intramuros through archways in the walls. Most of the buildings along the straight but narrow streets were old, two-storied residences with tin roofs. In the south-eastern corner were large barracks, used by American troops but still keeping their Spanish names. Five blocks in the northwest corner were occupied by Spanish-built churches and Catholic schools. Fort Santiago was at the western end, with its back to Manila Bay, and USAFFE (United States Army Forces in the Far East) headquarters were at No.1 Calle Victoria.

The entrance to MacArthur's headquarters was down a fifty-yard passageway flanked by the plaster walls of buildings. The building on the left was the Sisters of Charity Catholic nunnery, one of the oldest in the Philippines. The passage ended in a garage, which was occupied by a brilliantly polished black Cadillac limousine. Its license was red with the three silver stars of a lieutenant general, and later the four stars of a full general. Behind the garage was a bomb shelter for the USAFFE staff, with underground desks and switchboard. MacArthur's spokesman met us in a small room at the right of the garage. Its walls were whitewashed and undecorated except for a hat stand of Philippine mahogany and a large stag head and antlers. The spokesman. Major LeGrande A. Diller, stood on the stairs which led to USAFFE headquarters upstairs and to MacArthur's flag-bedecked office.

Diller arranged for two daily press conferences, and for the issuance of credentials. There was not much news as yet. He told us to come back at 4 P.M.

War came home to most Manilans that morning when the air raid siren blew for the first time. Its menacing sound swelled and wailed out over the flat roofs of the city, and swirled around the skyscrapers and church towers and into the slum section down by the bayfront. Police whistles blew and traffic came to a standstill. Crowds flocked out of trolleys and buses and automobiles, and rushed under cover of the nearest trees or arcade. Carretera and caleza drivers took their stone hitching anchors out of their vehicles and snapped them to their horses' bits.

Constabularymen and Filipino troops patrolled the streets. The police wore the constabulary uniform of khaki with khaki sun helmets and carried .45 automatics and short clubs. The troops, most of them recent recruits, carried Springfield and Enfield rifles which they fired on the slightest provocation. They were dressed in coarse blue fatigue uniforms, with a few of them in khaki.

The reporters printed cards with the words "police-press" and we pasted them on our windshields, so that we could drive around the streets during air raids and alarms. We would go fast, with the horn blowing full blast, to make the police believe we were on official business.

The siren went off eight or nine times that first day of the war, but no enemy planes appeared. We learned that Boy Scouts were operating the warning system; that there was no adequate lookout network around the city and that the air raid wardens depended on telephone calls from isolated villagers who couldn't tell a friendly plane from an enemy plane. Of course that was no problem of identification after the first few days, when every plane in the sky was invariably Japanese.

In the next few days the alarm kept going off at intervals, but seldom in advance of a raid. Usually the first warning would be three loud bomb explosions. I told Brines, "The fellow blowing that siren has lost so much face by his false alarms that he'll keep on sounding it every few minutes until he happens to coincide with an actual attack." It worked out exactly that way. Meanwhile, people lost faith in the alarm system.

The Manila Hotel had its own siren. Sometimes it beat the city's alarm and sometimes it lagged behind. MTB's (U.S. Navy motor torpedo boats) starting up at the dock in front of the hotel would frequently cause the alarm to go off. The MTB's, popularly called PT's (patrol-torpedo) were sleek and powerful and noisy. Whenever the air raid siren sounded, and sometimes in advance of it, the PT's would roar off across the bay, out of the dock area. They would dodge around out there until the raid or alarm was ended, and we envied them their mobility and speed and ability to get away from the danger areas.

Three or four Q-boats belonging to the Philippine Army would follow the PT's away from the dock. The Q-boats were smaller and less sinister than the American naval torpedo boats and represented the nucleus of a fleet of Q-boats with which General MacArthur had hoped to defend the coasts of the Philippines. He had purchased one in England, and had had three replicas built in Manila, but no funds were available to build up a sizable fleet.

Until the first bombs dropped the following night everybody was more curious than scared when the air alarm sounded. The police and street patrols had difficulty in keeping people from poking their noses out of doorways and windows.

Throughout that first day of the war, press telegrams kept pouring into the Manila Bulletin office. The first Japs set foot on Philippine soil in the Bataan Islands north of Luzon. They first landed at Aparri on Luzon two days later and quickly overcame units of the Philippine Constabulary, which withdrew to the south. Even when the Japs landed at Aparri, which was 250 miles from Manila over rough country, nobody worried very much.

There was not much fear because everybody thought the Jap planes would come over Manila and our boys would knock them out and it would be pretty as hell to watch. We said to each other: "The minute that first bomb fell on Pearl Harbor the United States got moving. From all over the United States those big bombers are flying to San Francisco. They'll hop to Hawaii and then on down to Australia and up here. They'll be here within a week. The aircraft carriers will ferry pursuit planes out from Hawaii."

At 4 P.M. that first day I went back to USAFFE headquarters. Major Diller looked serious. He said, "Japanese planes which bombed Aparri this morning and later bombed Tuguegarao continued on the way to Manila.

They were met and turned back at eleven this morning by fighters from Clark Field.

"However, at about one this afternoon Clark Field was badly bombed. Many planes were destroyed and it appears that casualties were heavy."

We asked for further details.

"I don't have any," he said. "There is only one telephone line to Clark Field and that has been cut."

That disturbed me. I said to Mel Jacoby, "Haven't these people ever heard of the radio or the automobile? Can't they send up there and find out what happened?" Of course, the fact was that MacArthur and Diller and the others at headquarters knew the truth, but it was too grim for public dissemination at that time.

At six in the evening a very scared Manila physician came into our office at the Bulletin. He had been driving past Clark Field. "I saw planes diving through the sky and heard explosions. I thought it was practice. Then I saw planes blazing on the ground and a wounded man ran past me and crawled into a ditch and a plane came down and sprayed the road with machine-gun bullets. Santa Maria, I was terrified!"

His story precipitated our first skirmish in what was to be a three weeks' battle with the Navy censorship. The censorship had been set up early in the morning, after news of Pearl Harbor, and was operated by naval reservists who had no experience in their jobs. We had many a vituperative fight with them as to whether or not the people of the United States should be told the truth about what was happening in the Philippines.

We wanted, especially, to report that our soldiers were clamoring for planes and to tell the people back home that without planes the Philippines would be lost. Then and later in the war the correspondents objected not to the idea of censorship as a means of keeping military information from the enemy, but to the inefficiency, inconsistency, and lack of understanding with which censorship was administered.

The Manila censors kept our work pretty closely limited until the last week before Manila fell. Then they relaxed the censorship completely and everything went through. Those last days the censors were urging us, "Get the people of the United States to wake up and get going and send some airplanes out here. Tell them we must have help or we'll go under." Later, on Corregidor and Bataan and elsewhere in the Philippines we became friendly with the censors. In the midst of danger we forgot all our previous ill feeling.

The telegrams that were coming into the Bulletin office sent us scurrying for maps. The Japanese had bombed Vigan, San Fernando, and Iba Field, and a number of other places in northern Luzon. Most of us had never heard of them. But the messages in each case said the enemy concentrated on the airfields, and in that way we learned for the first time that our Air Force had built and was building a number of outpost and dispersal fields down the eastern coast and in the northcentral areas of Luzon. In another ten days the fields would have been completed and our planes dispersed from Clark Field and Iba. The Japs had obviously known about it all along.

A blackout was ordered in Manila. There had been several practice blackouts and most of the city was already prepared with dark window curtains and dim lights. Roy Bennett, editor of the Manila Bulletin, worked all afternoon blacking out part of his city and press room, so that we could have lights inside. It was sweltering in the Bulletins low-ceilinged office, and next day we moved over to the TVT (Tribune-Vanguardia-Taliba) newspaper building where it was a little cooler, even with the window covered with black paper.

That night the only light in the streets was from the stars and from the flashes of shots fired by nervous police and soldiers. Those were the first shots we heard in the war—the rifles and revolvers fired at automobiles with dimmed headlights or at windows through which a crack of light was shining. Sometimes, machine guns chattered nervously. Every night thereafter, until Manila was declared an open city and the blackout was lifted, the nights were never still.

The AP hired an old Plymouth with a tiny chauffeur whom we named Butch. Butch possessed a calm nature and a pair of cat's eyes. We would come out of the light in our office and be completely blind in the blackness of the streets, unable even to see the automobile a few feet away. But Butch drove us safely through the inky, narrow streets. He could spot a sentry a hundred feet away and halt in time to save us from getting shot.

It was ticklish approaching the sentries. We would hear the command, "Halt!" but couldn't see where it came from. Every sentry had a different method of challenging and a different accent in speaking English. Some would shout, "Dismount and advance to be recognized." Butch would interpret the command for us. Usually we would say "Press," and the sentry would let us go on. Sometimes sentries would fire from a distance at any car, and most of the automobiles which had to be on the streets at night had one or more bullet holes in them.

That first night we worked until 3 A.M. winding up the story as well as possible and getting it on the way to New York. Butch drove me back to the hotel. I had just tumbled into bed when the siren sounded. The torpedo boats outside started up and raced away across the bay. I decided if the planes came they would attack the docks, just outside my hotel, and that I'd rather get killed in the open air than buried in a building.

I crawled exhaustedly into some clothes and walked down three flights of stairs and through the hotel. Most of the guests were heading for the basement air raid shelter under the air-conditioned dining room. Many of them spent most of their time there until Manila fell. There were American women, with their babies, and English women, and American and English men of all ages. They made themselves as comfortable as possible on narrow benches in the shelter which was about one hundred feet long and thirty wide. The hotel boys kept fresh ice-water pitchers filled. The only other civilian shelter in town was under High Commissioner Sayre's residence on Dewey Boulevard.

I walked out of the hotel and across the Luneta and Dewey Boulevard to the statue of Jose Rizal, martyr of the Philippine fight for independence from Spain. There were four young Filipinos sitting on the stone railing. They were singing, "I'm Nobody's Sweetheart Now."

No planes came, so after a while I went back and to sleep.

*The Patrol Bomber, designation Y - or PBY - was the Navy's go-to twin amphibious aircraft of the war, produced by Consolidated Aircraft. The 'Canso' as it was called by the Canadian Troops, was retired in 1957.

Following image: A 'Canso' PBY in flight, c. 1941-1942.

5

IN THE NEWSPAPERS OF THE NEXT MORNING, Tuesday, December 9, there was nothing to cheer us up, but the rumors were all encouraging.

I heard that within four hours after the Pearl Harbor attack American planes had located and sunk the Japanese carriers which had launched the bombing and fighting planes against Hawaii. That sounded like the way the United States would do things, and we all believed it.

Another rumor had American forces on the way to Wake Island, where U.S. Marines were besieged. We boasted, "They'll knock hell out of those Japs and sink all their ships, quick."

Someone said that a convoy had left the Hawaiian Islands for the Philippines. The problem looked simple to us in Manila: All the United States had to do was load those ships, put soldiers and guns aboard, and get them started out here. Of course, they might run into trouble, but the United States had never dodged a fight and this was American territory under the American flag.

Meanwhile, the Philippine government called up more recruits. Hundreds and hundreds of them were drilling outside the Walled City as I drove to the office. Troops in blue denim dungarees were digging in under the trees along the wide avenue which bordered the grassy former moat, installing machine guns. There were also machine guns on the walls of Intramuros, with American soldiers manning them, but those guns looked pretty small and ineffective.

Along the waterfront the ships which had arrived in the last convoy were still being unloaded. I watched them from my room, and the work seemed to be going very slowly.

Additional ships arrived in the harbor most of them inter-island vessels and some freighters of various allied nationalities. The S.S. Anhwei arrived from Shanghai and Hong Kong with three hundred British women and children who had tried at the last minute to make a run for the safety of India. They were one day out of Hong Kong when war broke, and their captain was ordered into the nearest friendly port. With not enough room to tie up, twenty-two of the ships were anchored in a straight line, extending from in front of the Army and Navy Club diagonally across the bay toward the distant Mariveles mountains.

Occasionally a P-40 roared overhead, approaching or taking off from Clark Field, and as it passed over the city hundreds of rifle shots would be fired at it by our Filipino recruits, who couldn't tell one plane from another. A few Navy planes were buzzing around over the bay, and we could see PBY's circling over Cavite, nine miles across the bay.

There seemed to be a great deal of coming and going, and considerable confusion, around MacArthur's headquarters. The officers we talked to were serene but uncommunicative. They didn't have much information from the areas where the Japs had landed.

The USAFFE communiqué reported some patrol fighting in progress around Vigan.

News from other parts of the Orient didn't look so good. The Canadians were being pushed back in Kowloon toward Hong Kong Bay. Thousands of Japs were landing in Malaya. Guam was definitely finished.

Dispatches from our correspondent in Bangkok, where the Japanese allowed radio transmission for several days, indicated that the Japanese had bought their way into that country. Only a few days before, the premier had been loudly proclaiming that the entire country would fight to the last man against invasion, but there had been only five and a half hours' fighting before the Thais had quit and arrangements had been completed for the Japanese to occupy the country.

Brines said, "It looks like the work of our old friend Jiro Saito." I added, "Our bull-necked buddy has done it again." Lieutenant Colonel Saito* intermittently, for years, had been Japan's advance agent of conquest in the south. Educated in Honolulu, speaking flawless English, Saito had spent three years in Bangkok in the early 1930's as military attaché. He had been rushed to Indo-China in August of 1941 to pave the way for complete Japanese occupation of that French colony, and then had gone on down to Bangkok to reap the crop he had sown years earlier.

Saito had been a pupil of the then Colonel Kenjichi Doihara, "Lawrence of Manchuria," back at the time of the Mukden Incident in 1931 when Japan started on the path of conquest and gave Hitler and Mussolini a few lessons in how to bluff the other powers. Saito had told me the whole story of the Mukden Incident—a full confession of Japan's premeditated guilt—in Shanghai some months earlier. He knew the story well, because it had been he who transmitted the orders for the Japanese troops to march that snowy September 18,1931, which is actually the date when World War II started.

There were stories of fifth column activities in Manila, but as far as I can recall General MacArthur never made any official mention of them in his communiqué and it seems certain that the number of Filipinos actually in the pay of the Japanese was small. For every traitor at least a hundred Filipinos died for the American flag. There were one or two confirmed cases told me by officers of the Army and Navy. A secret radio transmitter, with beam director to guide the enemy planes, was found near Cavite Navy Yard and the operators, an American with a Japanese wife, were arrested. A similar transmitter was found near Clark Field in the restaurant of a Japanese whose customers were chiefly American fliers and ground troops from Clark Field.

Cafés and bars and restaurants near every one of the American military and naval establishments in the islands were run by Japanese undoubtedly sent to the Philippines for the specific purpose of spying, just like the Japanese Army and Navy officers, either reservists or on active duty, who came and went freely in the Hawaiian Islands for years before the outbreak of war.

Filipino fifth columnists, or paid traitors, set fires which guided enemy planes in night attacks and the Japanese unquestionably had pipelines right into MacArthur's headquarters. A week or two after the war started, fifth columnists attempted to create a panic by starting rumors that the water supply of Manila was poisoned, but the rumor was quickly spiked and its effects nullified. Most of the Filipinos working with the Japanese were members of the outlawed Sakdalista and Ganap organizations, which wanted freedom from American rule at any cost, and they probably considered themselves not traitors but patriots.

An American naval officer vouched for a romantic story of spy intrigue. He said that an attractive Japanese-Filipino girl employed in a trusted position at the Cavite Navy Yard had been caught red-handed in an act of treachery. It was decided that she must be executed on the spot and the officers present drew lots to see who should carry out the sentence. The task fell to a young officer who had been enamored of the girl. Without hesitating he led her outside and shot her.

Most of the Japanese in Manila were rounded up the first few days of the war. Soldiers arrested some five thousand of them in Manila alone and found them ready to be taken to internment camps. They all had purchased small suitcases of similar size which were packed with clothing, toilet articles, and food, proving that they had been warned that trouble was coming.

From everything we could learn, the first few days, Japanese forces that had landed in northern Luzon were not very large. But they were reported to be building a landing field at Aparri. We wondered why our planes weren't chasing them out. We studied the maps with civilian strategists who pointed to Lingayen Gulf and told us: "The south shore of the gulf is the obvious point for a major landing and attack on Manila. We have known about it for years and are prepared to fight there. It is the most strongly defended area of the island, with the exception of Corregidor."

During the day the Japs bombed Davao again and other isolated small places here and there in the islands.

That night, after midnight, the planes came to Manila. I'd just gone to bed when I heard motors. They weren't the motor torpedo boats. They sounded different—more menacing, more purposeful. They seemed to be coming in from the northwest, directly across Manila Bay. I went to the window and tried to follow the planes by the uneven sound of the motors.

Down to the left, where Dewey Boulevard left the bay and curved inland, there were many explosions. Although more than two miles away, they shook the hotel. Within a few seconds, a huge fire sprang up, and from that minute on until late in January there was not a time when the night skies of Manila were not brilliant with fires, and the skies blackened in daylight by clouds of smoke. Watching the fires eat down homes and offices and churches and piers, I thought many times of Genghis Khan and his hordes of terror spreading death and ruin over the earth.

That night the planes made only one run on their target, then circled and headed out across the bay. They had been guided by flares and small brush fires ringing Nichols Field, and they hit their target squarely. One 1,100-pound bomb went squarely through a hangar, wrecking the planes inside. Several parked planes were destroyed.

I telephoned Cronin, who was on duty at the office, and dressed and went out into Luneta Park across from the hotel. The fires were blazing higher. Trucks and gun mounts were turning into Dewey Boulevard and going toward Nichols Field. Across the boulevard I saw that two guns had been set up. I approached them gingerly and the crews greeted me.

They were Americans belonging to the 200th New Mexico National Guard, an anti-aircraft regiment of the coast artillery which came to the Philippines in September. Their guns were 37-millimeter rapid-fire weapons; "America's answer to the dive bomber."

In the darkness we introduced ourselves. The sergeant was Joe Smith, the corporal, Gene Davis. There were Gene Davis's brother, Dwayne, and Paul Womack, Leon Beasley, Charlie James, Sam Buse, Lieutenant Frank Forni and Lieutenant J. A. Oden, Jr.

"We were at Clark Field yesterday," they said.

"For God's sake, tell me about it. I heard the Japs knocked off a few of our planes."

They said, "Yes, and that ain't all. It was lunchtime and our officers had gone to eat. We had been listening to the radio and knew the war was on, but we didn't think the Japs were going to hit us. We were sitting by our guns and chewing the fat.

"A bunch of planes started to come over, with the sun shining on their silver wings.

"We said, 'Look at them U.S. Navy planes. Goodness me, but ain't they purty!'

"Somebody was counting: 'Fifty-one, fifty-two, fifty-three—My, God! They ain't ours!'"

Just to verify the story they called over their mate who had been counting.

"Then the bombs whistled down. One of our guns was hit squarely. We started to shoot right away, without orders, but I don't believe we hit many of those bombers. We think they were four-engined bombers. They hit the hangars and set them on fire, and a lot of our planes.

"Just as the bombers cleared off the fighters dove down on us. Somebody counted eighty-six of them. They really came low. They dove up and down the line of planes and set fire to most of them with bullets. They were firing 20-millimeter cannon, too. They gave me a few of the empty 20-millimeter cases for souvenirs.

"The planes came straight at our guns and when they passed by the pilots would shake their fists. When they got too close we'd duck into our foxholes and then shoot at them going away.

"We shot down six of them altogether."

They stopped the story to show me what a foxhole was. Some had already been dug behind their guns. The best way to visualize a foxhole is to dig a hole six feet long and two feet wide and three feet deep. Lie down in it, fold your arms on your chest, remember the smell of lilies, and you'll get the idea.

They went on with the story. "Two of our fighters got in the air. They jumped on the Japs and got one apiece. One of them got on the tail of a Jap fighter way up in the sky and rode him down into the ground.

"We picked up some of the bomb fragments. A lot of us recognized pieces of our old Fords. Some were hunks of Singer sewing machines. We said to each other, 'And to think we sold it to 'em.'

"The crews of the bombers had been eating lunch but lots of them ran out and got in their planes and started shooting. One sergeant sat at the nose gun of a B-17 while it was on fire, and shot and shot at those Japs. He never tried to get out. Another did the same thing and shot until his cockpit was on fire. Then he ducked out.

"Lots of our pilots and crews were killed running for their planes.

"The bombs hit the barracks and mess, too, and killed a lot there.

"Some of them fell in the woods, near Camp Stotsenberg, where our tanks were parked. But nobody was hit. The planes strafed the quarters at Stotsenberg, which adjoins Clark Field.

"We heard about three hundred and fifty were killed or wounded.

"We figure we lost twenty-four bombers, out of thirty-six, and all of our fighters except a half-dozen or so. There's not much left of our Air Force."

*This Colonel Saito is not connected to the (apparently) fictional character of Colonel Saito, the sadistic head of Japan's Allied POW camp in the 1957 movie The Bridge on the River Kwai.

6

LATER I FOUND OUT MORE ABOUT HOW OUR AIR FORCE was destroyed, but I never established to my entire satisfaction why it was on the ground when the Japs came over, more than ten hours after we had received word of the Pearl Harbor attack.

As nearly as I could determine, the situation was this:

The pursuit planes had been up patrolling in the morning, and the pilots had come down to eat and refuel their planes all together, instead of a few at a time.

The bombers were on the ground because it would have been impossible for them to fly around aimlessly while awaiting orders to bomb objectives in Formosa or Hainan Island.

Such orders could not be issued in the Philippines because we were not yet officially at war with Japan.

The planes were lined up in straight rows and not dispersed because our fliers had not had any experience and did not understand the necessity for dispersal. Underground hangars were being built, but were not yet finished.

Radio detecting equipment was inadequate.

Shortly after the Clark Field attack, I ran into some of the survivors of the B-17 crews of the 19th Bombardment Squadron, who said:

"That first day of the war we went up in the morning, got our planes running perfectly, and then came down again. The pursuits had also been up and had come down to refuel and to let the pilots get lunch. For weeks we had expected that if war came we would bomb southern Formosa. We knew just where and what to hit.

"Right after lunch we pilots were called to the office. I heard our commander, Colonel Eugene Eubank, arguing over the telephone with someone in Manila. He was insisting that we be allowed to take off for Formosa, but apparently he could not get an okay.

"Anyway, Eubank hung up the phone and turned to a map on the wall. He was just pointing out our objectives on Formosa when someone came running in. The messenger shouted, 'The Japs will be here in twenty minutes.'

"We started to get out and get to our planes. Two minutes later the bombs crashed down around us.

"We had about twelve heavy bombers left when it was all over. We flew most of them down to the field at Del Monte, on the island of Mindanao.

"From then on we were under the orders of General Wavell. We heard several times that MacArthur begged for us to come up and give his troops a hand during the early days of Bataan, but instead Wavell sent us to attack the Japs at Borneo and other islands once or twice. Then we were ordered to Java, and then to Australia."

I questioned them further about why we were surprised at Clark Field. That was one of the most crushing blows in the whole Philippines campaign. It lost us any chance to gain air control, and without air control we never had a chance to win.

"Then it is your impression," I asked, "that someone in Manila headquarters ordered our planes to remain on the ground?"

"That is what we understand," they said. "We were told that we were forbidden to bomb Formosa because the Japs had not yet attacked the Philippines, and perhaps did not intend to. Inasmuch as the Philippines were a commonwealth and not an integral part of the United States, we had to wait to be attacked first."

That last part didn't add up to me, because many hours before the Clark Field bombing we knew that the Japs had bombed Baguio and Aparri and Davao and many other points in the Philippines. I told one of the high officers on MacArthur's staff what the pilots had said.

"The truth is that as soon as MacArthur knew Japan had attacked Pearl Harbor he ordered our pursuits into the air and instructed that our bombers be dispersed to other fields, part of them to Del Monte," the officer replied. "Apparently those orders went astray or at any rate were never carried out."

Another factor in what happened at Clark Field was undoubtedly the fact that, at the time the Japs hit, we were not officially at war with Japan. Congress did not declare war until the following day. In the Philippines we knew that the Japs had attacked Pearl Harbor but, from the record, even that did not necessarily mean that we would go to war with them. They had sunk the U.S.S. Panay near Nanking four years before and no war had resulted. It seemed incredible, but there was always a possibility that they could apologize for this attack too.

In any case, the disaster at Clark Field was another chapter in the tragic story that shows we were not, as an army, navy or nation, prepared militarily and psychologically for the shocks of war. Even individuals had a hard time realizing it when they came into combat for the first time.

On Bataan in January, Lieutenant L. E. McDaniel, who had lost his plane and was attached to the anti-aircraft at that time, told me more about the Clark Field raid.

"I was flying my P-40 from a field near Clark and was up on patrol when the Japs came over. I saw a plane on my tail, way back. When he first opened up and I saw the blue flashes of his guns, I thought he was signaling to me. Then I snapped out of it and got in there and fought him. The sky over Clark was full of Jap planes and it looked like the entire field was on fire."

A pursuit pilot who had been at Iba Field, which was designed as a pursuit field to protect the bombers flying from Clark, told what happened there.

"They caught us flat-footed. Our warning system failed but the main thing was that we were all green and inexperienced. The Jap high-level bombers took one pass on their way to Clark. Then the fighters dove low and strafed our parked planes. Naturally they were all lined up in pretty rows. We didn't know any better then. We never had time to get one in the air. Only a few were still flyable after the attack."

The pilots whose P-40's were still flyable, soon found out that they wouldn't fly so well, that in a combat airplane there is no substitute for soup—for power. The P-40-B, the model they were flying, proved to be very much underpowered for modern war conditions. It was far too heavy and unmaneuverable to dogfight a Zero, although it had a good score against the Japanese Army's older type airplanes, the T96 and T97 in Burma. The Zero was light and fast and it had the horses in its engines to take it upstairs fast. It would turn twice while a P-40 turned once. The only advantage our planes had was greater firepower and armor protection for the pilot.

The P-40 was useless against the high-altitude Jap bombers. It would only climb 1,000 to 1,200 feet a minute when fully loaded, if that, and the bombers would come over way up, at between 20,000 and 30,000 feet. The P-40's never bothered them.

Our pilots quickly learned not to dogfight. They found the only chance they had was to take one pass at enemy planes and keep on going down fast, using their weight and diving speed to get away. They saw that the Japs had built a plane which could outfly anything we had in the air and finding that out made them very angry.

Those who lived through the early days of the war used to come into the Manila Hotel in the evenings. "It's high damn' time our airplane manufacturers stopped wasting advertising space trying to prove to our people that we have the world's best airplanes," they said, "and started producing them instead. The Japs can't be convinced by those beautiful ads. We've got to have more horsepower in our engines. We can't fight them in those planes."

Even so, our pilots fought in the Philippines in the few planes they had left.

Through a mutual friend in Honolulu, I met Captain Colin Kelly a few days before the war and he told me he had come out to the Philippines prepared to fight. Before he left Hawaii to ferry his B-17 out to Manila he spent three days studying the data on the Japanese Mandated Islands and other Pacific islands gathered by John Williams, a Honolulu newspaperman. The B-17's were to fly from Honolulu to Wake, and then across the Japanese Mandated Islands at night and land at Rabaul in New Britain. From there they were to go to Darwin and then up to the Philippines.

For three days Kelly studied and made notes and copied maps. When he had finished he stretched his long legs out in front of his wicker chair and ran his big hands through his thick black hair.

"We're sure in a hell of a fix out there, aren't we," he said.

"What are you going to do about it?" Williams asked.

"Well, I'm going out and bomb the first thing I see and blow it to bits," said Kelly.

They started rehashing the old argument as to whether airplanes could sink battleships. Kelly had some decided ideas about that. He promised, "I'm going to put an end to that argument personally by sinking one of those Jap ships."

Kelly got his chance on December 11, and dropped his bombs on the Japanese battleship Haruna and left her blazing, although, apparently, she did not sink.

On his way home two Zeros dropped out of a cloud and got on the gunless tail of his plane and shot it up so badly that it wobbled, on fire, toward the ground. Kelly stuck at the controls until the rest of the crew had parachuted. Before he could jump his plane exploded in the air.

Captain Jesus Villamor of the Philippine Air Force fought too, in a nine-year-old plane that proved a better match for the Zero than did the P-40. Villamor and six other members of his squadron were flying P-26's which the U.S. Army had long decided were obsolete. Those were the only planes that MacArthur could get for the Philippine Air Force he was trying to build.

Villamor, short and thick-set and a fine pilot, was a graduate of West Point and had learned to fly at Kelly Field and Randolph Field. In the first two weeks of the war he flew his P-26 so well that he won two Distinguished Service Crosses. Once, with one of his two guns jammed, he tackled a formation of thirty-six enemy bombers and brought down two of them. Another time he tangled successfully with a cloud of Zeros.

All together Villamor and his squadron had about six airplanes and they flew them as long as they held together—which was about ten days. After the first few days they ran out of ammunition for their machine-guns and the pilots took the useless guns out of the ships, to lessen the weight, and flew them on scouting missions. I saw a lot of Villamor and his fellow pilots during the first three weeks of the war and many times, at their request, I took out my notebook and wrote: "Try to get the U.S. to send some decent planes out here quickly." I wrote stories, too, but the censors killed them.

The young American pilots who still had P-40's performed epic feats of heroism in the early days of the war. Lieutenant Boyd Wagner became the ace of our Air Force, destroying many Japanese planes in the air and on the ground at the airfields which the enemy quickly built in northern Luzon. During one such strafing attack, Buzz Wagner's wingman, Lieutenant Russell M. Church, was hit by anti-aircraft fire over the Jap field at Vigan. Church dived his burning plane over the field and released his bombs. Then he crashed, making no attempt to jump out in his parachute. Even the Japanese were impressed by his courage and determination and they honored him with a hero's funeral.

Lieutenant Samuel H. Merett attacked Japanese transports, landing troops in northern Luzon. He strafed the landing boats and, when his plane was hit by anti-aircraft fire, dived into the side of an enemy transport. The plane and transport both blew up. Joseph Moore and Jack Dale, Carl Gies and Randolph Keator, and a dozen other of our young pilots fought the Japs in the air as long as they had planes.

By the time our forces completed their withdrawal into Bataan on January 1 we had about ten P-40's still in fairly good condition despite the terrific beating they had taken. They operated from two runways which had been leveled off in the rice fields on the southeastern tip of Bataan. Brigadier General Harold George set up his headquarters in the woods near one of the runways, and directed the mechanics who nursed the planes along and the pilots who flew them.

The most planes that we ever had in the air at one time during the battle of Bataan was six—five P-40's and an old Philippine army biplane piloted by Captain Villamor. The five pursuit ships escorted Villamor on a photographic mission over Cavite, where the Japanese were installing artillery to shell Corregidor. After Villamor landed safely the P-40's tangled with a flock of Japanese dive bombers.

I saw the fight in the air over Bataan and Manila Bay and I remember the USAFFE communique on that engagement. "Our planes shot down six enemy planes and damaged three more. We lost one plane." That sounded like a victory and it was. But the loss of one P-40 left us only four, and we had no replacements coming. General George treasured and hoarded his planes, trying to save them for occasional decisive actions, but one by one they were shot down or damaged on the ground by Jap bombs, or simply wore out.

It was a great occasion for our troops when they saw one of our planes in the air. But nobody saw the planes the night they carried out one of their most audacious actions. The pilots were angered at the daily poundings they were taking from Japanese planes based at Nichols Field, where only a few weeks before our fliers had lived in comfortable quarters. Without orders from USAFFE, the pilots worked out a plan to bomb Manila. They rigged bombs on the three P-40's which were in flying condition that night and took off one evening late in January. They flew into Manila and bombed and strafed the Japanese planes on the ground at Nichols and Zablan airfields.

Some of our intelligence agents were in Manila that night and on their return to Corregidor they told us that the raid spread panic among the Japanese, who threw down their guns and ran into homes, seeking shelter under beds and tables. The Filipinos rushed into the streets and cheered. Some of them dug up their rifles and bolos they had buried and got ready to slaughter the Japs. They thought our counteroffensive had started at last.

It was a tremendous let-down when the raid was not repeated.

In another night attack with rigged-up bombs and with machine guns our planes helped drive off a Japanese force attempting to land on the west coast of Bataan late in January; and again in March, when the Japanese were putting troops ashore in Subic Bay for their final overwhelming assault on our lines, the planes dived on their vessels and sank or damaged six ships, including a large transport. They showed what could have been done all over Luzon if we had had enough planes.

Most of our Air Corps troops fought without planes. The trained pilots and expert mechanics and skilled bombardiers were given rifles, machine guns, and hand grenades and fought for their lives on the ground in Bataan. Among them was the entire personnel of an army attack-bomber squadron. They arrived in the Philippines on the President Coolidge about two weeks before the war. Their fifty-four planes—planes which might have made a decisive difference in the battle of Luzon—never arrived. The planes were within four days of Manila on an army freighter on December 7. Someone ordered the ship to turn around and it eventually got to Java.

7

AT NOON ON WEDNESDAY, DECEMBER 10, Manila got its first close up of the Japanese Air Force.

The planes were almost overhead when we saw them from our office on the third floor of the TVT building. We looked out the window and there they were, flying high and straight in, from the north. We counted them. There were fifty-four in three tight "V's," the whole formation making one big "V." Their wings were silver in the noonday sun and they were barely distinguishable against the white wisps of clouds far up in the blue sky. Seeing how high the planes were flying we realized the Japs knew all about the use of oxygen for the crews of high-altitude bombers.

I jumped over the city editor's desk and onto the fire escape which led to the roof. I got up a few rungs on the iron ladder and suddenly found it difficult to hold on. My knees were doing a combination jitterbug-rhumba. We didn't know whether the Japs were going to bomb the whole city or concentrate on definite targets, and in either case the TVT newspapers, which had been extremely antagonistic to Japan, were a legitimate target.

I finally made the top and looked down on the surrounding wooden buildings, each of them a firetrap. From the roof of a nearby building a .50-caliber machine gun started chattering. Rifles crackled from the streets, although the planes were far above the range of any ordinary anti-aircraft gun, to say nothing of rifles. Then black puffs blossomed high in the sky and I looked down toward the bayfront where my new friends of the previous night, Sergeant Smith and Corporal Davis and the others, were firing their 37-mm. guns. But their shells were bursting at 10,000 feet, only halfway up to the planes.

Most of the people in the TVT editorial and press rooms had run down to the first floor when we shouted that the planes were in sight. Down in an alley alongside the building a bunch of newsboys were unconcernedly pitching pennies against a wall. The police were having difficulty keeping the crowds off the streets. After the first raids, when the people saw the Japs weren't bombing the center of the city, it became even more difficult, and in the TVT and other offices the workers kept on with their jobs during attacks.

The planes went right on past, out of sight, into the sun. There were distant, fairly loud, explosions. I got down from the roof and went to the rear of the building. From a window I saw fires in the direction of Nichols Field and Fort McKinley. The smoke was black and fierce, and the flames were high, and it looked as if the gasoline dumps had been hit.

The planes turned out over the bay and were lost to view. Fifteen minutes later from the direction of Cavite, we saw smoke, and knew that the naval base was being attacked.

Inside the TVT people asked, Where are our fighters, sir? Why do they not attack the Japs?" We couldn't see any fighters in the air.

Jack Percival, the Australian reporter, and I climbed into a car and sped through the center of the city and out Dewey Boulevard along the bay.

Two tremendous fires were burning in Cavite, punctuated by explosions. But from the distance of nine miles across the water it was impossible to distinguish individual buildings or tell whether the naval base itself or the town had been hit. We saw one minesweeper speeding in toward Cavite. It seemed to be running right into the flame and smoke.

We went on out to Nichols Field and drove through back roads to the nearest fire. Nipa shacks were burning hotly, while their occupants aided the firemen in trying to put out the flames. Nipa, which is coconut fiber, throws up a dense black smoke when it burns and very much resembles an oil fire, and this fact caused frequent reports and rumors that oil dumps around Manila had been hit by bombs when actually the bombs had missed their targets and landed in Filipino villages.

In the large grounds of an American-owned estate there was a deep crater thirty feet wide behind the servants' quarters. On the lawn a five-year-old Filipino girl was lying, her abdomen ripped open by bomb fragments. Her father was bandaging a wound in his leg. "Those damn Japs, sir, have killed my baby," he said. Nobody was crying or showing signs of grief.

The homes of Americans on Harrison Boulevard had also been hit. Bombs seemed to do more damage to buildings of concrete and steel than to the nipa shacks on stilts. Frequently, part of a shack would be torn away by a direct hit and half of it would still be standing. There were bomb craters in the Elizaldes' polo field, across from Nichols Field.

At Nichols Field no damage had been done to our planes or hangars or barracks. We saw several planes that had been ruined the night before by a direct hit on a hangar, but most of them were old Martin B-18's, twin-engined bombers which had been on their last wings even before the war started.

Neither the Army nor Navy would give us any details about the bombing of Cavite, except to intimate that it had been "very bad." Russell Brines, who lived on Dewey Boulevard near Nichols Field and facing the bay, had seen two dogfights in which Jap planes were shot down. They belonged to a fighter escort accompanying the bombers and they dived on the airfields and strafed our fighters in an attempt to pin them to the ground. Despite those excellent tactics, a few of our fighters got into the air and fought successfully. Brines, his wife, and daughter had spent an hour crouched behind the seawall in front of their home, sheltered from machine-gun bullets fired by the planes zooming above their heads, and from shell fragments from the anti-aircraft guns at Cavite.

One U.S. Marine fighter pilot had succeeded in taking off from the field at Cavite, but had been riddled with bullets before he was five hundred feet up.

That night I learned of the sinking of the British battleships Repulse and Prince of Wales, under command of Admiral Sir Tom Phillips, off Malaya. Jap torpedo planes and dive bombers had gotten them, and I recalled the party in Hongkew when the Japanese captain said, "If your ships come out here, we will dive into them and sink them with bombs and torpedoes."

General MacArthur told me additional details about the sinking of those ships several weeks later on Corregidor, and, as he told it, it seemed that Phillips had lost his ships in a magnificent gamble, and not through any blunder. MacArthur always referred to our Japanese enemy as "the Jap."

"The morning of December 8," MacArthur said, "Tom Phillips telephoned me from Singapore. He told me the Jap was approaching Malaya in eighty ships. He said he was going out and get in among them and sink them. That was his only chance to save Malaya, since the British didn't have the forces to stop an invasion once the Jap landed.

"Tom Phillips said he was going out without an air umbrella, but he had to take the chance. The weather was overcast and if it would remain that way, the Jap could not use his air.

"Tom Phillips steamed out of Singapore and headed north and a little east. He steamed for nearly forty hours and the sky remained overcast. Then the Jap sighted him through a hole in the clouds and just two hours before he would have been in among the Jap Fleet, the weather cleared.

"He wired for air assistance but the Jap dive bombers and torpedo planes hit him and in a few minutes his ships were wrecked and burning.

"The first British fighter planes arrived overhead just as Tom Phillips was sliding down his bridge into the sea."

It wasn't until four days after Cavite had been bombed that we learned how damaging the attack had been. On Sunday, Rear Admiral Rockwell summoned us to Cavite, where he was stationed as commander of the 16th U.S. Naval District. He wouldn't let us inside the base to see the damage but received us at the entrance, inside of thick, Spanish-built walls. Rockwell was tall with a stiff white pompadour. His face was tanned, lined, and strained.

"The bombing was accurate and devastating," he said. "It was perfectly planned and executed. The planes divided into four groups and flew systematically over our heads from east, south, west, and north. They hit the fire station and the power plant, which made it difficult to fight fires. The firemen who were in the streets after the raid were machine-gunned by fighter planes, and everyone was killed.

"One bomb hit the dispensary and killed everybody in it. However, we are still able to operate.

"I am proud of our American naval and civilian personnel and of the Filipinos. They conducted themselves magnificently, as did our nurses."

Admiral Rockwell said, "We found out that if you get down and keep down, preferably in a shallow trench, you are safe from anything but a direct hit. Even direct hits within a relatively few feet won't harm you, as the shrapnel spreads out and up. It is not pleasant, but it's safe." He did not give us the casualty figures, but we understood that some six hundred sailors and officers and civilian personnel were either killed or wounded. The week after the first bombing the Japs went back to Cavite again. I saw the whole raid through a telescope from the Manila waterfront with the boys of the 200th, who had meantime moved their guns from the Luneta to positions directly on the bay in the park between the Manila Hotel and the Army and Navy Club.

This time the attack lasted even longer and the fires were even fiercer. At least one oil tank was hit and burned for days. At night its flames lighted the entire bay. Through the glasses I saw one of the three giant radio towers at Cavite topple and crash from a direct hit. Again destroyers were buzzing around just outside the flames.

The boys of the 200th asked, "Where are our fighters?"

I didn't know.

I told them their 37-mm. guns were shooting far under the Jap planes. They answered, "These guns are for use against dive bombers. They won't shoot over ten thousand feet. We clocked those babies as they went over just now at close to thirty thousand feet. The Japs certainly have a good bombsight and know all about using oxygen.

"The best we can do is to keep them up fairly high."

Keeping them up seemed to help a little.

The Japs bombed the twenty-two ships anchored in the harbor, all in a line. They cruised up and down the line three or four times. We saw the big fountains of water spout up. After it was over one ship was sinking fast, and another was on fire. There had been only one direct hit.

After that the ships were scattered over the bay to present less of a target and those with passengers aboard came in and unloaded. One of the ships tried to make a run for it to a southern island in the Philippines. It was the S.S. Corregidor, now an inter-island steamer but formerly His British Majesty's ship the Engadine and as such the first seaplane carrier in history. The Engadine had survived the battle of Jutland. As the Corregidor it was less fortunate. Trying to sneak through the minefields off the island of Corregidor on December 17, it hit one of our own mines and exploded and sank within a matter of seconds. Three hundred were saved by PT boats and other vessels from Corregidor Island, but five hundred persons, including many prominent Philippine political figures, lost their lives.

Most of the other ships successfully negotiated the minefields, with the assistance of pilot boats, and made it through to Singapore, Java, or India, and then to relatively safe waters.

But they went out without passengers, including the China coastal vessel, the Anhwei, whose three hundred British women and children were put ashore at Manila where they later went to the internment camp.

8

TOWARD THE END OF THE FIRST WEEK THERE WAS A BRIEF LULL in air attacks. We thought maybe the Japs were concentrating on Hong Kong, intending to knock it out before tackling Manila; but later we learned that they had been moving their planes from Formosa down to bases on northern Luzon, at Aparri and other points.

We kept asking each other, "Why doesn't our Air Force knock them out?" Even after hearing the stories of Clark Field, I still thought we had planes at other fields—and so did our soldiers.

When they got their bases set up the Japs came back to Manila again. They came almost every day, usually at noon when the sun was directly overhead and their targets were unshadowed.

Their bombing was erratic. Sometimes, they hit their targets on the nose as they did at Cavite. Other times they would miss by as much as a couple of miles. They concentrated on Nichols Field and Fort McKinley, which was the barracks for American troops in Manila, on Zablan Field where the midget Philippine Air Force was based, and on the dock area. They didn't waste bombs on hospitals, churches, or schools.

I developed a routine for covering the bombings, after we had worked out a schedule for the office. Cronin worked from 6 A.M. to 6 P.M.; my shift was from 11 A.M. to 11 P.M., and Brines from 8 P.M. to 8 A.M. At least, that was the schedule, but actually each of us worked about twenty hours daily. I'd get up at ten in the morning and shave and have breakfast in the hotel, then pick up the eleven o'clock USAFFE communiqué from Major Diller or from Major Carlos Romulo, publisher of the DMHM newspapers, who was appointed to MacArthur's staff after the beginning of the war. I immediately began a private war with Romulo. His papers were clients of the United Press, our rival news agency, and several times his papers published news in advance of the official communiqués. I suspected that Rommy was a newspaperman first and an officer afterward and that through his papers the United Press was gaining access to official news before its release to the rest of us.

After several such instances I complained to Major Diller about it in the presence of Rommy, saying, "Major, there seems to be a leak and it seems to be right in your office." Diller promised, "We'll check up on that." Rommy, with a twinkle in his eye, added, "Yes, Clark, we will certainly look into it."

When I got the morning communiqués, I'd take them over to the Press Wireless office in the Crystal Arcade and file them and then go on to our office.

The siren would usually sound about noon. I'd say, "Come on, Joe," to our photographer.

We would run down the stairs of the TVT building, sprint 150 yards to an alley which led to the back of the Avenue Hotel, the biggest building in that section of the city, and then run up seven flights of stairs taking two steps at a time. The elevators stopped during raids. That running and climbing proved good conditioning for what was to come later.

The planes usually came from the north. They would circle over Nichols and Zablan, and drop a half-dozen or dozen bombs. Sometimes they would attack the docks.

We watched from the Avenue's seventh-floor roof garden. The first day I went clear up to the top of the water tower with Joe, but soldiers in the streets mistook us for fifth columnists and cut loose with their rifles. We crawled around the water tank, dropped down to the roof and then to the roof garden itself. Whenever the planes came over the soldiers would fire at them with rifles and machine guns and revolvers, even when they were at 25,000 feet.

From the top of the Avenue Hotel the city sprawled beneath us in a panorama of color and beauty. The modern buildings along the waterfront loomed high against the blue background of the bay, and to the east the city trickled off to the foothills in streams of tinted roofs.

We had lots of company on the hotel roof garden. For several days I watched the raids with W. H. Donald, the Australian newspaperman who had been Generalissimo Chiang Kai-shek's adviser in China for many years.

Donald said, "This reminds me of the first days of this same war back in Nanking in 1937, when we watched bombers like these wreck China's capital."

Donald had left China six months before with the intention of writing his memoirs.

"Chiang Kai-shek kept wiring me in Tahiti to come back to Chungking. I temporized, but he was insistent so I went up to Honolulu and caught a freighter, the Don Joss. We were four days out of Manila when the Japs attacked you here, but we kept coming and made it all right."

I suggested to Donald, "Why not get in touch with General MacArthur and see if he can't get you on to Singapore by airplane."

"I'll take my chances here," he answered. "If necessary, I will take to the hills later on." I did not see him again.

The photographer and I would watch where the bombs fell, and then run back down the stairs and over to the office and get our car and go out.

One day at Nichols Field we were stopped at the gate and then escorted around by a sweat-soaked sergeant of the Air Corps. From the city it had looked as if Nichols was badly hit, but the flames and smoke were from a single gasoline truck and from an officer's home and a corner of the barracks.

The sergeant was still shaking from the excitement of battle. He'd been firing a .30-caliber machine gun at the enemy

"For Christ's sake," he said, "you people are reporters; tell planes. the people back home to send us some anti-aircraft guns and some airplanes that'll fight those Jap fighters and climb high enough to knock down those bombers. All we can do now is sit here and take it and it's a hell of a lousy situation. Tell them this isn't only our war, it's the war of every American."

At his insistence, I took out my notebook and wrote, "Try to impress Roosevelt and Washington that we must have planes here!" The book, by that time, had many such notations.

Another day Russell Brines and I reached Zablan Field as the dust from the bombs was still settling. Under the trees dividing the field from the Wack golf course we met Colonel Backus, American commander of the Philippine Air Force, and a group of his officers. One of them was Captain Villamor.

The colonel said only two men had been killed in the raid. "Both of them failed to duck, or get down in a foxhole, and were cut to pieces."

He showed us a fragment of the Jap bombs, a wickedly jagged, shining piece of the casing, about a foot long.

"When the bombs burst, they throw out the casing fragments like whirling saws that cut to pieces any man they hit."

One old B-10, out in front of the hangars, was still on fire, and the pilots were laughing about it. It had been wrecked in a landing a month before the war, but the Japanese pilots dive-bombed it.

I asked, "How big is the Philippine Air Force?"

"There it is," was the reply. "Those four old P-26's scattered around the field. We have one other like it, and a couple of Beechcraft. One of them is going to take General George Brett to Mindanao."

Later General Brett's pilot took off from a highway in the Beechcraft and landed safely in Mindanao. Then the general got a bomber to the Netherlands East Indies where he served as Air Force commander before going to Australia.

Everybody we talked to who had been in a bombing and narrowly missed being killed seemed badly shaken. No one was casual about it.

I couldn't understand it at first. I thought that if you happened to be in an area where the planes were bombing, you would just watch until they came near and then duck into a foxhole or gutter and lie there calmly until it was all over. If you got a near miss you'd just say like the nonchalant British, "Rather close that one, what!"

Stories about bombings, whether told by word of mouth or written, don't include the sound effects and the sound is what makes bombing terrifying. That and the fact that there is no way to defend yourself against bombs and no way to fight back against the planes that are dropping them. I learned this through personal experience.

The people of Manila were taking the bombing well. With the exception of those who had been shell-shocked by near misses, they were more puzzled than scared—puzzled that our Air Force was not keeping the bombers away from the city or at least making some show of tangling with the bombers. It was grim to see the enemy planes cruising overhead, far above the anti-aircraft bursts, and taking their time to pick their targets.

The Americans in Manila were beginning to sense that something was wrong. The USAFFE communiqués were worded optimistically, but not much fighting seemed to be going on. If the Asiatic Fleet was in action, we didn't know it, and the Army didn't seem to be doing anything to chase the Japs out of their air bases on Luzon.

In the Manila Hotel there were still nightly dances in the blacked-out, air-conditioned dining room. Lunch was served in the big outdoor restaurant right on the waterfront and the more carefree of the guests could sit there, eating and drinking, and watch the bombs falling around Pier 7, only a couple of hundred yards away.

Many preferred to sit out the raids in the small, low-ceilinged, dark-paneled taproom. There was so much noise inside that even with the bombers overhead it was difficult to hear them. Bombs falling within a quarter of a mile made only a faint whoomph inside.

To the Americans and English people living in the Manila Hotel the greatest annoyance was the nervous watchmen assigned to enforce the blackout. If you lit a cigarette in your rooms a bullet from a 45 revolver or a .30-30 carbine might come whistling through the window and plunk into the ceiling. The only light in the rooms was a dim blue bulb in the bathroom. Even when the whole city was lighted by fires from oil tanks or buildings ignited by Jap bombs, the blackout guards at the hotel discharged their duties—and their guns—conscientiously.

The Americans in the hotel adopted the anti-aircraft men of the 200th New Mexico National Guard. They would load their arms with sandwiches and soft drinks and stumble through the darkness across the Lunetta to the gun emplacements. Then they would chat for several hours with the gun crews, recalling their own experiences in the last war and passing around cigarettes and listening while the youngsters told stories of their own homes. When the boys from the guns weren't busy firing at Jap planes they would come into the hotel to get their hair cut or have a Coke or a sandwich.

One evening, a week after the war had started, we sat around a table in the hotel and talked things over. Most of them thought the Japs would go for Singapore and not attempt a major invasion of the Philippines. They were optimists.

The General Motors man had the best news of all. "This is confidential, but it comes from a high source. There are two American aircraft carriers off Corregidor. They'll be here within a few days."

Chappie, who had bet there wouldn't be any war, had heard that one too. He bet drinks for the crowd that the reports were true.

All of them said, "We were in the last war, some in the Army and some in the Navy. We'd like to get in this one. We've been around to Army Headquarters but nobody seems to know what to do about us."

I said, "Look, you fellows. This may be 'fifth columnism.' But here's the way I've got it figured out and I've been talking to everybody in town. You all heard Sayre's frantic appeal for help today in which he said "Time is of the essence!"

Pearl Harbor has stunned us. Wake Island is the tip-off. We have planes that can fly easily from Midway to Wake to give those Marines a hand. Our ships could have reached there by now to fight off those Japs.

"But we're back on our heels, now. Most of our admirals are punch drunk. We have lost our old dash and recklessness. The U.S. is going to play this thing slowly and cautiously and take no chances. This means they are going to let us go out

Chappie laughed at me. He was a fountain of rumors and optimistic reports in those days. "The Lexington is off the coast," he said. "We are getting planes tomorrow."

In those splendid rumors that planes were on the way it was always the Lexington that was bringing them. Probably because she was our best-known aircraft carrier.

After I saw MacArthur for the first time* I tried to force myself to believe that maybe, after all, the Lexington was on the way. I hadn't seen him before because I was constantly on the move getting first-hand stories of the bombing, and he didn't have time to attend the press meetings.

MacArthur didn't speak. He just walked with long strides through the room at No.1 Victoria where we were waiting for the press communique, and up the stairs to his office.

He nodded confidently to us on the way past. His gold-braided cap was tilted jauntily. His shoulders were back. He was smoking a cigarette in a long holder, and swinging a cane.

He looked so young that I nearly asked, "Is that MacArthur or his chief of staff, General Sutherland?"

Then I saw the four silver stars gleaming on the shoulder of his neatly pressed shirt.

He looked completely sure of himself. He looked like a man who couldn't lose.

9

ON DECEMBER 10, THE JAPANESE LANDED AT APARRI on the north coast of Luzon, 250 miles from Manila, and at Vigan on the northeast coast, 200 miles from the capital. They sent a few boats in to land at Lingayen Gulf but they were driven away. Then they landed in force at Legaspi, southeast of Manila on December 13.

The first news of the Japanese landing at Legaspi came from the stationmaster who telephoned the Manila railroad's central office. From there the call was switched over to USAFFE headquarters.

Stationmaster: "There are four Jap boats in the harbor, sir, and the Japs are landing. What shall I do?"

USAFFE officer: "Just hang onto the phone and keep reporting."

Stationmaster: "There are about twenty Japs ashore already, sir, and more are coming." A pause. "Now there are about three hundred Japs outside the station, sir. What am I to do?"

USAFFE officer: "Just sit tight."

Stationmaster: "Sir, a few of those Japs, with an officer in front, are coming over here."

USAFFE officer: "See what they want."

Stationmaster: "Those Japs want me to give them a train to take them to Manila, sir. What do I do now?"

USAFFE officer: "Tell them the next train leaves a week from Sunday. Don't give it to them!"

Stationmaster, hanging up, "Okay, sir."

The landing at Legaspi sent us scurrying for our maps again. We saw that to reach Manila the Japs would have to cross the swampy and mountainous narrow neck of Luzon southeast of Manila and we heard that the only crossing was over the railway bridge which was being blown up.

Neither then nor later did the USAFFE communiques tell much about the war in southern Luzon. I asked an officer at headquarters about a report that, within a few days of their landing, the Japanese had advanced forty miles inland.

He said, "To tell you the truth we don't know much about it. Our communications are not so good down there."

The best source of information about what was happening in the south proved to be Don Alejandro Roces, owner of the TVT newspapers. White-haired, tall, red-complexioned Don Alejandro had a friend who was manager of the Manila railway and whose station agents kept him informed of the Jap movements. He never tired of telling a story about the day Dewey's fleet sailed into Manila Bay.

He had been standing on the bayfront where the Manila Hotel is now located.

"Nearby was a group of aristocratic old officials of the Spanish colonial regime. They said to me, "Young man, whose ships are those far out in the bay?"

I replied, "Those are American ships, senores."

They said, "Nonsense, boy, your young eyes deceive you. Surely you can make out the Spanish flag?"

"I said, "Senores, the flag is that of the United States of America."

"They became extremely indignant. "Well," they said, "we do not believe you. But if that is the American flag, by the Holy Mother we will never let it sail out of this harbor again."

"And," Don Alejandro would chuckle, "so faithfully did they keep their word that the American flag is still flying over Manila today, some forty-four years later."

The flag was not to fly much longer. Following the occupation of Manila by the Japanese, Don Alejandro's TVT newspapers—the English language Tribune, Spanish Vanguardia, and Tagalog dialect Taliba—were the only ones to continue to publish. They printed Japanese official announcements and abandoned their editorial pages. The Tribune's editor, Dave Boguslav, was locked under "special detention" in Santo Tomas University, together with Roy Bennett of the Bulletin and Ford Wilkins, Bulletin city editor and New York Times correspondent.

Perhaps Don Alejandro decided, from the depths of his experience, that the Japanese flag would fly over Manila for some time and that he might as well make the best of things and keep on doing business.

SHORTLY AFTER THEIR LANDING AT LEGASPI, the Japanese put large forces ashore at Atimonan and Mauban, also on the east coast of Luzon, but farther north and nearer to Manila.

One Filipino soldier arrived in Manila from Mauban. He had been captured by the Japanese, who broke his foot by smashing it with a rifle butt, but he had escaped anyway.

He said, "Our forces were dug in on the beach at Mauban and were fighting very well with machine guns. We killed many Japs. But then their airplanes came over and killed many of us in our trenches. Where are our own airplanes, sir?"

He reported that the Japanese moved with lightning speed. From Mauban the road climbed steeply upward in a zigzag to a mountain pass leading toward Manila, but within four hours after their first landing the Japanese had brought trucks ashore and had already reached the top of the pass. They came in fast from Atimonan too.

I was at USAFFE headquarters when two young Filipino soldiers came in. An officer asked, "Where did you come from?"

"From Legaspi, sir."

"Legaspi! How did you get here and where are your guns?"

"Our officer told us to withdraw, sir, so we withdrew to Manila. Our guns were very heavy and we threw them away. Our homes are here, sir, and we have been to see our families. We are now reporting for duty."

"How long have you been in the army?"

"About ten days, sir."

"Okay, you can take your uniforms off and leave them here and go home and stay with your families."

Two other youngsters came in from northern Luzon. "We were on outpost duty, sir," they said, "when some Japs came near us. If we had stayed there those Japs would have killed us, sir. So we retired to Manila."

That happened time and again in the first two weeks of the war and witnessing incidents like that we began to see MacArthur's problem and to understand why the communique were guardedly reporting Japanese advances and not much fighting.

The trained Filipino soldiers who saw the Japs land in the south did not think much of the enemy. Some of the prisoners who fell into our hands were youngsters of about 18. They said they thought they were being sent on maneuvers and had no idea that Japan had gone to war with the United States or that they were to attack the Philippines. Our Filipino troops reported the Japanese were raggedly clad; some wore big civilian caps, some "baseball caps"—which actually were the uniform of the Japanese infantry; only a few had steel helmets and many of our troops were hit by their .25 rifle bullets and lived to tell the tale.

The story, as we got it in snatches then and later on, was that there was not much fighting to the south and east of Manila. We had very few troops there and they were quickly outnumbered and forced to withdraw or be annihilated. Our forces at Legaspi withdrew to the north under orders. When they passed the narrow neck of Luzon and proceeded toward Manila they found the roads already blocked by Japanese who had come overland in trucks and on bicycles from Mauban and Atimonan. On orders, the American officers disbanded their recently recruited troops and with a few Filipino Scouts made their way as best possible through the enemy lines. Some of them reached Corregidor after January 1, by which time the siege of Bataan had begun and the enemy were in control of most of the main highways in Luzon.

There were some isolated patrol contacts in the south, mostly delaying actions fought by small groups of our forces.

It seemed that MacArthur sent some of his men to the south in an effort to check the Japanese advance. On Sunday, December 20, we saw many light tanks going south through Manila. One of them stalled near the Jones Bridge over the Pasig River while Brines and I were having a sandwich in Ben's restaurant nearby. We went out and talked to the crew of the tank. Some of them were from Minnesota, others from Kentucky. They had been at Clark Field during the Japanese attack and only that morning had been ordered south. They understood that a big battle was to be fought a few miles south of Manila.

On December 25, some of the tanks went into action near Lucena, 60 miles south and east of Manila. Sergeant Robert Mitchell of Salinas, California, who was wounded by shrapnel, told me about it later on Corregidor where he was in the hospital.

"We met our own forces on Christmas morning," Mitchell said. "A Filipino major was in charge. He told us we were to lead a company of infantry in an attack which was intended to check the Japanese advance. As far as he knew, the Japanese had no anti-tank guns.

"The attack was to be made along a curving road through rice fields. The Japanese were in the hills about a half mile from the bend in the road.

"We started down the road in six tanks, with a group of infantry behind each tank.

"As we rounded the bend, an anti-tank gun in the hill opened fire.

"The first shot was a bullseye on our first tank. It was knocked off the road into the rice fields. The second one hit my tank squarely. The mechanism became jammed in reverse and we backed off the road into the fields. The third shot hit the third tank. The others managed to turn around and get away.

"We crawled over to the first tank and found our commander, Lieutenant Noli of Salinas, badly wounded in both legs. He said, 'Go on, boys, this is as far as I'm going.' But we stayed there and made him as comfortable as possible until he died."

"Nearly all of us in the first three tanks were wounded, many of us from rivets which the shells knocked loose. We hope they build the new tanks without rivets."

Mitchell and five or six others hid from the Japs and eventually got back to Manila and Corregidor. In a Manila hospital they left one of their companions, who had been wounded by a rivet through his throat.

Apparently, after that abortive attack, there was not much more fighting in the south. From December 26 on we noted in Manila that the trucks and buses and guns which had been rumbling past the city every night to the south had suddenly turned around and were headed north.

We couldn't find out where they were going nor could we determine what our forces were doing.

Don Alejandro Roces kept in constant communication from the TVT building with his friend in the railway and gave us all the available information about the Japanese advance. One or two Americans succeeded in getting through from mines and plantations in southeastern Luzon. They told us that the Japanese were coming fast without much opposition and that our troops were withdrawing toward Manila.

About December 30, the Japanese passed the last blown-out railway and highway bridge and were within forty miles of the capital. They had apparently expected the bridges to be destroyed, because they carried complete equipment for crossing ravines. They had guns which shot heavy iron arrows, with ropes attached, across the gaps. Soldiers pulled themselves hand over hand across the ropes and within a few hours the Japanese had built bridges and their main forces were crossing.

The Japanese obviously didn't know it because they waited outside the city until January 2, but from December 31 on there was nothing between them and Manila but a few miles of excellent highway.

10

THE SAME DAY THAT WE SAW THE TANKS GOING SOUTH through Manila, I determined to go up north to Clark Field and investigate for myself whether or not we still had an Air Force. I still thought we did—despite what had happened on the first day of the war—and couldn't understand why it wasn't attacking the Japanese transports and landing parties.

I arranged with a Spanish-Filipino university graduate in his early twenties, whom I shall call Carlos, that he drive me out in his automobile, a fairly new Ford sedan that was in good shape. He wanted to see the war and asked only money for gasoline. A Filipino reporter named Juan thought he wanted to come along too. Next morning, on Monday, December 22, I went to USAFFE headquarters to pick up the morning communique before starting out. Major Diller kept us waiting a few minutes and then came down and stood on the stairs. He ran his hand nervously over his bald head.

He said, "Ladies,"—the ladies being Annalee Whitmore Jacoby and Mrs. Arch Royal Gunnison, both the wives of correspondents—"and gentlemen. I have a bulletin here for you. I shall pass it out. There is no additional information and no comment."

The bulletin was brief and startling. It said that an enemy flotilla of eighty transports and warships had been sighted early that morning off Lingayen Gulf, headed for the shore. Everybody breathed a little faster. We ran for our cars and rushed for the wireless offices to get off urgent flashes to New York. But first I had a word with Diller.

In my story I reported that the Army made it clear "there was no doubt this was the beginning of Japan's major drive on the Philippines."

I went up to our office and told Ray Cronin, "The Japs aren't going to bypass this flank after all."

"Well, at least," Cronin said, "they are hitting us where we are most ready for them. Our defense plan has been prepared for years. I understand that the south shore of Lingayen Gulf is strongly protected with barbed wire, trenches, and heavy field artillery. We have a flock of tanks at Stotsenberg. It is a defense in depth."

I said, "I'm going up to Clark Field anyway and have a look at our Air Force, if any, and try to find out what chance we have of stopping them. If we don't have any planes left, we haven't got a hope in hell."

Carlos and Juan and I finally got away shortly after noon. Just as we stepped into the car the air alarm sounded. We debated momentarily whether to stay and cover the raid or get going. We decided to go on. We drove out Rizal Avenue at fifty miles an hour, passing the cars and horse-drawn vehicles which had pulled over to the side of the street, and left the wailing siren behind. We saw the dive bombers plunging low over Zablan Field, and then circling in strafing runs.

The Japs were wasting bombs and bullets, because as we already knew there were no planes left at Zablan.

Manila ended abruptly, except for scattered homes and small factories. We stopped outside the city and fastened a big cardboard placard with the word "PRESS" to the radiator with adhesive tape. But the wind soon blew the tape loose and we didn't bother to put it on again. The road headed straight north, through level rice fields. Up on the right, loomed Mt. Arayat, with the mountains of Zambales on the left. That was the country of the tiny Negritos, whose king had brought in three trussed-up Japanese aviators to Stotsensberg a few days before and had sworn a blood feud against the enemy.

Those mountains looked reassuring. "The Japs can't land on the west coast there and climb over those mountains," I said. "They'll have to come right down the middle from Lingayen, through this flat country and the plains of Pangasinan Province, and squarely into our defenses."

The Filipinos along the road had heard news of the landing at Lingayen and they apparently thought we were reinforcements for the front, because they waved at us and held up their hands, with their first two fingers separated in the V-for-Victory sign. There were Filipino sentries every few miles along the road, and air raid wardens in each village. Numerous times they stopped us by blowing whistles, and we got under the trees or sheltered in ditches as Jap planes passed overhead. The Japs strafed various parts of the road throughout that day, but we missed all the attacks.

When the first enemy planes roared low over us Juan decided that he had made a mistake in coming, and with every mile he became more frightened. That afternoon, for the first time, I heard the sentence that he was to repeat at least a thousand times in the next four days: "I'll never forget his voice, tremulous with panic, "Xeeeeee. Let us go back." Carlos and I laughed at him and I said, "Juan, que nos maten si puedan, pero no vayamos a morir de miedo." The Spanish is probably bad, but what I meant was, "Let's not die of fright before we ever see a Jap."

After so many years of traveling through China's dusty, dirty landscapes I enjoyed the ride through the clean countryside. The rice had been cut and was stacked in the fields. We passed one large town, San Fernando, but the only other settlements were small villages of fifty or sixty nipa huts, with one or two frame buildings.

In an hour and a half we reached Tarlac, capital of Tarlac Province and the biggest Luzon city north of Manila. We drove down the wide main street and I telephoned Cronin from the Tarlac exchange. All the other public phones along the road had been closed and most of the buildings in Tarlac, like those in the villages, were boarded and closed.

"The telephone lines to the north have been cut but I'm going on up," I told Ray. "You probably won't hear from me for a few days but I'll get the story in as soon as possible. Where we go will depend on how things look ahead. We'll probably spend the night in Baguio. I've always wanted to see it."

"Okay, but you better look out," Ray said. "Baguio is past our extreme right flank. Army communications seem to have broken down and we have no news here up to now."

We drove on, expecting momentarily to come to our third lines. I expected to see trenches like those in France in World War I. But there were no lines and only a few sentries. One of them stopped us a few miles north of Tarlac and we showed him our press cards and went on, wondering now when we would come to our second line.

The road went straight north, frequently passing over bridges spanning wide and stony river beds. The rivers were mostly dried up, with only a small stream in the center. Philippine Constabularymen guarded the bridges, but we drove past them fast and they had no chance to challenge us.

Cars from the north were speeding down the road. We saw one that had stopped to repair a flat tire and went over to talk. An American woman, with a baby in her arms, was weeping.

"We went up to Baguio when the war started," she said, "thinking we would be safe. But they have been bombing all around us. Last night we heard the noise of big guns, over at Lingayen Gulf, all night long. This morning the Japs bombed Camp John Hay at Baguio again. We seem to be surrounded. What shall we do?" I advised her husband to keep going until he got to Manila.

Trucks were loaded with beds and chairs and all the people who could crowd aboard. Filipino families told us they had seen the Jap ships in Lingayen Gulf that morning, and the planes had come over, and many people had been killed in Lingayen City and the other towns along the south shore. We reassured them, "Our army is fighting them now. Within a short time you will be back in your homes."

Traffic to the north was sparse and we noticed that the nearer we got to Lingayen, the slower it was moving. Traveling fast, we overtook a few jeeps and army trucks and motorcycle riders. Some of the occupants were Americans.

Approaching the gulf at about five in the afternoon we reached a fork in the road. The left-hand road led out to Da Mortis, four miles away on Lingayen Gulf. The right-hand one went to Baguio. We could see the waters of the Gulf, but no ships. The Japs were further over to the west. An American soldier rode up and stopped his motorcycle.

"Those Japs are pretty smart," he said. "They made a feint at landing on the south shore of Lingayen, where we have strong defenses. Then they sent their main forces along the eastern beach from Da Mortis, over here to Bauang, which is about twenty miles north. The Twenty-Sixth Cavalry is fighting them a couple of miles up this left-hand road." He advised us to turn back and then rode on, slowly, toward the fighting. We had about two hours of daylight left and had to decide fast.

Juan wanted to take the soldier's advice. Carlos was neutral. "Let's go on up to Baguio, where headquarters for this area are located," I said, "and find out what the score is. I want to see Baguio, and this might be my last chance. We'll have a good sleep in the cool air and get going in the morning."

Juan objected, "But the Japs may cut this road in the night."

I said, "Hell, amigo, they are fighting the American Army now and the American Army will hold them on the beach forever. Hirohito's boys will die right where they land."

11

THE ROAD TO BAGUIO LEFT THE GULF AND RAN LEVEL toward the foothills for a half mile and then started to climb and turn, following the course of a river that had cut a deep gorge in the mountains. In most places, the cliffs on the inside of the road rose almost vertically, and on the outside dropped down steeply to the river. A retaining wall kept automobiles from plunging into the stream. Four or five times the road crossed the river on suspension bridges, and the last few miles into Baguio were a steep zigzag which had to be driven in second gear.

There were sentries and boxes of dynamite on the bridges. A few miles from Baguio a toll gate barred the road, and the conscientious gatekeeper was still collecting one dollar for admission to the national park, even with the war just over the hills. He couldn't have collected much that evening, for we saw no other cars on the road.

As we started up the road and rounded the first bend we saw a 75-mm. gun mounted on a truck equipped with wheels in front and tractor treads in the rear. It was manned by Filipino scouts. They had been fighting the Japs at Da Mortis in the morning, and a few minutes before we sighted them a dive-bomber had located them and dropped three 100-pounders in the hill over their heads. We saw where the dirt and rocks had fallen into their truck.

"Those Japs are not so tough, sir," they said. "The Filipino Scouts and especially our regiment, the Twenty-Sixth Cavalry, can defeat them at any time."

I asked why they were not at the front. They said, "It is rather difficult to determine exactly where the front is, sir. We were ordered to withdraw to this position by our commander, Colonel Pierce."

We drove up the winding road and over the zigzag and into the outskirts of Baguio. Through the pine trees we could see the wooden buildings of Camp John Hay on a nearby hill. It did not look badly damaged. There were some American army trucks drawn up at the side of the road with a few officers standing beside them. One of them had a blood-soaked handkerchief wrapped around his head. His left sleeve was cut off at the shoulder and his arm bandaged. In the twilight he looked like the drummer in The Spirit of '76.*

He was Major Joseph Ganahl of Shaker Heights, Cleveland, a West Pointer and in peacetime a polo player and hunter. He and Major Williams and Major Noble and their Filipino Scouts had been fighting the Japanese advance from Vigan, down toward Lingayen, with a few mounted 75's.

"We've been fighting these fellows for the past two weeks and holding them pretty well. Day before yesterday the Japs hit us with a large force, including tanks, and we started to withdraw slowly down the coast road to the cut-off to Baguio. Last night they surrounded us. We found them holding a bridge behind us, but we shot our way across, then turned into a road to our left, away from the beach and toward the mountains. All last night they were firing at us with rifles and machine guns.

"At daylight this morning we could see their ships out there. A bunch of them landed on the beach and set up some 88-millimeter guns. We shot back and forth for quite a while, with considerable damage on both sides. Finally, only one of my guns was firing and only about twelve of us were still alive and unwounded. The Japs were on the beach and on the road to the south of us, and we couldn't draw back through the mountains.

"We were sitting there, exposed, in the middle of the rice fields. Then their dive bombers came over, to add to the merry hell of it, and I stopped a piece of bomb and a fragment of a shell and a rifle bullet. Nothing serious, though.

"We decided our only chance was to try to fight our way out to the south. I put the survivors in the two trucks that were still running. There weren't many survivors, and most of them were wounded.

"We drove back onto the road without getting hit, and turned south. About a half mile up ahead the road passed through a cut-out in a hill, which rose to about twenty feet on each side. The Japs opened up on us from the top of the cut with machine guns.

"Our leading gun-truck was badly shot up and was limping along at only three miles an hour. The second one couldn't pass it on the narrow road.

"When we reached the cut-off we ducked low in the trucks and held our breath. Machine-gun bullets bounced down on us and a few of us got new wounds. We got through because the Japs were too stupid to drop a couple of hand grenades into our trucks. If they had been experienced soldiers we wouldn't be here."

Ganahl told me that story many weeks later in Bataan. That evening he was too exhausted to talk much.

That night I asked him only one question. "What happened to the rest of our northern forces?"

He said, "Hell! WE are the northern forces, what's left of us."

Colonel Collyer, who was one of the officers talking to Ganahl and who had just driven up from a lookout post overlooking Lingayen, told us that a few minutes before he had counted fifty-six Japanese ships off the coast. He said the main Japanese landings had been made at Bauang and at Da Mortis. We wanted to go to the lookout but had to make plans for the night.

We drove on into Baguio, and it was already so dark that all we could see were wide streets and big homes surrounded by bougainvillea and other flowers, and a huge cathedral outlined against the overcast sky. I was cool for the first time in a month.

We found our way to the home of Major Joaquin Garcia of the Philippine Army, who was in command at Baguio, and told him what we had seen on the way up. I asked him what was being done to stop the Japs.

"We have lost touch with Manila," he said, "and I have no recent orders. My last orders were to send four hundred recruits down to Manila to be enrolled and I am trying to get buses for them now. When they get past we will blow the bridges on both roads leading up here."

"That lower road, at least, looks like an ideal place to defend," I said. "We should be able to hold it forever with a few machine guns. The Japs can't climb over those hills."

"We should, my friend," the major answered, "if we had anything to hold it with. There were only a handful of troops under Major Horan at Camp John Hay. I have nothing but recruits. And don't overlook the Jap dive bombers. They've been swooping up and down that road all day, picking off our trucks and troops. Their dive bombers co-operate very efficiently with their infantry."

We drove on over to the big, blacked-out Pines Hotel and as we walked into the bar I immediately thought of the play Idiot's Delight. The bar and lobby were expensively and tastefully furnished and decorated, and the people sipping their cocktails in front of the fireplaces were very composed and very sure of themselves. There were about a dozen; a handsome English woman and her daughter and son-in-law; some suave, elderly people of the world-traveler type, and a doctor with a Teutonic accent and a face which made it immediately apparent why he had to leave Vienna.

They were listening disinterestedly to the Manila radio broadcast. They said, "Most of the Baguio people have gone on down to Manila. We are staying here, as we believe the Japanese will not bother to come. After all, there is nothing here for them." We didn't tell them that the Japs were only about eighteen miles away.

The manager apologized because a buffet supper was being served in place of the regular dinner. The supper was excellent, with cold turkey and goose liver, and several kinds of salad and wine, and we realized we hadn't eaten since morning.

While we were eating, our local correspondent came in. He knew a little more about what was going on, but not much. He told us the almost unbelievable story of Major Emil Speth, ex-U.S. Army, who had obtained release from an internment camp for A. H. Nagatoni, Japanese businessman, and had gone out with Nagatoni to meet the Japanese Army in northern Luzon and arrange a separate peace between the Japanese Empire and the resort city of Baguio. They had been intercepted by American officials.

"Of course," the correspondent said, "that was a foolish move, but we have another plan. When the Japanese approach the city I am going out with the chairman of the Japanese chamber of commerce in Baguio to meet them. We shall arrange for the Americans here to continue to live in their homes."

There was no use reminding him how the Japanese Army had conducted itself toward the conquered Chinese, nor that Japan was purposefully attempting to humiliate the white man in the eyes of the Oriental people.

The correspondent, an American who had come to the Philippines many years previously, invited us to ride with him a few miles down the Nagilien road, the northernmost of the two roads from Baguio down to the Lingayen Gulf shore. "They have just set fire to Jan Marsman's oil storage tanks," he said, "to keep the oil from falling into the hands of the Japs, and it is quite a sight."

Juan refused to go, but Carlos and I rode on down, past numerous sentries who challenged us in the blackness. We saw the fires from a couple of miles away.

The road curved sharply down the mountain, and as we rounded a corner we pulled up short to keep from hitting a truck parked in the middle of the road. By the light of the fires we could see a long line of trucks and buses stretching around the bend past the burning tanks and then out of sight down the hill. Filipino soldiers were standing quietly by the roadside, or sitting impassively in their trucks and buses.

We located two American officers. They were both young and one was tall and dark and the other medium-sized and blond, with his trousers torn off at the knees and one shirtsleeve gone. We put our feet on the retaining wall and leaned our elbows on our knees and looked at the fires. Finally, the officers started talking.

"MacArthur has sure got us slewed, stewed, and tattooed with these green troops," said the tall one.

"Those airplanes have really got us switched, twitched, and bewitched," said the other.

"What happened?"

They told the story, each supplementing the other.

"We were sent up here a while ago and stationed on the beach at the junction of this road and the one to Vigan, to the north up the gulf. This regiment was formed three days ago, and most of the troops hadn't been in uniform for more than a couple of weeks.

"We dug in on the beach as well as possible, and got our guns set up. We had a few one-fifty-fives and a couple of seventy-fives and some fifty-caliber machine guns. We sat down to wait.

"Last night we saw lights on ships a long way offshore and this morning the gulf was thick with ships. They were anchored in a straight line, about half a mile offshore, directly in front of us at Bauang and all the way down to Da Mortis.

"About seven-thirty, when it was fully light, the Japs started coming ashore in landing boats. Meantime, as soon as we could see, our guns opened on them and we sank one or two of their ships. They were small, about three thousand tons.

"These green troops had never heard shooting before, and when our one-fifty-fives fired for the first time we looked around and saw about half of our forces heading for the hills. They just left their rifles and machine guns and took off.

"While the landing boats were still coming in the Japs hit us from the air. They came low and bombed and strafed, but didn't do very much damage. Most of their bombs went wild.

"As the Japs hit the beach the planes went away.

"We opened with our fifty-calibers and started mowing the Japs down. The Japs didn't seem to know what to do when they ran into our fire. They looked like bewildered young kids. Every third one had a baby machine gun. Even though the first ones were cut down the others kept coming, like men in a hypnotic trance.

"Those Japs may be first class troops, but if we'd had five thousand American soldiers or Filipino soldiers, and fifty airplanes, the gulf would be full of floating bodies tonight and we'd still be sitting there on the beach. Those Japs looked like frightened kids to me. The only trouble was, our own kids were more frightened. That and the fact we didn't have any airplanes."

I asked, "How many warships were with them? Did they cover the landing with a barrage?"

"They didn't shoot hardly at all from the ships," they said. "We saw only two ships that looked like destroyers. The rest were transports."

I asked, "Didn't some of our ships get in among them and muss them up? Where were our submarines?"

"We haven't seen one of our ships since the war started. And we heard that Tommy Hart has taken his submarines down to Java."

"Where were our airplanes?"

"We saw one about ten days ago, but that was the last."

They called over one of the Filipinos, a green youngster who had stuck and fought, and I questioned him. He said, "It is very difficult to fight airplanes with rifles, sir."

The blond lieutenant said, "Those airplanes have really got us tripped, stripped, and whipped. For God's sake, if you get a chance, tell them back home that we need airplanes." By the firelight, I made one more notation in my book.

The officers said the Japanese had kept coming ashore for hours, despite their losses, and that finally our forces had to withdraw. By that time it was afternoon and the Jap planes had returned either to their carrier or to one of the fields they had seized in northern Luzon, and had refueled and come back. Our troops dumped everything they could carry into their trucks and drew back up the road to Baguio. Bombs dropped all around them, but they did not lose a man or a gun during the retreat.

"What are your orders now? Where are you going?"

"We were just told to sit here and wait. We haven't heard anything directly from Manila since the war started. If the Japs cut that south road down the mountain from Baguio we'll probably have to take to the hills."

I asked, Where in hell are the American troops?"

They snorted and answered broadly, "Don't rightly appear to be none hereabouts, stranger."

Driving back to Baguio I was still optimistic. I thought the big battle, Americans versus Japs, was still going on at Da Mortis. But the correspondent said: "If they cut the south road tonight, there are a couple of ways out by trails over the mountains. They are easy to find and the natives are friendly. At least, they have been up to now."

We went back to the Pines Hotel and studied our Standard Oil road map. It showed no roads out of Baguio except the north and south routes down the mountains to the shore, and a partially finished highway to the northeast. But that meant a two days' drive into territory more than likely held by the Japs. There was also a spur road, fourteen miles long, which ran down past the gold mines to the south and ended in the mountains.

The correspondent said, "From there, there are two trails. One leads to the west over the back of the sierras and comes out on the road to Manila—the one you drove up today. It is about a three days' walk. The other goes east and joins the highway from Cabanatuan down to Manila. It is also three days. A lot of Baguio people have sent their wives and children up to a place in the mountains called the Saw Mill, where they have stored food for six months. That should be long enough, don't you think? If you get cut off you can go up there and sit it out for the duration."

Carlos and I thanked him and were getting ready to turn in when Juan came running into the room.

"Leeeeee," he quavered. "We must go. I have been back to see Major Garcia and he tells me all the bridges will be blown up by morning. His troop convoy has departed and we can follow it down the south road and maybe get through."

I telephoned the major. He confirmed what Juan had said. We paid our bill and hurried out to the car.

With lights off we crept through the streets of Baguio and onto the main road down the mountains. Elsewhere in the Philippines the moon was shining, but not in Baguio. Dark clouds were down below the tops of the mountains, and it was impossible to see more than a few feet ahead.

It was raining slightly. That was the only rain I saw in the Philippines from the first day of war until I finally left the islands. We prayed for it many times, but our prayers were never answered.

*"... he looked like the drummer in The Spirit of '76."

Artist Archibald MacNeal Willard (1836-1918) famously captured the early American spirit in his work, a section of which came to be known as 'The Spirit of '76.'

12

WE STARTED DOWN THE MOUNTAIN, BARELY CRAWLING, and in the first twenty minutes we made only a couple of miles. No light at all came through the clouds and the trees lining the road.

I tried standing on the running board watching the roadside and calling directions to Carlos, "Hard right, slow, straight, slow, slow." Then I steered with my arm through the window, while he operated the clutch and brake. In that way we negotiated the sharp turns of the zigzag and finally came to a fairly open portion of the road.

We decided it was hopeless to go on without lights, and taped some wrapping paper over the headlights. The paper soon blew off, but we left the lights on dim and kept going at about fifteen miles an hour. Juan kept asking, "Do you think we'll make it? Will we get there before the Japs?"

With only a mile or so to go before reaching the main road to Manila we rounded a corner and our lights illuminated the rear end of a bus halted in the middle of the road. We saw eight or ten more buses ahead of it. The buses were in the middle of the road and we couldn't get around them, so we turned off our lights and coasted to a stop.

Carlos walked up ahead to investigate. He reported that it was the convoy that our friend Major Garcia was sending to Manila. It was commanded by another major. They had stopped while a scout car went ahead to investigate if it was still possible to get through, or if the Japanese coming inland from Da Mortis had already reached the junction between our road and the main highway to Manila. It was about one-thirty in the morning.

On our left, on the inside of the road, the hills rose perpendicularly for a hundred feet. The river, which we could hear but not see, was some thirty feet below the level of the road on the right, and the retaining wall dropped steeply down for that distance. We could see the tops of the hills across the river about a hundred and fifty yards away, dimly outlined against the sky. We got out of the car and sat on the wall and chatted with the Filipino boys, who were smoking cigarettes and enjoying themselves. Only a few had rifles and they told me, "We are Filipino Scouts, sir, of the Engineers. There are sixty of us. The rest are recruits."

Twice the convoy started and we got back in our car, but each time it moved only a few feet and stopped again.

The second time the soldiers remained in their buses, while the three of us got out and sat on the wall. Juan was the first to hear it. Across the river, up on the hill, there was the noise of breaking bushes and of someone or something descending the mountain. He quavered, "Leeeeee. What is that?" I said, "Just a couple of deer." Then we heard it again. Suddenly, I remembered flying over Ningpo, on the China coast, six months before, and watching the Japanese Army land. In six hours their leading units had advanced some fifteen miles inland from the coast. I thought, "This is only six miles from the Lingayen shore and it's been eighteen hours since they landed. Maybe that isn't deer, but Japs."

In the darkness Carlos located the major and called him back to our car. We all listened and heard the unmistakable sounds of many people, or animals, coming down the hillside.

I remembered my ROTC training, many years before. I said, "Look, major, deploy your forces along the wall here. If you have any machine guns put them on top of the buses. We'll turn on the searchlight on our car and you challenge whoever is over there. Maybe they are some of our troops withdrawing from the battle on the beach yesterday." I was thinking of the blond officer and the dark one, and what had happened to their forces when our 155's went off for the first time.

The major was excited, "I have only sixty men with rifles. No machine guns. We had better run on and take a chance of making it."

Just then, we heard a loud explosion from up ahead. "They must have blown the bridge at Klondike," Carlos said. "We can't get through now. We'll have to fight."

"Major," I said, "this looks like a good position to defend. Nobody can come down this hill on the left, except human flies. We can tip our car over on its side, and a few men can control the road from the upper end, since they'll have to come straight at us. They can't climb this wall from the river. We can hold until nearly dawn and then set fire to the buses and get back up the road and into the hills before their dive-bombers get here."

The major, by this time, was jumping with nervousness, and Carlos took over. He ran to the nearest buses, and in Spanish and Tagalog, plus a few words of Igorot, told the boys to pile out and crouch behind the wall. The major saw him and snapped out of it.

He disappeared, running, down the line of trucks and in a few minutes came back. The soldiers piled out, scared and excited, and bumped into each other as they ran to the wall and knelt down. In the darkness they were just shadows.

The last I saw of Carlos was his white shirt, over near the last bus. He seemed to be thoroughly enjoying himself and I knew that he was waving his tiny .25-caliber pistol in his hand and shouting orders. I thought, "Maybe Carlos is a descendant of some great Spanish admiral and just needed this experience to bring out his fighting blood. I can't let him outshine a Lee."

The major came back and stood by the car and said, "O.K." I switched on the light and focused it on the hillside. It was much nearer and lower than it had seemed and the slope down to the stream was only about thirty degrees.

The hillside was covered with trees and brush. We couldn't see anyone moving.

The major challenged, in a loud shout: "Halt, who goes there?" Immediately, from about a dozen places on the hillside, came back grunts and shouts, "Hai," "Ha," "Ho," "Hai," "Ha." Then we heard the sing-song call, "A-tu-ta," which we learned later was the Jap password.

To the right of the car, covering our right flank, I could see about twelve boys crouched beside the wall I snapped out the searchlight.

The major ran back a few steps and pulled out his .45 and fired three quick shots in the air. The recruits who had been alongside the car evidently mistook the shots for the starting pistol of a fifteen-mile race back up the mountain to their homes in Baguio. They stampeded up the road. Juan, who had been in the back seat, jumped past me and took off behind them. He disappeared almost instantly, a thin streak in the darkness.

Our soldiers started firing their Springfields and Enfields, rapid fire. The sound echoed back and forth across the canyon and sounded like thousands of shots. I could hear the bullets smashing into the brush on the hill across the river.

There was a pause while the soldiers reloaded, then another volley. Leaning back against the cliff, with the car between me and the hill across the river, I couldn't hear any shots coming back, nor see any flashes. I thought, "This engagement will go down in the minds of these boys as the Batalla de las Sombras—the shadow fight."

I walked the few feet back to our car and saw the rear door was open and three pair of boots were projecting. Three tiny figures crawled reluctantly out. One of them still had a rifle. He knelt down on the road, while I sat on the running board. He said, "I am wounded, sir." I felt his arm and got blood on my hand. He had another wound in the shoulder. "Kindly do not make me shoot any more, sir." "It's all right," I said. "You do not have to fire anymore."

The second recruit said, "I, also, have been wounded in the arm."

Panic had untied the tongue of the third figure. He chatted on, quietly and continuously. "Oh, sir, I am not a soldier. I am but the pobre caminero from Baguio. I was warned not to take this trip. I wish to return to my home and my wife. I am the poor bus driver, sir, and I do not like wars."

I didn't know where I was going, if any place, so I took all three of them over to their bus, where they crawled onto the floor. I was still not thoroughly convinced there were Japs across the river, and I thought it was possible the two recruits had been wounded by our own fire, in the first confusion.

The firing had ceased for a second time and then suddenly it started up again. There were no flashes from alongside the car, nor behind it. I realized suddenly that I and the Ford were our right flank and rear guard.

The darkness back up the road took on shapes and my imagination created figures which came charging down toward me. They weren't the ragged kids that our officers at Baguio had described to me as landing earlier in the day, but the Japanese landing-party troops I had known back in Shanghai, the husky, blue-uniformed marines with their white puttees and polished bayonets.

I said to myself, crouching there beside the car, "Lee, think how angry your wife would be with you if you were killed here, all uncovered with glory and without killing a single Jap. You know you have to die sometime. You cannot refuse to die for your country. But do you want to die here, now, on this lonely road, bayoneted by a Japanese marine without a chance to fight back?"

The answer was easy. It was "No!" and the indicated action was to get the hell out of there.

There remained the question of Carlos. I had last seen him in the middle of things, running the show, waving his arms and giving orders. I made myself walk down to the left, stumbling along the wall, looking for him. I went about 150 yards, past most of the buses, and couldn't find him or anybody who had seen him. Finally I bumped into the major. He told me, "The muchacho with the white shirt ran up the road when the firing started."

Our troops were still firing sporadically, but apparently some of the Scout sergeants had taken over, because there was less wild shooting and things seemed to be pretty well under control.

I went back to the car and saw that it was on a slight slope to the rear. I left the door open, got behind the wheel, and pushed with one foot. The Ford rolled back, slowly and then faster. My imaginary Japanese marines had disappeared, and the chief danger was that if I started the engine our own troops would shoot at me. I coasted about two hundred yards, and then the decline ended and the road began to climb. I started the engine.

I made several attempts to turn around, but the road was too narrow, or I was shaking too much, and I couldn't negotiate it. So I turned on the lights and backed up, holding the door open and keeping close to the wall, and stepping hard on the gas. Several times the fenders scraped the wall. After at least two miles, I saw a break in the wall and backed into it. There was a level space, apparently a dump or fill-in, projecting about fifteen feet out over the river. The car sank down into the dirt as I jammed on the brake, but before it could slide backward into the river I yanked the gear into low and pulled back onto the road and headed up the mountain toward Baguio.

There were shots for the next five minutes, which sounded as if they were coming from across the canyon. They may have been echoes of shooting farther down, but more likely they were fired by some of our own recruits who had run up the road and were crouching in the brush.

Five miles up the road the headlights illuminated a prostrate figure on a grassy bank at the right of the road. I guessed it was Juan even before I heard his terrified shout, "Leeeeee, for God's sake, stop!" I halted the car, he climbed in, and I drove on.

"Where is Carlos?" I asked.

"He passed me back there, running. Lee! For God's sake! Hurry up Go on!"

"Are you sure he passed you? How did you recognize him?"

"I saw his white shirt, and he shouted at me. I was running as fast as possible but he is an athlete and he passed me."

By this time my conscience was giving me hell. I thought, "Here I am running away and leaving that kid back there." I was driving slower and slower, and finally I stopped in spite of Juan's frantic pleas.

I turned around to him in the back seat and said, "Juan Garcia, kneel down and raise your hand and swear by the Holy Roman Church that you saw Carlos pass you."

He knelt and leaned against the seat and said, "I swear."

"Maybe you aren't a Catholic," I said. "Swear by your mother."

He swore, "By the memory of my mother, I swear he ran by me on the road. He was with five or six soldiers. They overtook and passed me and went up a slope and into the brush. I saw his white shirt and he spoke to me."

"The major told me the same thing," I said, "so it must be true. But if you're lying, cabron, I'll cut off your ears."

Then I drove full speed up the deserted road toward Baguio. All the sentries had disappeared from the bridges, except one. He motioned to us to stop and I asked what he wanted. "I have been ordered to Baguio, sir."

"Whose orders?"

"My captain came down in his car and told me to come back." He climbed in with Juan.

There was no one at the tollgate, but the gate on the left-hand side of the road, our side, was down. I almost smashed into it before we saw it, and then I backed up and circled around the little tollhouse in the middle of the road and went through on the right.

I dropped the soldier in the center of Baguio and drove straight to Major Garcia's house. He woke up after I had pounded on the door for a few minutes, and came down in his dressing gown, carrying a flashlight. We went up to his rooms, on the second floor, and after Juan had calmed down I told the major what had happened.

"Where is the other muchacho?" he asked. Juan told him, and the major said, "He will show up here in the morning.

"I don't know how you got back. I ordered those bridges blown at one o'clock. Well, in any case, we are very nicely cut off here now."

Wearily he pulled on his pants and boots. He said, "If you are going to walk out in the morning, you better get some rest." Juan sprawled on his bed and I lay down on the couch.

The major picked up the telephone and called his office.

"Captain Hernandez? The Japs are on the south road, now, as well as the north. Our convoy seems to be cut off. My orders to blow the bridges have not been carried out... What am I going to do? I am going to fight... With what forces? Well, we have those fifty ROTC cadets. They have six machine guns and I believe they know how to shoot them. Wake them up and tell them to get ready. Get two buses and take them down the road... I'll be right over."

I went to sleep before he went out. The air raid siren woke me in the morning. It wasn't as loud or as startling as the sirens in Manila. It sounded more like the fire alarm they used to blow on bad days back home to tell the kids that there wouldn't be any school.

13

WHILE THE SIREN WAS STILL BLOWING, ONE SINGLE PLANE CAME OVER, flying low through the overcast sky, and dropped one bomb, up by Camp John Hay.

I saw it from the major's dining-room window, which looked out over all of Baguio. I also saw that the town was in a shallow basin, with pine-covered mountains all around. Over to the northeast, toward the Lingayen Gulf shore, there were puffs of anti-aircraft shells. Over the mountains, with the guns out of sight and the planes hidden by clouds, the shell-bursts looked like parachutes cracking open.

"So that's why we've been getting these reports of Japanese parachutists landing in Luzon," I thought. "It was probably anti-aircraft all the time."

We knew our troops were no longer on the beach, and we figured it must be Japanese guns shooting at one of our few remaining planes. We felt sorry for the pilot, but we were glad to know we had a plane left.

There were two second lieutenants of the Philippine Army having breakfast with the major. They told us they had come up the north road during the night, and that most of the forces we had seen there the previous evening had gone on down the south road and gotten through safely. They themselves were taking to the hills and were going to try to walk out and come in behind the Japs and get on to Manila.

They told us they had been in the rear guard fighting down from Vigan, with Major Ganahl. "Our scouts have been outsmarting the Japs, who don't seem to care for night fighting. They don't like hand-to-hand combat either, and in our skirmishes with them we had the best of it. The trouble is that there are too many of them, and they keep coming in behind and cutting us off. But the real reason we are still here, instead of fighting at Vigan, is that they have airplanes, and we don't."

Major Garcia said some of his buses with the recruits had got through to Manila the night before and the remainder had returned to Baguio, a good many of them with wounds. He thought it possible that the road was still open.

He told us Major Ganahl and his troops had driven east into the mountains, where they were to destroy their guns and then walk on out to the Cabanatuan road and try to get buses to take them down to Manila.

Just as we finished breakfast the phone rang. It was Carlos—at the Pines Hotel. "I took to the hills with some soldiers when the shooting started," he said, "and early this morning we got a ride up in one of the troop buses."

"Get ready to walk," I told him. "We are going to try to drive down the road, but if we can't we will leave the car at Itogen and walk over the mountains to San Nicolas."

We said goodbye to Major Garcia. "If you get out and I don't," he said, "please go to headquarters and tell them what is what up here. Tell them to radio some instructions and if they have a spare plane to lend it to us long enough to make a reconnaissance."

I drove up to the Pines Hotel, hoping it would still be possible to get through down the south road. The streets were full of people, running excitedly, and down near the big park in the center of the city a group of young men with knives and rifles and clubs were gathering. Some had uniforms, but most were in civilian clothes. At the hotel we saw forty or fifty cars in the driveway, and others coming in. An excited, frightened group of men and women and some children, most of them Americans, was standing under the portico. They were bewildered, and indignant that the United States would let this happen to them. I talked to some of the men. "We tried to drive down to Manila, but there is fighting on the road. The lower bridges were blown up at six o'clock this morning."

"What will you do now?"

"We are all residents of Baguio, engineers in the gold mines, so we will stay here in the hotel. It has been arranged for foreigners to gather here. Our Japanese business friends are being released from the internment camp. They will meet the Japanese Army officers and arrange for us to have good treatment."

I went back to the car and told Juan and Carlos, "The bridges have been destroyed. We have to walk."

We drove back to the main street and stopped at a Calcutta Indian store, which was about the only one still open. I bought three pair of socks each for Carlos and Juan and myself. We had already filled the tank with gasoline, getting it by showing our press cards just before the service station closed for the last time.

We drove south through the town and up the hill and turned into a side road leading down the mountain to Itogen. There were a number of army trucks and buses and cars, all moving slowly in our direction. I passed one car, after blowing my horn. An American major motioned me over to the side of the road and got out.

"Damn you," he said, "don't blow your horn. Don't you know it is the signal that airplanes are overhead?"

I apologized and we went on, falling in line with the army vehicles. The macadam soon ended and we drove on a dirt road down the steep slope of the mountains, past the entrance to the big gold mines, and a huge refining plant. There were many people walking down the road, Filipino miners and their families. With their battered suitcases they looked more as if they were off for a fiesta and thankful to have a holiday from their work underground than as if they were fleeing.

Curving steeply downward the road came abruptly against a hillside. A side road swung off to the right, straight west. Army buses were parked for a half mile along it and the map showed it was a dead end. Another road curved to the left. The soldiers told us it ended a few hundred yards down and that it led to the trail to San Nicolas and Tayug.

An American major was in charge of the soldiers, who were mostly Filipino Scouts, and I tried to convince him to take over our car, which was no longer of any use to us. I wrote out a receipt, dated December 23, 1942, "Received of Carlos, one Ford sedan, 1938 model, reimbursement to be made after the war." He was holding it in his hand and looking at it, when someone shouted, "Planes!"

There were three of them, twin-engined Navy "96" bombers, flying low and straight up the valley. The soldiers scattered for cover. Juan and I ran a few yards down the left-hand road. He scrambled up the bank and I jumped to the left, off the road. The slope was much steeper than it looked and I started to drop. I grabbed a bush, but it tore out in my hands, and then I grabbed a rock, and it held. The planes looked us over and then went on without dropping any bombs or strafing. Juan came down and gave me a hand to get back up to the road. It was the first and last time I saw him worried about anything but his own safety.

We went back to talk to the major when a lieutenant colonel drove down and called the major over to his car.

"What are you doing here? Your orders were to go down the south road from Baguio and join our forces behind Lingayen Gulf."

"I started down, sir, but we ran into Jap machine guns at the bridges and turned back."

"Where are your seventy-fives?"

"Some of them we destroyed by pushing them into the rivers on the south road. The others are here."

The colonel lowered his voice. "Well, I suppose you did right. But I believe I would have tried to fight my way through."

I left them discussing what to do next. Later I learned that most of them were cut off in the hills, where they were operating as guerrillas for the next few months and may possibly still be fighting.

We couldn't sell our car to the major, so we drove on down the left road. Around the bend we ran into more buses and trucks. Soldiers were pushing them over the bank into a 250-foot ravine on the left. We went through the car and took the things we thought we needed. The new socks, Carlos's .25 pistol, a jacket and a box of crackers, and the Standard Oil map. Everything else we left in the car. My camera had disappeared during the night.

Carlos sprinkled some gasoline on the car, and threw a lighted match while Juan and I gave it a push. Flames shot up as it crashed over and down into the gully. Carlos said, "Adios, Fordcito."

We walked on down the road, crossed a stream by jumping from boulder to boulder, and started up the path on the other side. Our map showed that the trail we wanted followed the course of the San Nicolas River most of the way. The river, down on our left, seemed to spring out of the mountains behind us, somewhere near the smelter. There, and for miles downstream, it was discolored with oil which the American engineers had dumped from their tanks at the mines.

Before we had gone a mile Carlos and Juan ran into a friend from Manila, a college student, who told us to take the right-hand path, up the hill. He was headed for the sawmill, where his mother had taken refuge.

For the next two miles the path climbed steeply, then it leveled off and ran the same distance from the summit of the mountains while the river and the valley floor dropped steadily away beneath us. The mountains had been stripped of trees and we could see for miles ahead where the path wound around the hills. Little groups of people were strung at intervals along the path. We overtook a party of American Army doctors, with two American nurses and several Filipino Scouts. They had been ordered to evacuate Camp John Hay. As far as we could learn, they never reached Manila but remained somewhere in the hills to sit out the war.

The path was so narrow that when we overtook a group of people they would have to crowd back against the hillside while we inched past, trying not to look at the steep drop beside us. At one place, where the path had partially crumbled away and the hill dropped sheer for more than five hundred feet, I became suddenly dizzy and Carlos had to give me a hand across the break.

The next two days are a confused jumble of impressions: vividly beautiful vistas of terraced rice fields and the river far beneath us; heat and fatigue and hunger; the blessings of cool streams flowing out of the mountains every few miles, where our fellow refugees stopped to cook and rest, and where we drank greedily and bathed our faces and wrists; whole families of Filipinos trudging drearily and steadily along the trail, the women carrying babies on their backs and the men bent over with the weight of huge packs; miners with their pith helmets, most of them carefully carrying their pet fighting cocks under their arms; the fact that everybody, everywhere, spoke some words of English and with it the realization that our occupation of the Philippines had given us obligations; withered Igorot women wearing horizontally striped skirts of faded cotton, and nothing else, and their men wearing shirts, and nothing else; jaunty Igorots riding sure-footed horses at a trot along that narrow trail, one rider wearing a smart, heavy tweed jacket and a stock around his neck, and no pants; villages of four or five grass huts built on stilts, with the dogs sharing the interior with the family and the pigs dozing underneath; Juan's haunting fear.

Those people were fleeing from a terror that had come on them out of the skies. We were racing for our freedom. We rested only a few minutes at a time, while we bathed and drank, and then kept going, putting one weary foot ahead of the other.

That first night we stayed in a small village by the riverbank, as guests of the village headman. The friend whom Juan and Carlos had met back at the start of the trail had sent word on ahead, in some manner unknown to us, and we were accepted, if not welcomed. At twilight, which lasted only a few minutes, we sat in front of our host's home and watched the young girls threshing rice, while boys and chickens and pigs raced around the stone enclosure that bounded the village. The houses were of nipa and built on stilts, except for the headman's home which was three stories high, built of lumber, and with a tin roof. The sliding windows reminded me unpleasantly of Japanese homes.

The headman spoke a queer Spanish, consisting mostly of infinitives, but we could converse. I was amazed to learn that he knew the war was going badly for us; that the enemy had command of the air. He said, "Aviones Americanos no estar aqui. Porqui?" The same question, "Where are our airplanes?"

A Belgian priest lived in a tiny combination chapel and home outside the village wall. He told us, "These people are suspicious. They think perhaps you were sent to bring airplanes against them. They have already heard that airplanes spread death and fire. So you had better hope no planes come tonight."

We hoped hard, until exhaustion closed our eyes.

We started walking again shortly after daylight, with a guide furnished by the headman showing us the way. We were told that by hard walking it was possible to reach San Nicolas by sundown. The guide was relieved at the next village by another young man, and so on. These boys spoke English and proudly wore their silver badges of the National Guides organization. They were friendly and helpful, but I grew to hate them for the effortless way they walked, setting a pace that at times had us running to keep up. They knew every step of the way and where the path frequently led through rice fields and over fences, they knew exactly which fence rail or which boulder to step on and would go up and over the obstacle without breaking stride. Their bare feet, of course, made no noise, but as the hours went on it seemed that each of their steady, unfaltering steps was a hammer pounding at the back of my head.

The second day we forded the San Nicolas River sixteen times. Once the water was nearly to my shoulder and we had to struggle to get across. Once we crossed on a rickety suspension bridge, fifty feet above the riverbed. Almost all the wooden flooring was rotted away and shook unsteadily on the wires.

When one of us stopped to rest or put on a new pair of socks, the others kept going and the straggler would have to run to catch up. Once I plunged, clothes and all, into the river to cool off and was refreshed until the sun dried me out.

The worst part was climbing over the last hump of the sierras that second morning. The top looked deceptively near. Toward the summit it was like climbing an interminable ladder with every other rung missing. The trail consisted of long steps chopped out of the hillside. At the last we were making only twenty or thirty of these steps before having to rest. We overtook an American mining man near the top. He joined us and shared some tinned soup he was carrying.

"I left Baguio yesterday afternoon and kept walking most of the night, with my flashlight. The garrison was ordered to abandon Camp John Hay. Some of the miners dynamited the equipment there. We also destroyed our own supplies and flooded the gold mines. It will be a long while before the Japs can use them."

That climb was the worst, until later in the afternoon, when we thought all the climbing was behind us. Wherever possible the path followed the river winding over and between boulders, but in some places the hills came right down to the river's edge and the path climbed steeply up one side and down the other. We made many of those climbs on hands and knees.

By four in the afternoon there were unmistakable signs that we were approaching the lowlands. The river widened and flowed more slowly. We hoped that every hill we went around or over would be the last, but always there was one more behind it.

It was nearly 6 P.M., when the last guide left us at the last fording place. He said, "San Nicolas is just ahead." By that time there were people coming up the trail in the opposite direction, headed for the mountains, and they told us the Japs were already close to Tayug. They said, "San Nicolas is just ahead there." But it wasn't. There were rice fields, and some sugar cane and flatlands. But not San Nicolas.

When we finally came to a village, over across the rice fields, it was Santa Maria. But it was good enough. There were ten or twelve houses along the single street, and a few horse-drawn calesas. We breathed a prayer of thanksgiving at being back once more in civilization—meaning vehicles.

Carlos ran up the street, sprinting, and in a few minutes came back with two calesas. We were afraid that the weight of the four of us in one vehicle would hoist the tiny horse off the ground in his shafts.

The calesa drivers said they could take us to San Nicolas, three miles down the road, but no farther. "This road is now our front line and our soldiers are on it, closer to Tayug. There has been fighting all day a little to the north, with many airplanes and much noise of guns."

Carlos said, "Well, if our army is still on the road it means we've made it. If we can make it to Tayug we can get through to Manila." None of us had dared to mention the goal of our flight before now. Carlos was riding with me in the calesa, and we studied the Standard Oil map again. If the road to Tayug was blocked we decided to hike across the fields to Victoria during the night and try to get on in the morning.

We reached San Nicolas with surprising speed and pulled up in the tiny plaza in front of the rickety church. I argued with the drivers.

"Ten pesos to Tayug."

"I regret, sirs, that it is impossible to go further."

"Fifteen pesos for a few miles. Surely it is more than you have made in one day in your life, viejo."

Finally they gave in. For fifteen pesos they would take us as far as the first sentry, and no farther. Going west again, with the bony horses trotting, we passed many calesas and carabao-drawn carts fleeing toward the mountains. The drivers were urging on their animals, hoping to reach shelter before night which was only a few minutes away.

Over to the right, toward Lingayen Gulf but much nearer, was the smoke of two huge fires. "From the airplanes, this afternoon," the driver explained.

We were watching for the sentries, with our eyes on a carabao cart a quarter of a mile ahead of us. Suddenly it disappeared in a crashing explosion. When we reached the wreckage our drivers refused to go any farther. There were two dead men and a dead carabao in the road, and a small group of people had gathered around them. They said, "It was a landmine, sir."

A few hundred yards further on we reached the sentries. Only a faint flush of light was left in the sky. We showed them our press cards and told them:

"We come from the northern front. It is imperative that we be taken to your headquarters to report."

One of them led us down the road toward a car which we could see dimly a quarter mile farther on. In the near darkness it was impossible to make out the black dust covering the landmines planted in the road. I would have stepped on one except for the sentry, who grabbed my shoulder and pulled me back when my foot was already in the air and descending. I was too dead beat to worry about it and the incident seemed unimportant, although neither before nor since have I come any closer to being killed.

The car turned out to be a light truck, with red crosses painted on its sides. The driver was a young Filipino, not over fourteen, and his mother was in the seat beside him. The sentry jumped on the running board and ordered the boy to drive us to headquarters.

We drove to headquarters and found that headquarters was not there. It had just moved five miles to the south, at Victoria. The driver took us to the hospital.

"I am sorry, sirs, but I cannot leave. My duty is here and I may be of some use."

A large, open truck drove up and a group of patients who were not badly wounded came out of the hospital and climbed in. The driver told us he was going to Victoria and there was room for us. The wounded boys were boasting about fighting the Japs at Vigan and along the Lingayen Gulf. "Those Japs are no good, sir," they said. Many of them had four or five wounds from the Japanese .25 caliber rifles and one had ten wounds in his back from a Japanese machine gun of similar caliber.

The driver backed around and headed south, following the roads by the light of the moon which was now shining brightly on the Pangasinan plains. The miner suddenly said, "So it's Christmas Eve. And instead of Saint Nicholas coming to us, we've been to San Nicolas."

My own thoughts were, "And this is the night I was going to walk up Fifth Avenue in the snow."

14

THERE WAS NOT MUCH TRAFFIC ON THE ROAD, except tanks. We had to pull over while some tanks overtook us. Then other tanks passed going the other way, northward toward the front.

Once, when we stopped, I had a few words with an American boy whose head was sticking out of a tank turret. He told me he was from Harrodsburg, Kentucky. "How is it going?"

"Not bad, except for their planes. When we pull under a tree and hide, and get everything camouflaged, it doesn't seem to take twenty minutes for their planes to find us."

"Sounds like it's all done with mirrors."

"You said it. Somebody is tying mirrors or pieces of steel to the trees around our positions. The pilots see the flash of sunlight on them, and dive down and strafe and bomb us."

"Where are you heading now?"

"Looks like everything is moving gradually south. We've been fighting delaying actions, holding bridges and shooting the Japs when they come down the roads, while our infantry withdraws behind us. When their tanks come, or they surround us, we are ordered to get out to the south."

"Merry Christmas!"

The tank threw up clouds of dust in the moonlight as it pulled away.

At Victoria we were arrested by the constabulary and taken to the police station. Our miner companion had a German-sounding name and no identification papers, but we quickly convinced the sergeant that all of us should be taken to Army Headquarters.

Headquarters were in the village market building, which was open on the sides with a concrete roof. Troops were moving about the yard and others were asleep on the concrete floor.

A sentry took me to the intelligence officer, a major whose features I could not make out in the darkness under the roof.

I told him about the 71st—the regiment of the blond officer and the dark one—and about Major Ganahl, and the south road to Baguio being blocked, and the troops cut off in the hills at Itogen, and the nurses and doctors hiking through the mountains. He thanked me, but wasn't especially interested.

"What is the situation here?" I asked.

"It has been necessary to order a general withdrawal to the south from Lingayen Gulf, to prevent the Japs who landed on the east shore of the gulf from coming around in the rear of our forces. Here we are on the right flank of the line, which extends all the way westward to the Zambales mountains."

"What's up in front of us?"

"Twenty-sixth Cavalry is holding the right flank. They have been fighting magnificently and have held up the enemy by rearguard actions. They are now bivouacked for the night in Tayug."

The major said, "Excuse me, there's General Wainright." He went over to greet a tall figure stepping out of a car. The officers surrounded him and took him aside before I could speak to him.

Our sentry led us back to the police station and we inquired about transportation to Manila. "There is a train in the morning."

We wanted to make sure whether or not we were under arrest.

"If you don't mind we will go over to the station tonight and sleep there to be certain we do not miss the train."

"Certainly. The sergeant will show you the way."

Near the station we heard a train whistle and broke into a run. An engine, pulling a single caboose, was just about to start for Tarlac. We climbed into the caboose and stretched out on the floor. There were a few soldiers, Americans and Filipinos, and one of them opened a can of beans and we had a spoonful each. During the night the miner woke me several times. "Look at the moon," he said. "It has shifted to the wrong side. Are you sure we aren't going north?" I was too tired to care much where we were going, but I assured him we were headed south. Under the bright moon the rice fields looked golden and peaceful.

We awakened in Tarlac, at about four in the morning, and piled out onto the station and promptly fell asleep on the benches.

When the train for Manila came in, at 8:50 A.M., the long station platform was jammed with people. There were many American miners who had hiked out over the hills from Baguio, and Filipino families with bulging suitcases. Many of the Filipinos had come from Lingayen Gulf towns, where their homes had been bombed. Everybody had one idea in mind: to get south, to Manila, and away from the invaders advancing from the north.

The train backed and went forward, and picked up and dropped cars, for nearly half an hour. When we finally started south the station clock said 9:19 A.M.

Just twelve minutes later, as we learned shortly afterwards, Japanese planes dived low over the station. They dive-bombed first and then raked the platform with their .25 caliber machine guns and 20-mm. cannon. Twenty-seven people were killed and some fifty or sixty wounded. We saw photographs showing where one bomb hit, just where we had been sitting.

There was an aging American woman schoolteacher in our crowded first-class compartment. "I have been in the Philippines for nearly thirty years. I was principal of a school at Lingayen City. We were forced to close our school by the authorities and I left there yesterday. Up to then the Japanese had not landed, but we heard they were coming down over to the east." She was indignant because the U.S. Army had taken the school fence to build barricades out in the gulf. She wanted me to put a story in the papers about her fence.

The train got more and more crowded, so Carlos and I pushed out onto the platform and stood there. We spotted smoke in the distance and climbed to the swaying top of a box-car which was coupled on behind the first-class carriage. The train came rapidly abreast of the smoke and we saw it was at Clark Field. There were two huge columns, the black smoke of burning oil, with high flames shooting up through the smoke. We could see a few wrecked planes on the wide runways, and the hangars seemed to have been badly hit. There were other, smaller fires in the barracks and houses at Camp Stotsensburg, which adjoined Clark Field.

The train stopped at a station just opposite the fires. U.S. soldiers were on duty on the platform. I called to one of them.

"They bomb you again this morning?"

"Hell, no! Set it ourselves." Then, proudly, "There's two hundred thousand gallons of aviation gasoline burning there."

"It's a pretty fire but what in hell did you set it for? Isn't this our main airfield?"

"It was, but a field's no damn good without airplanes. And we are slightly short of airplanes."

"Where you fellows going from here?"

"Don't know yet. South somewhere."

We told him that a huge, inflated inner tube for a bomber tire had bounced off a flat car a few miles up the track, and he promised to send someone to investigate. There were other tubes in the car, and two boxes marked "Wright Cyclone Airplane Engine."

Carlos scrambled down and bought a newspaper and we read a statement by General MacArthur: "In order to spare Manila from any possible air or ground attacks, consideration is being given by military authorities to declaring Manila an open city, as was done in the case of Paris, Brussels, and Rome during this war." Somehow, that didn't sound like MacArthur.

In the next two hours the train stopped five or six times for air raid alarms. Watchers along the track waved to the engineer when they spotted planes overhead. He blew the whistle and everybody got out of the train and scattered into the fields. When the planes passed over the whistle blew again and we climbed back aboard. Near the small station of San Marcos about thirty-five miles north of Manila the alarm turned out to be the real thing. By that time we knew of the bombing of Tarlac station.

The planes came over from the direction of Manila. They were the lowest that I had seen Jap heavy bombers flying, so low we could easily see the Rising Sun and the retracted landing gear. They couldn't have been over eight thousand feet. There were nine in the first "V" and they flew straight over the train.

Suddenly, from all around us, anti-aircraft batteries opened up. Three inches and 37-mm.'s and even machine guns peppered the sky around the planes. We crawled out from the ditch where we were sheltering and cheered.

"Hit the god-damn' bastards! Knock them down!"

The shells burst all around the planes. Finally they broke formation, and the last three swung out and away to the south. Then, when they were out of range, they joined up again. Nine more came over, then nine more. These last two flights also broke formation, but as far as we could see none was hit.

Those planes had been to Olangapo, where they plastered the American naval station and pounded the 4th U.S. Marines who had come down from Shanghai just before the war started. They also hit Fort Wint and as a result of their attacks our forces were driven out of Olangapo and Fort Wint and the shores of Subic Bay were open to the Japs. But fortunately, the Japs never found it out.

We rode all the way into Manila on top of the freight car and all along the way the people were still cheering and saluting with the "V" signal and shouting, "Keep 'em flying!"

I went straight to our office in the TVT and just as I walked in the telephone rang. It was from Admiral Hart's office. The admiral had a "Christmas present" for the people of America—and of the Philippines, One of his subs had sunk a ship, or damaged one, in a harbor on Luzon. After what we had seen it didn't seem very important. After all, the Japs were already ashore in force and sinking or damaging one of their ships now wasn't going to affect the battle of Luzon very much.

It was dark by the time I finished writing my stories and went back to the Manila Hotel for a shave and bath. I was pretty ragged and dirty, but the people sitting around the big Christmas tree in the lobby crowded around and begged for news. I told them everything was going all right, that the 26th Cavalry and our tanks were doing wonders, and that as soon as our airplanes arrived from the United States we would get busy and push the Japs back into the sea.

"But why didn't our Asiatic Fleet and our subs sink their ships before they reached the Philippines?" they asked. I didn't know the answer to that one, at the time.

Mel and Annalee Jacoby came over for Christmas dinner, and Russell Brines came by from the office and joined us. We had turkey and a bottle of champagne, and they told me what had been going on in Manila. The Japs had bombed the waterfront the day before, and had killed thirty people in one of the big buildings opposite Pier 7. They didn't know any reason why Manila should be declared an open city. The people were still full of fight and confidence.

Brines asked Annalee to dance and I said to Mel, "It looks like everything is folding up, fast. Time to get moving somewhere. Especially you, as you are on their blacklist for your work for the Chinese government in Chungking."

"I hear that your name is about third on their Navy's blacklist," Mel said. "You better not stick around too long either."

I spread out my Standard Oil road map on the table and we began looking for ways out. We puzzled over the names of islands we had never heard of before. The only way seemed to be south, first to the island of Mindoro and then on down through the Philippine Archipelago and eventually to the Dutch East Indies. We didn't know if transportation was available, but we agreed to investigate in the morning.

When the Jacobys left, Brines and I went up to my room. I had moved from the air-conditioned section of the hotel to the fourth floor, where I had a wide window and an unobstructed view of the docks and bay. We sat in front of the window, in the blackout, looking at the bay, which was lighted by a few bomb-lit fires along the shore and by the moon and Venus, whose path was clearly visible even in the moonlight and firelight. Corregidor, looking like a huge whale looming out of the water, seemed only a few miles away.

I told Brines our experiences in the last four days, and a number of things that can't be written even yet.

He said, "Write it."

"Not a chance," I said. "Not even Hollywood would go for it. All the fires and falling of the cliffs and nearly stepping on landmines, and just not getting killed at Tarlac, and the rest of it. It's too melodramatic."

I was about to say more when Cavite suddenly blew up right in front of my face.

15

THE FIRST EXPLOSION WAS A BLINDING WHITE FLASH which rolled and spread across the bay. There was blast after blast, which rattled all the walls in Manila, and then soaring columns of flame. There were no enemy planes in the air and we realized instantly that it was not an air raid but that our own Navy had decided the Battle of the Philippines was lost and was itself destroying stores and shore installations and ammunition to keep them from falling into the hands of the enemy. "Jesus!" Russell said, not irreverently, "we've been building that place up for more than forty years. Now we blow it up. That's the end of the U.S.A. in the Philippines for a while."

Just to see if we could do it we picked up a newspaper and read some of the small type by the light of the explosions nine miles away. The white flashes of burning powder were punctuated by red streaks as exploding shells shot into the air.

"Since Dewey sailed in here a lot of people have watched a lot of spectacular sunsets across this bay," I said, "but nobody has seen any like this before."

"That's a sunrise, too," Russell said. "The Rising Sun of Dai Nippon."

Too dazed to do anything but just sit and watch, I told Russell, "You write the story." He took my portable typewriter and began to write by the light of the explosions. His story was a masterpiece, not only for its description of the scene but as an account of the general public bewilderment at the way things were going in the Philippines. When I got to New York I went to The AP office to look up the story in the files, but it had never come through. Apparently the censors killed it.

That same night Admiral Thomas C. Hart, commander in chief of the U.S. Asiatic Fleet, climbed over the deck of one of his submarines and stepped down into the conning tower.

With his piercing eye, which his subordinates said could drill a hole in the armor of a battleship, he looked around at the men he was leaving behind. He said, "Goodbye and good luck," and then he told the captain of the submarine to set a course for Java.

Hart had tried to get away the previous night in one of the few PBY patrol planes that were still flying. I met the pilot later in Bataan. He told me: "I had the plane wide open and running along the water for a take-off when I saw a small boat crossing my course. I tried to swerve but one of my wings clipped the boat. We worked all next day to repair the damage but then the admiral decided to go by submarine. So here I am with a rifle." Later, the pilot was taken out by submarine to Australia.

With Hart, in other submarines, went Rear Admiral William Glassford and a number of other staff officers. Only a few high ranking naval men stayed behind. Rear Admiral Rockwell went to Corregidor and set up headquarters for what was left of the 16th Naval District. Captain Ray and Captain Hoeffel and a number of communications men accompanied him. There were also some torpedo experts who, while the torpedoes lasted, supplied the PT boats and the submarines that occasionally came into Corregidor. These men and the sailors who fought with rifles in the jungle, and all the other naval personnel that Hart left behind, fought bravely and well during the Battle of Bataan.

But the Asiatic Fleet as a whole was never an important factor in the fight in the Philippines. It was unable to halt the enemy landings on Luzon or to cause any considerable damage to the Japanese Fleet.

That was not the fault of the American naval men. The fact was that the Asiatic Fleet was not a fighting force. It was an ineffective symbol of naval power, a little stick which the United States carried while talking loudly in the Far East. Soon after the war started most of the Fleet went to Java.

From time to time before he left for Java, Admiral Hart called in the reporters in Manila or telephoned to give us some news of the activities of the units under his command. A number of his patrol planes had been caught on the water and destroyed by Japanese fighter planes at Olangapo, but the planes that were left did what they could in defense of the Philippines before they too were withdrawn to the south. The PBY's carried out several scouting and bombing missions despite the fact that they were too big and slow to defend themselves successfully in combat.

At one press conference in his headquarters in the Marsman Building on the Manila waterfront. Admiral Hart told us about what his PBY's had done. "One of them sighted a Japanese battleship of the Kongo class and got a direct hit with a bomb. When last seen the ship was out of control and its steering apparatus was obviously crippled."

"Do you think it was sunk?" a reporter asked.

"Ships that are out of control usually have a difficult time getting home," the admiral answered. But that one apparently

We heard later that the PBY's that Hart had taken south to Java with him had continued to fly until all but three were shot down. They made one raid on Japanese shipping at Jolo. In the final days of the Battle of the Philippines some PBY's flew into Corregidor under the muzzles of Japanese guns on the shores of Cavite and Bataan, and succeeded in rescuing a number of American nurses.

Hart's submarines didn't have very good hunting in the days when the Japanese were landing on Luzon. One submarine went into Lingayen Gulf on the morning of December 22. It drew a bead on the nearest Japanese transport and fired a torpedo. The sub commander pinned his eye to the telescope and watched the wake of the torpedo headed straight at the enemy ship. Nothing happened. The torpedo had gone under the shallow-draft vessel. The submarine submerged.

Then a Japanese destroyer raced over and dropped depth charges around the submarine. The waters of Lingayen Gulf are only eighty-six feet deep in that area and the "ash cans" burst all around the sub. For three days it was pinned to the bottom, after which it finally escaped and got back into Manila on Christmas Day.

I met one of the crew, a husky, bearded veteran chief petty officer who had spent twelve years in submarines. We were in a restaurant and he was telling about the experience in Lingayen, when the air raid siren sounded. The sailor rushed to the door and looked frantically for a taxi. "Take it easy," I advised him. "The Japs have never bombed this part of the city."

"To hell with this," he said. "Don't you realize that this is dangerous? I'm going back to my submarine where it's safe."

That submarine and its crew were still in action many months later. It made at least one trip into Corregidor to bring supplies and to take out naval personnel, and on its way out it attacked three Japanese destroyers in the narrow waters of the Philippines. Lieutenant Vince Schumacher who had served with the PT boats was on board the sub and told me about it:

"We spent three days on the bottom after firing our fish and were bounced around the whole time. The lights went out and the paint was knocked off the hull but the skipper never stopped grinning. He actually liked it. Said that after the experience in Lingayen he didn't feel good unless a scrap was going on. His feeling must have been catching because I've decided that I prefer subs to PT boats. I'm on my way home now to get training for submarine work."

Outside of the press conferences called by Hart, as spokesman for the "silent service," we didn't have much opportunity for contact with the Navy during the days when our Army was withdrawing into Bataan. We soon realized that our concept of the Asiatic Fleet as a "suicide" force which would rip into the Japs before they reached Luzon was erroneous. What Hart did was to keep his force intact and to use it to protect ships which fled from Manila to Malaya and Java. The surface force remained nearly intact—until the battle of the Java Sea.

En route to Java, the U.S.S. Marblehead was bombed for hours by Japanese planes which left it lying helpless in the water. Those of the crew who were not killed patched up the ship somehow and finally brought it safely to New York after an epic trip halfway around the world.

The Houston, and the American destroyers Pillsbury and Pope were sent to the bottom in the Java Sea battle, but two other destroyers succeeded in escaping past Bali and reached Australia.

Months later I went aboard one of the destroyers in a tiny port in the South Seas to which she had just escorted a convoy. Officers told me that prior to the Java Sea battle four American destroyers had encountered a Japanese convoy in Macassar Straits and had damaged four of the enemy transports in a night sea battle.

That, they said, was all there was to the so-called Macassar Straits battle, which was hailed in Allied newspapers at the time as a great victory for our forces.

16

THE MORNING PAPERS OF DECEMBER 26 ANNOUNCED that General MacArthur had proclaimed Manila an open city in a declaration dated December 24. The Tribune and Bulletin headlines said, "Manila Open City." The Spanish language papers headlined, "Manila es Ciudad Abierta." In Tagalog and Ilocano and Viscayan the dialect newspapers made the same announcement.

When I went out of the hotel in the morning I saw that the troops of New Mexico's 200th had departed and taken their anti-aircraft guns with them. Only the pits they had dug and their foxholes remained along the bayfront. The machine guns were gone from the walls of Intramuros. The fires at Cavite were billowing white and black smoke high into the morning air, and there were oil fires at Nichols Field.

In the streets and in restaurants and offices I heard the people of Manila discussing this new turn of events.

"What is this ciudad abierta, this open city?"

"It means that we are removing all our forces from the city and asking the enemy not to bomb it. The purpose is to safeguard lives and prevent destruction of that which we do not have the forces to defend."

"It is what they did in Paris before the government fled and the Germans came in."

"Does it mean that the enemy is coming here? What has happened to our Army?"

"Our Army is fighting well. Have you not read the communiques?"

"It means, in effect, that we are throwing ourselves on the mercy of the enemy."

"Yes, of an enemy whose soldiers spread murder and rape throughout China."

Where is the American Navy and why does it not smash their invasion fleet?"

"Maybe it would be better if we would fight the Japanese in the streets and from our houses, as they did in Odessa. Maybe we should fight them with our knives and bolos and clubs. Maybe it would be better to die fighting than to let them kill us later, at their leisure. After all, if we hold them for a few days, help will be here from our big brothers."

By that time I had begun to realize that we did not have the forces to defend Manila and to suspect that the path to the capital was being thrown open to the Japanese in the hope that when they arrived in the city without having to fight, they would be well under control of their officers and would observe discipline; whereas if they came in fighting and overwhelmed our forces they would be more likely to rape and kill and loot.

We were still hopeful that the tide would turn, even though the Japanese had poured more men into the battle in northern Luzon and on the 26th reached a point less than one hundred miles from the capital. MacArthur and his staff had "taken the field" on the 24th. Rumors spread that MacArthur was massing his forces north of the capital on the plains of Pampanga and that a decisive battle would be fought there. The hope of the populace rose, because the people loved MacArthur and believed no enemy on earth could defeat him.

Secretary Knox gave fresh encouragement when he announced that the United States Navy was taking definite and positive measures which would result in aid to the Philippines. But the optimism lasted only until the people read President Roosevelt's promise that the freedom of the Philippines would be "redeemed."

"Redeemed!" That meant that the war was lost.

Fear spread through Manila and the rate of exodus from the city increased. The roads back into the hills were black with people striving to reach their native villages before the murderous armies overwhelmed them. The few trains still running into the provinces were literally jammed to the car tops. The business district, which, despite the air raids, had been crowded with shoppers on December 24, began to look deserted. The Japanese stores had been closed the day the war started, and now many Filipino, American, and Chinese establishments closed their doors.

High Commissioner Sayre tried to restore the confidence of the people. He declared that the declaration of an open city did not mean surrender in the Philippines. "We will fight to the last man!"

The military authorities ordered that the blackout be terminated and the city's lights turned on in keeping with the "opening" of the city. That first night, police had to go through the streets and threaten many residents with arrest unless they tore down their blackout curtains and lighted their lights. The people clung to the darkness, fearing that lights would invite night attacks by the enemy airplanes.

The Japanese considered the opening of the city a cynical and "unilateral" act, without binding force on themselves. They considered it an invitation to bomb. They came in mid-morning of December 27, while we were at the USAFFE press conference. The conference had been shifted from No.1 Calle Victoria to a convent school around the corner. Lieutenant Colonel Herb Harries, a West Pointer who had been recalled to active service, had replaced Major Diller as spokesman.

Colonel Harries was cool and a little sardonic at times and he spoke firmly and decisively. He was reading the morning communique in a slow, clear voice when the first bombs hit the waterfront only a few hundred yards away. When the bombs burst one reporter started running and then there was a general stampede into the patio where some threw themselves on their faces and others crouched behind pillars.

When the planes passed we climbed shamefacedly to our feet and went back to the office. Colonel Harries was still seated at his desk. He looked at us over his glasses.

"You were saying, Colonel—"

The colonel picked up where he had left off and finished his statement deliberately. He told us the Japs advancing from the north had reached Moncada, only eighty-five miles from Manila.

We waited out the rest of the morning raid in a big trench in front of the barracks across from No.1 Victoria.

The planes came back again about three in the afternoon and for two hours they plastered the waterfront area where members of the Army Quartermaster Corps were forced to abandon their work of loading supplies into barges and trucks. The supplies were being sent to Corregidor. I noticed that the big freighter Don Josi had departed. The Japanese bombing was erratic that day and most of the bombs landed in the water between the piers. Some holes were torn in the street along the waterfront and a few fires started.

Jacoby and I watched the bombing from my hotel window.

"What have you found out about ways to get out of here?"

"The best way seems to be to go from here to Batangas by car. It is about forty miles due south. From there we can probably get a motor launch to the island of Mindoro, then pick up a banca and sail a short way down the coast, get another banca and make our way from island to island."

Bancas are small canoes carved out of tree trunks and equipped with double outriggers to give them stability. Many of them have sails.

"If we can make the island of Mindanao," I said, "we can probably get a bigger boat, a Moro fishing vinta, and run through the straits between Zamboanga and Jolo and get to Borneo and then to the Dutch East Indies."

"How about going around the east coast of Mindanao and trying to reach Australia?"

"That is another possibility, but we'll have to sneak past Davao at night. The Japs have Davao now."

We decided to wait another day or two.

When I got back from the office late that evening I found Captain Villamor of the Philippine Air Force sitting alone in the Bamboo Grill at the Manila Hotel. None of the Americans there recognized him as the aviator who had just received the DSC and the Oak Leaf cluster for his two air victories over the Japanese. Jess looked like a lonesome man with no place to go. There were two beds in my room and I invited him to spend the night there.

Out of his airplane, there was nothing of the daredevil about Jess. He was serious, sincere, and thoughtful, a student of his people, and he was worried about them now. Several other pilots from his squadron joined us and we talked things over for a couple of hours.

In the morning I awakened in the middle of a nightmare. I had dreamed that bombs were dropping somewhere nearby. I opened my eyes. Jess Villamor was gone, the sun was shining, and there was no noise. I went back to sleep.

Then the dream started again and I jumped out of bed. I was just in time to see huge columns of water spurting up around two ships, both new freighters of about 3,000 tons, which were anchored inside the breakwater directly in front of the hotel and about eight hundred yards from my window. The planes went away and nine others came over, very low. They were twin-engined bombers.

For over an hour they attacked the ships in relays of three "V's," each consisting of nine planes. Finally their bombs hit just alongside the ship farthest from shore. It began to settle immediately and in a few minutes it was resting on the bottom with only its masts and the top of its bridge standing above the shallow water. Then the bombers went after the other ship.

I took a few pictures with my movie camera as the bombers made their runs and then I dressed and went down to the lobby. There were people sitting on the wide stairs and in chairs, and others walking around. You could hear the airplane motors clearly and each time they approached, the people drew up their muscles tensely. When the bombs hit and burst, everyone made an instinctive protective motion to duck. If two people were sitting side by side, one would duck to the left and the other to the right. Others would crouch down close to the floor.

One plump blond woman in pink slacks kept walking about the lobby. With each series of explosions she would throw herself flat on the floor and roll frantically over and over until the noise subsided. Then she would rise and pace back and forth again.

I walked through the lobby and the huge dining and dance pavilion. A group of Spanish jai alai players were sitting on the railing on the bay side watching the bombing, and Frank Hewlett and Bert Covitt of the United Press. We watched the bombers come over again and again, trying to hit the remaining ship. Finally they got one direct hit on the forecastle and it started to settle. In twenty minutes it was on the bottom. It did not catch fire and we didn't see anybody get off.

During the bombing the hotel waiters placed a large table in the center of the dance floor and served a buffet lunch, with apologies for not producing the usual menu.

In making their runs on the target the bombers came directly toward us sometimes, and sometimes from back over our heads. But we had a fair amount of confidence in their bombing by then and were pretty sure they weren't trying to hit the hotel, so we stayed and watched. After the bombers laid their eggs and went over the city we heard the brief tack-a-tack-a-tack-a of machine-gun fire. The tail gunners in the planes were apparently trying to hit the trucks along the waterfront, or maybe just keeping their hands in.

Usually the planes came nine by nine by nine, but sometimes all twenty-seven would drop at once. They had a beautiful maneuver for turning and regaining formation. The middle nine would fly straight ahead while the right-hand nine broke away and climbed and the left-hand group turned off and dived slightly. The three sections would make their turns independently, and the middle one fly straight back toward the target. Then the right-hand group would dive and the section on the left climb, both coming back into position by the leader simultaneously. They had so many bombs that it was obvious they were flying from bases pretty close by, probably at Aparri, and didn't have to take up much of their load with gasoline.

After sinking the second ship they stayed away so long that we thought they had gone to rearm and refuel. Hewlett and Covitt went back to their office and I went inside to get a sandwich. By that time Mel Jacoby had come over. Mel and I heard the planes again. There were forty-nine now. They flew in from the bay, over the waterfront and MacArthur's headquarters without dropping, and then let go their bombs over the northwest corner of Intramuros. The whole corner of the walled city seemed to rise in the air. Flames and smoke shot up.

Jacoby and I got in his car and drove over. All of our soldiers had gone from Intramuros and when they left the Filipinos had become frightened and fled to the hills. The stores and houses were closed tight.

We parked a block from the fires and walked over. The streets were littered with dust and rubble, and wooden slats and sheets of tin from the roofs. Several buildings were caved-in completely. Two Catholic schools had been hit squarely. From the dust in the streets I picked up a school copybook, with English phrases in it, and a small American flag.

Flames were licking an upper corner of one of the twin towers of the Santo Domingo Church and the firemen were trying to get their hoses connected. The firemen had rushed in unhesitatingly even though they had heard of the Cavite bombing where all the firemen were machine-gunned by Jap planes and killed in the streets. For a while they seemed to get the fire in the tower under control. Then their water pressure failed, and the flames ate around the base of the yellow stone tower and it toppled into the streets. The upper part crashed through the roof of the Santa Catarina girls' school, which had received a direct hit and was already burning inside.

Several nuns of the order of the Sisters of Charity rushed out through the doorway into the street. Priests were walking about, dazedly. It was their church of Santo Domingo which had been most active in raising funds for Fascist Franco. One of them told me, "Our table was set for us and we were just going to dine. A bomb crashed through the roof and showered the table with wreckage. None of us was hurt."

We went into another school around the corner and saw the body of a young boy who had been killed by shrapnel. An attendant told us, "It is fortunate that most of the children were sent home a week ago."

Around the corner, facing the Pasig River, a bomb had crashed through the roof of the Intendencia building, the old treasury. Thirty people crouching on the floor were killed. In front of the building was a cremated body in a burned out automobile.

We saw what the Japs—possibly—had been aiming at. The target possibly was four small ships, anchored in the Pasig River 150 yards from the nearest part of the Walled City. If that was the Jap target they released a quarter of a mile too soon. If they had made the same error on the other side all their bombs would have plunged into the heart of the business district across the river. As it was, only one did. It hit a fire station.

The next day it was the same medicine, only more so. The Jap bombers came so low that it was insulting. I watched most of the raid from the Bayview Hotel, on Dewey Boulevard and opposite Sayre's residence, where I had gone to confer with Mel and Annalee about the chances of getting out.

Most of the morning the bombers plastered the waterfront. They made their runs up Dewey Boulevard and right over Sayre's residence so low that we could see the bomb bays open and the wheels retracted into the fuselage. We estimated they were at 6,000 feet. We thought they might hit Sayre's residence, so when they reached the likely release point, directly opposite our hotel, we would duck under a bed or against a wall. But they kept pounding Pier 7 and got one hit, near the end of the pier. The other bombs landed in the water.

They were bombing in nine-nine-nine formation. Then they swung out over the bay and all twenty-seven lined up in a single big V. They flew straight in from the bay and over the waterfront and released over the Walled City. Their bombs crashed into the same northwest corner which had been devastated the afternoon before. The fires started at once, and flared up tremendously.

Jacoby and I went over. We found that Santo Domingo Church had been hit again, and the Intendencia, and there was one direct hit on the DMHM newspapers building. It set fire to the newsprint and flames swept through the building. Two of the ships in the Pasig were sunk, but even on the bottom their superstructures projected well out of the shallow water.

We went over to USAFFE to get the afternoon communique. I offered condolences to Major Romulo for the loss of his newspapers. Somehow, he managed to grin. "Oh, it doesn't matter. I was planning a new building anyway." My personal feud with Rommy was dead from that moment on.

Rommy took me aside. "The newspaper is nothing," he said. "I have just received word that the Japanese machine-gunned the native town of my mother. I have no word from her. My oldest son who is a captain in the Army is reported missing and probably dead."

Then he handed us the communique. It said, "Lines holding firm on all fronts."

I said to Jacoby, "Somehow these communiques don't sound right to me. Let's go see for ourselves."

17

Before starting out next morning, December 29, Jacoby and I stopped at No.1 Calle Victoria to see Colonel Harries and try to find out what was going on.

"Where are General MacArthur's field headquarters?" I asked. "We want to go up and have a look."

The colonel wanted to help us, but he was in possession of secrets which meant success or failure to our forces and he couldn't tell us too much. While we were talking Major Diller came in. We were surprised to see him, as he had left town with MacArthur and the rest of the staff.

"Look," he said, "all I can say is this. If I were in your position I would try to locate headquarters on Bataan. I am leaving Manila myself in a few minutes."

We tried to detain him long enough to get some more definite information. He seemed to us our last link with the Army and we didn't want to lose contact completely.

"Bataan?" we said. "We thought headquarters were at the Lingayen front. And where the hell is Bataan?"

"Look at Mariveles on your maps and you'll find Bataan," the major said.

We found Bataan was a peninsula, shaped like a miniature Florida, whose southern end pointed at Corregidor. On the eastern and southern shores it was bounded by Manila Bay and on the west by the China Sea. We had heard that Mariveles was a naval base. We figured that possibly General Wainwright, as field commander, was going to set up his headquarters there to direct the battle on the Pampanga plains, which by that time we felt sure would be the scene of the big United States versus Jap showdown.

Manila looked empty as we drove out to the north. There was less traffic and more stores were closed. Smoke was still surging up from Cavite and from the fires that our demolition squads had set at Nichols Field, Zablan Field, and Fort McKinley.

A few miles out of the city we started to run into traffic, all going north. It was mostly convoys of buses, with Philippine Army troops in their blue denim uniforms, with a sprinkling of khaki. Jap planes were patrolling over the road and we wondered why they didn't dive down and strafe the convoys. Four dive bombers were circling over the bridge at San Marcos where I had witnessed the anti-aircraft firing on Christmas afternoon. We drove across as fast as possible. On this bridge and all the others we saw wooden boxes piled up at each end. They were stenciled in red "Dynamite. DuPont," and were camouflaged with tree branches.

Four or five times the air raid wardens in small towns along the road signaled us to stop, and we dived into ditches. The towns consisted of only a few huts on stilts lining the road and possibly a wooden general store and a few streets extending away from the main highway. Most of the buildings were closed.

As we passed the big sugar mill and neared San Fernando the road was choked with northbound traffic and we had to slow up. We looked at our map and saw that the road into Bataan branched off to the left from San Fernando and curved southward, finally ending at Mariveles. To get onto the north road to Baguio you made a right turn in the center of San Fernando and then a left turn.

A staff car drew up behind us and we saw an officer we knew.

"Say," we questioned, "where are General Wainwright's headquarters? We heard this morning that they were at Tarlac, and now they tell us he is ten miles farther back in this direction."

"You'll probably find him even ten miles nearer now than when you heard that last word," the officer said. I knew General Wainwright's reputation as a fighter who led his troops.

"You can bet your bolo," I said, "that Wainwright is at the front, wherever it is. If Wainwright is coming back this way that means that the front is moving this way."

Jacoby said, "It looks like the front is moving back toward us faster than we are going toward it."

"This calls for a little investigating."

We pulled into San Fernando and parked just south of the old arched bridge and the cathedral. Where we stopped there was suddenly no more traffic, and we saw that all the trucks were turning into the left-hand road a few hundred yards behind us, the road that our maps showed led to Bataan. We went back and stood there and watched the buses and trucks go past.

A Filipino officer got out of a Chevrolet in front of us and I recognized Major Garcia who had been in command at Baguio. We swapped delighted abrazos.

"So you made it," he said.

"And you. Felicidades! How did you do it?"

"I walked out over to the Cabanatuan road and then got a bus down into Manila. We blew up the bridges on both roads into Baguio but I have heard the Japs are already there."

"What is going on now?"

"I was assigned to another regiment and ordered to Batangas down south of Manila where it appeared the Japs were about to land. They have been bombing all the small towns down that way and strafing the markets just for the hell of it. They didn't land and last night we were ordered north. We have been traveling all night and here we are."

"And where are you going?"

"To the Bataan Peninsula. That is where we are to fight."

"Buena suerte."

Again Bataan. We studied our map. Most of the area seemed to be mountainous and there were only a few towns, most of them on the Manila Bay shore. We debated going there and decided against it. Some American officers came up.

"If you fellows are looking for news we suggest that you drive about five miles east along the dirt road to the town of Mexico. The Twenty-sixth Cavalry is bivouacked there, and they have been fighting the Japs since they landed at Lingayen."

A few miles along the road we met a chaplain attached to a Filipino Scout field artillery regiment, under American officers. He led us to one of the batteries, which was stationed just off the road and well concealed in a thicket of trees.

We performed mutual introductions. I remember only two of the officers' names. They were Major Vepsala, the battery commander, and Lieutenant Larry Smarr, an ex-reporter for the St. Louis Post Dispatch. There was another youngster, a captain, who was the son of an American general. I believe his name was Wood.

Larry said, "Our guns—seventy-fives—are up ahead there. We are just firing some test shots. The Japs seem to be quite a ways north still, some forty miles or so, but they are coming down fast. We are getting set to go into action here."

Filipino Scouts were operating the field telephone and range-finding apparatus in a big truck. I asked the major about them. "No better soldiers in the world," he said.

Several of the officers had seen Captain Colin Kelly's death plunge after Jap fighters hopped his big B-17, and they told us the story. I borrowed Larry's portable typewriter and wrote it there. We offered to take back New Year's messages to be sent to their families and their girls back home, and Larry typed them out while the others dictated. I charged them to my personal account at Mackay Radio but I never got a bill. Maybe Mackay won't mind not being paid for them until after the war.

"If you want some real stories," Larry said, "go on down the road to Mexico and find the Twenty-sixth."

Mexico was another typical lowlands town, with a few dirt streets laid out in squares, nipa houses on stilts, and trees everywhere. In none of these towns were there any sidewalks.

We found two officers of the 26th bivouacked along a stream. One was from Boston, tall, with high cheekbones flushed a healthy red. He was as dapper and immaculate as if he had just stepped out of Abercrombie and Fitch's. He gave us some coffee but he wouldn't talk about the war without permission of his colonel. The other officer told us he had been stationed with a squad of men as a lookout at a small town on the east coast of Luzon. They got orders to withdraw and blew up the radio station. Then they rode their horses over the mountain and joined the regiment. The Japs had bombed them, but not hit them. Fifth columnists had given them plenty of trouble and seemed to have some means of disclosing their whereabouts to the enemy bombers.

We found headquarters in another street in the open air. The officers were just sitting down to mess and they asked us to join them. They introduced us to their commander. Colonel Clinton Pierce. Pierce was stocky, with black hair parted in the middle and a strong, leathery face. He hadn't spoken two sentences before we guessed his home town.

"Are you a Dodger rooter, Colonel?"

"Have been all my life," he said.

"I don't know whether I'm bad luck for you fellows, or vice versa," he said. "Anyway, there's one of you here already." We shook hands with Franz Weisblatt of the UP, whom we had difficulty recognizing under his black beard. He had joined the 26th the day after their battle at Tayug and had been with them since. He stayed with them all the way into Bataan, where he was cut off and captured, after being wounded while throwing hand grenades at the enemy. Tokyo decided that throwing hand grenades deprived him of his non-professional status and treated him as a prisoner of war instead of a civilian to be interned.

"We hear you fought the Japs for four days at Lingayen, Colonel. What do you think of them as scrappers?"

"Hell," said the colonel, "you can hear anything. You can even hear that I'm a hero. None of us are heroes. All we did was fight the bastards. That doesn't make us heroes. It's our job."

Little by little he told us the story, and we could see he was choosing his words deliberately in order to play down his own part in it.

"It was a week ago this morning that the Japs came ashore at Da Mortis, where we were stationed. Da Mortis is a town like this one. We fought 'em in the streets and under the houses, with rifles and machine guns. We stopped 'em cold all morning and most of the afternoon. By 2 P.M. we had beaten back their first attack and had them on the run.

"Somewhere further up the beach, at a place which must have been un-defended, they got some tanks ashore. We were supposed to have tanks backing us up, but they never showed up. The Japs drove into Da Mortis in their tanks and we peppered them with rifles and machine guns. They didn't seem to know what to do next. But we couldn't stop their tanks, and they were coming in behind us, so we had to withdraw.

"We got back to our horses and during the night we retreated to Rosario, We threw a circle around the town, taking positions in rice fields, behind the irrigation ditches, and sat down to wait for them. They hit us again the next morning.

"They came walking up the road and across the fields, little guys in brown uniforms. We waited for them to get close and then let them have it. We mowed down the first ones and the others flopped on their bellies. They threw a ring around us. They shot and shot and shot at us all day long and so help me God they never hit a damned thing. Our casualties were one man hit in the hand and one horse killed.

"Then the troops which had come around in our rear withdrew, leaving the way open for us to draw back. But our horses were bivouacked over to the left. We could have gone away and left them, but all of us love horses so we fought our way over to them. In the afternoon we pulled back to Pozomibio."

He told us about Major Trapnell of the 26th "who set fire to a bridge and saved a lot of us from getting killed out on the road. We were riding down the road and the Japs came after us with tanks, firing their 37-millimeter guns onto the concrete pavement so they exploded among our rear guard. We couldn't turn into the fields so we just had to take it. Trapnell drove a truck back onto the bridge and set it on fire. The bridge burned down and stopped the Jap tanks." Neither Jacoby nor I understood Trapnell's name at the time. We thought Colonel Pierce was saying "Chaplain."

"The next day it was the same damn' thing," Colonel Pierce went on. "They shot and shot and fired a million shots and made a hell of a lot of noise and couldn't hurt us at all. Then in the afternoon their tanks came. Our lines were along the road through the center of the town. Two of their tanks got on the road. Two others parked around the corner of the nipa huts and started shooting at nothing in particular. Lieutenant Sid Marks, a youngster from Hollywood, crawled up to toss a grenade into the tanks. He got within ten yards before they spotted him and cut him down with machine-gun bullets. He was still crawling forward when he died."

Jacoby told the colonel that he had met Marks in Manila just before the war. Sid had told him, "I came out to get in on this war. I have a hunch that I'm going to get killed. But it's going to be a hell of a lot of fun while it lasts."

The colonel continued his story. "We withdrew a little ways, into the fields back of the town. The tanks followed us and spread out around us in a semicircle and began to pour it.

"Major Ketchum saw the fix we were in and went back and got one of our seventy-fives on halftracks. He drove down the road full tilt and right into the middle of their tanks. He started firing his seventy-five and knocked off the tanks right and left. But he got too confident. One of the Jap tanks fired a 37-millimeter shell that killed him instantly. For a wonder his driver was not killed.

"We pulled back again that night, to Binalonan, fought all the next day, and then fell back to Tayug. That was Christmas..."

I interrupted the Colonel to thank him for the fact that I was still alive, or at any rate not captured. I told him about our arrival in Tayug Christmas Eve, after the hike from Baguio.

"Well," he said, "it's a good thing we were out there in front of you."

Then he went on. "Next day we fought them all day at Tayug and held them until their tanks and planes came over. We couldn't do much against their planes with rifles. In those four days of fighting, we lost twelve of our thirty-six American officers and about two hundred of our men.

"Headquarters ordered us to withdraw to these positions. The situation is this. We are covering the right flank while General Wainwright straightens out his lines. In other words, we had to pull our main forces back from Lingayen Gulf to prevent the Japs from swinging in behind them from Tayug and cutting them off."

"What is your professional opinion of the Jap Army, Colonel, from what you have seen of it?" I asked.

"My professional estimate is that they are no damn' good on the ground. These fellows they sent against us were nothing but untrained kids. They are shooting pop guns and they are dressed like a ragged mob. To call their doughboys fourth-rate is being charitable. They can't shoot a rifle, and my Scouts were picking them off the right and left. They get confused easily and if you shoot at them they stop coming. On the other hand, their tanks and planes were too much for us.

"I don't know where the bloody blue hell our own tanks and planes were, but as soon as they get up here we'll chase those Japs back into the sea."

He asked a question: "How many ships did they land from at Lingayen?"

"The USAFFE communique said there were eighty-six ships there. The officers at Baguio counted fifty-six a week ago this afternoon."

"Well, that ought to give you a line on how lousy they are. There was only one regiment, the Twenty-Sixth, fighting them, and they must have had a good many thousand soldiers if they had all those ships. We whipped hell out of 'em on the ground, and if we had had any tank and airplane support we'd have slaughtered the whole lot.

"Their strategy was lousy too," the colonel went on. "We drew inland, to the east, and the whole damned crew followed us. If they had cut to the west they'd have surrounded our forces at Lingayen before we had a chance to straighten our lines."

All this was during lunch. The tin plates were heaping and there was fresh bread and some dessert and coffee. Once we were interrupted by the shout, "Planes." Nine silver bombers flew over us, but they kept straight on their course toward Manila.

The colonel arranged for us to interview a number of his Scouts who had been captured by the Japs and then released with an admonition to go home and live in peace away from the "white imperialists." Instead of going home, they had hot-footed back to report to the colonel, get new guns, and gone on fighting. While we went aside to talk to the Scouts a staff car drove up and a messenger handed the colonel a dispatch.

When we had the stories the colonel called us back. "I don't know what the hell is going on but we have orders to withdraw again. We are to move south and west and transfer all the way over to cover our left flank."

On the way back to San Fernando we stopped at the artillery position—I believe it was the 86th Field-Artillery—to pick up some more New Year's messages. The artillerymen had orders to move too, they told us. "Just when we were getting set up."

Franz Weisblatt drove back into Manila with us and we stopped along the roadside for a conference. Comparing notes, we decided that part of the army was moving into Bataan—though we didn't know why—and that there still would be a fight on the plains of Pampanga.

"In those rice fields, even though they are dry now, the Japs should have trouble using their tanks."

"By the time the fighting starts in earnest some of those planes should be here from the United States. They've had nearly three weeks now and it only takes about a week to fly them via Hawaii-Canton Island-Australia. The Navy should be getting into action soon, too—we hope."

"While we are getting those planes the Japs are going to give us an awful lot of trouble with their own dive bombers. As far as their infantry is concerned, everybody who has fought them agrees these are pretty poor troops. Looks like they sent about the third team down here and the first string into Malaya."

"Looks like MacArthur is pulling everything out of the south and will let them take Manila. We've got to get out in the field with the Army, or we'll be captured in Manila."

Weisblatt had been in trouble with the Japanese in Yokohama some years before and the last thing he wanted was to be captured. He decided he would stick with the 26th. Jacoby and I were already on the Japs' blacklist.

Back at the TVT we found out that the Japs had bombed Corregidor heavily during the afternoon. USAFFE announced nine planes had been shot down, and we thought, "Now they'll get it, the Jap bastards. They are tackling one place that is really ready for them. Just wait till they hit those American troops up in Pampanga."

Every day since the war started I had tried to cheer up the editorial workers in the TVT city room, but that afternoon I had difficulty smiling when I gave them the usual "V-for-Victory" signal. Don Alejandro Roces called me into his office and informed me that the Japs were advancing fast from the south, especially from Antimonan where they had landed on the 24th from forty transports.

From my window at the hotel I could see three new bomb-lit fires blending their flare with the sunset across the bay. They were far in the distance. One was at Mariveles and two appeared to be in the water off the end of Corregidor. I telephoned Carlos, my companion on the trip to Baguio, and asked him to come up to the hotel.

To my surprise he knew all about the bombing of Mariveles a few hours earlier. "The bombs burned down the entire town," he said, "but didn't hit any naval installations except an ammunition dump. One bomb killed a number of Marines manning an anti-aircraft gun."

"How in the world did you find all that out?"

"A friend of mine, a Spanish contractor, was over there this afternoon and just got back. He is helping to build two airfields on the southern tip of Bataan. He tells me there are a number of refugees from Manila living in the woods behind Mariveles, including many Americans."

I told Carlos that the Japs were closing in from the south and that we were looking for a way out. The Army had made no provision for us to go with them and we were considering taking a boat. I asked him to go with us. "You are brave and resourceful and you know the language. We want you along. You have no one dependent on you. We will, of course, pay your expenses and pay you for your services."

Carlos's answer surprised me. "Amigo," he said, "it is perfectly all right for you to go if you can no longer do your job and the end is near. I despise the thought of captivity as much as you do. But I am a Filipino and this is my country. If my country's fate is to go through hell I must remain hereto share it with my fellow Filipinos."

Then he said a lot more, which surprised me still further, as I had thought him only a young extrovert who loved adventure whether in a war or on the soccer field.

He said, "Look at me and tell me what you see."

"I see a healthy young man of medium size, with black hair and eyes, and a Spanish nose and mouth."

"And the color of my skin?"

"A healthy tan. The color that Americans spend hours in the sun trying to acquire."

"Well," he said, "you obviously don't realize it, because you don't feel that way yourself, but the color of my skin keeps me from living in your white world."

I protested. "In the first place, you are Spanish, and what does it matter anyway? You have eaten here in the hotel with me and you can go anywhere you want in Manila."

"I am not all Spanish. One grandmother was a Filipina. And because of that I cannot go with a white girl of my own station in life. Her parents will forbid it. I cannot marry one. In your country I would be looked on as an Oriental and a half-caste. There are two worlds. Your white one and the Oriental one."

"Are you trying to say that you subscribe to the Japanese program of Asia for the Asiatics?"

"Personally, I do not. I believe the Americans will treat us more fairly. But you must realize that such a program has a terrific pull for lots of Oriental people. As long as the Americans in the Philippines insist on living in their own world and keeping us in ours, the spiritual and psychological differences between us will continue to exist and to grow deeper. And if America doesn't send us help, who knows ... ?"

"I don't like to hear you talking like an underdog," I said.

He was firm. "That's the way it is," he said. "And if you still don't understand me, keep an eye on Malaya and Burma and on what happens in India if the Japs go into those places."

Following image: 100 Pesos note printed during the Japanese occupation.

18

THERE WAS A SUDDEN AND STARTLING CHANGE IN THE TONE of the morning USAFFE communique on December 30. Colonel Harries handed it to us at 11 A.M. It said, ominously, "Enemy dive bombers control the roads in northern Luzon."

Our forces had withdrawn from Lingayen Gulf and the "battle line" ran through Zaragoza, sixty-five miles north of Manila. The enemy forces advancing from the south reached Luisiana and Dolores, forty-five air miles southeast of the capital.

The people of Manila were frightened. Up until then the communiques, although reporting Japanese advances, had been optimistic. For all the people knew, we were winning the war and the bombing of Manila was something to be endured due to the temporary absence of pursuit planes. Of course, our pursuit forces would be replenished shortly. Help was on the way! Sayre, among others, had said it: "Help is surely coming—help of sufficient adequacy and power so that the invader will be driven from our midst and be rendered powerless ever to threaten us again."

That afternoon the USAFFE communique went back to the old line. It asserted: "Our forces are holding firm on all fronts." Next morning's papers said the same thing, and even on New Year's Day the people of Manila did not know that there were NO forces in front of them either to the north or south.

Later, on Corregidor, before he died of gangrene Colonel Harries called me aside one day. "You know," he said, felt like hell reading you those lies in a pontifical way every day. But it had to be done. We were trying to deceive the enemy and to conceal the fact that we were withdrawing into Bataan. And we were trying to keep the people of Manila from becoming panic-stricken. The Japs were going to take Manila anyway, and we decided that it would be better if the people didn't have time to worry about it."

The papers of the 30th and the 31st printed articles advising the populace to remain calm and stay indoors in the event that enemy troops entered the city. No resistance was to be offered. Even then, the people of Manila had difficulty in realizing that the peaceful lives they had known were at an end. They had suffered the bombing stoically, heroically, because of their overwhelming confidence that our forces would smash the invader.

On the morning of the 30th, members of the American community were called to a conference with Dr. Claude A. Buss of the high commissioner's office. Sayre had gone by then to Corregidor, where that same day President Quezon was being inaugurated for a second term, and Dr. Buss was in charge. Buss didn't attempt to soften the blow.

"In a matter of days," he said, "or perhaps hours, the Japanese will enter and occupy Manila. Our armed forces will not contest their entry to the city."

The reaction of most of the Americans was, "What! The Japs come here? By God, they can't do this to us!"

A half-dozen men clamored to be heard. Some of them wanted to fight. One said, "We will form our own police force and arm ourselves from the Cavite arsenal. Many of us have pistols, and with those we can maintain order."

Dr. Buss had difficulty convincing him that it was highly unlikely that the Japanese would allow any American to walk around the streets, let alone carry a pistol.

Another man suggested that they buy all the available food stocks in town and store them in their homes and simply remain indoors. Dr. Buss told them it would be wiser to pack some clothes and toilet articles and to prepare to be taken to an internment camp, just as the Japanese civilians in Manila had done a few days before the war started.

When the Japs finally did enter the city three days later.

Dr. Buss and Jorge Vargas, who had been left behind by Quezon went out to meet them under a white flag and arranged for their peaceable entry into Manila. Buss gave an inspiring example of fortitude and self-control during those last unbelievably nightmarish days. On the afternoon of the 30th, a number of correspondents met in the Jacobys' room on the sixth floor of the Bayview Hotel to try to decide what we were to do. I had learned that escape to the south was almost impossible. Small Jap infiltration squads were already on the road to Tagaitay, only forty miles away, and Batangas, the jumping off place for a banca trip to the southern islands.

There was still one possible loophole—to skirt the southern shore of Manila Bay through Cavite province and reach the China Sea shore to the south of Corregidor. From there it might be possible to get southward along the coast by banca, hiding by day and traveling out to sea and around Japanese-held areas by night. From my experience in China, I knew that it was impossible for an invader to occupy every foot of the country and if you could just learn in advance where their sentries and outposts were it would be quite easy to slip around them.

I determined to go to the southern front in the morning to check on how close the Japanese advance units were to the city and whether the road to the coast through Cavite was still open.

On the way to No.1 Victoria, I drove through the dock area. There had not been any bombing during the day and the waterfront was crowded with people. They were helping themselves to stores which the Army was giving to anybody who would carry them away. Laden with crates and boxes, the Filipinos were walking out of the waterfront section. It was fortunate for the Americans and Filipinos in Manila that these supplies were distributed free of charge.

In the days after the Japanese occupied the capital the canned goods which had been taken from the burning piers were about the only source of food in the city, and people bought them eagerly despite the exorbitant prices. All our armed forces had been withdrawn from the waterfront and the only representative of our military was an old man in his late sixties, a veteran of the American campaign in the Philippines, who guarded the entrance to the docks with an ancient 30-30 carbine.* He was obviously confused by the flight of our armed forces from the city.

At USAFFE headquarters I asked Major Diller for information, but he still was not in a position to reveal the movement of our troops that was in progress toward Bataan. For information about the southern front he turned me over to Colonel William Marquat, former Seattle newspaperman and a member of MacArthur's G-3. (G-1 is Personnel, G-2 Intelligence, G-3 Operations, and G-4 Supply.)

"Where are the lines in the south. Colonel?" I asked.

"Can't tell you exactly, Clark."

"Is it all right to go down there, and how far can I go without too great a risk of getting caught?"

"It's too late to go tonight. Come back and see me before you leave in the morning." He re-emphasized, "By all means, don't start out without coming here first."

The Jacobys and Rus Brines came over to the Manila Hotel for dinner, and we had another indecisive conference. I told them what I had learned about Bataan and Mariveles. I worked all night in the office burning the files of the stories we had sent since the start of the war, and turned over my room at the hotel to Ray and Mrs. Cronin.

At seven-thirty on December 31, I went to USAFFE and found Colonel Marquat on the second floor, studying maps. The big office was nearly deserted and there were evidences of preparation for further departures: papers stacked in boxes, packed suitcases sitting about, and the walls being stripped bare. The colonel was conferring with a tall, good-looking American captain. He introduced me and said:

"The captain here is the man for you to see. He has been fighting in the south."

From the captain, I learned more of the rear guard actions in southern Luzon. He told me that he and a squad of about fifteen Filipino Scouts had skirmished with the Japs on the road from Antimonan to Manila. He was wounded in the neck and had led his men up a trail into the mountains, where they camped for the night in a summerhouse. The Japs located them during the night and attacked, throwing hand grenades and making a lot of noise. The captain said: "Believe it or not their grenades are mostly noisemakers and don't spread shrapnel about, the way ours do. One of them hit my helmet, actually, and exploded without even stunning me. One of my sergeants was shot through the neck, the bullet going clean through. He clapped a couple of bandages on the wounds and kept on fighting. In the morning we attacked with bayonets, got around the Japs, and came here." He said a lot of our troops were still in the south but were taking to the hills and would join our forces around Manila.

I asked Bill Marquat whether I should drive on down south and see for myself.

"If you do," he said, "it will be the last thing you will see. The Japs are at Pasay, which is only a few miles from Nichols Field. They are definitely on the Batangas road and the road to Tagaitay. Don't go!"

I fully realized then that we did not intend to make a fight for Manila. The situation became entirely clear.

I drove back to the office as rapidly as possible and told Cronin the story. He had some information of his own: the wireless stations were to be dynamited by the Army at 11:30 A.M. and all communication with the outside world would cease. It was then about 9:15 A.M. We decided to try to inform our New York office that Manila was about to be captured. We wrote out a half-dozen urgent service messages, hoping one or more of them would get through the censor.

I worded one, "Just returned from southern front stop departed 6:30 by automobile returned 7:30 stop stories coming shortly if time."

In New York, they correctly interpreted the main import of the message: the Japanese were knocking at the gates of Manila and the city would fall shortly. However, the AP credited me with having gone to the southern front. Actually there was no front in the south,

I wrote another message, "Please include Manila staff in any negotiations involving Hill Harris stop we will shortly be same category." Max Hill and Morris Harris, our bureau chiefs respectively in Tokyo and Shanghai, were captured on December 8 and interned. We knew efforts were being made to obtain their release.

We also cabled New Year's greetings to all our colleagues, and "especially Lochner, Massock," two of the AP men interned in Europe. We could not ascertain how many of the messages were passed by the censors, but we knew if even one got through it would be enough to advise our headquarters of the situation.

Early in the afternoon we met again in the Jacobys' room in the Bayview Hotel. There were Mel and Annalee, Ray Cronin, Carl Mydans and his wife, Shelley Smith of Life Magazine. None of us had seen Arch Royal Gunnison of NANA, or Jack Percival, the Australian reporter, recently.

Mel had important news.

"I met a captain who is going out to Mariveles by freighter tonight and will take us along if we decide to risk it."

Nobody knew exactly what there was at Mariveles, except what Carlos had told me about a number of people from Manila already living in the hills behind the bay.

"I'm going," I said. "Anything to stay out of their hands, even if it's only for a few hours longer."

Carl said, "It seems foolish to go, and since Shelley is with me we will both stay here and be interned." Cronin and Brines made similar decisions, feeling that they could not desert their families. Mel was undecided until Annalee made up his mind for him. "We're going, Mel."

We voted to have a farewell drink together and then discovered there was nothing to drink. Both Annalee and Shelley had poured their liquor down the bathroom sink as a result of my telling them the day before that the Japs were inclined to get out of control after taking a few drinks.

It was decided that the correspondents who were remaining would all sleep that night in the Bayview Hotel with their families in the hope that the Japanese would allow them to remain there rather than intern them. We had read that American correspondents in Tokyo and the Japanese newspapermen in New York had been confined to their hotels instead of being taken to prison camps. Frank Hewlett of the UP telephoned that he was going to remain in Manila with his wife, Virginia, who was a stenographer on the high commissioner's staff. Later Frank and Virginia decided that it was his job to go to Bataan and hers to remain in Manila, and late that night he drove out to Bataan.

I went back to the Manila Hotel barber shop and had just gotten shaved and had one hand manicured, when Jacoby telephoned. "Get over here as fast as you can," he said. "We may have to leave at any minute."

I ran up to my room and grabbed a few pairs of socks, a shirt, and threw them into a canvas bag. I looked longingly at my golf clubs over in a corner and wondered if the Jap officer who occupied the room would use them to play golf or if he would send them back to Japan to be turned into scrap iron to be made into bombs to kill Americans.

From its neat wooden box, I took the vase which Lieutenant Colonel Akiyama had presented me the night before I left Shanghai, in appreciation for my having reported the "true intentions" of the Japanese Army. I put it on the dresser in front of a large picture of my wife. I took my portable typewriter and the canvas bag and went over to the Bayview.

In the dusk we sat in the Jacobys' room and tried to talk the Mydans into coming to Mariveles with us. A small Japanese biplane, an observation ship, flew over Nichols Field at about five-thirty and then swooped up and down Dewey Boulevard only a few feet above the treetops. Jacoby's friend, the ship captain, telephoned to say that he would be back for us at ten-thirty in the evening. The Jacobys packed one big suitcase with canned goods and a few clothes and wrapped up Mel's cameras in a package. Annalee was wearing a slack suit and had one more in the suitcase. Most of her wardrobe, her trousseau, had been on a ship which was en route to Manila but was diverted to Singapore when war started.

I was looking out the side windows at the plane flying down the boulevard when suddenly Mel shouted in an electrifying voice, "Hey, look!"

He was facing the rear window looking over the city. As he shouted a great wall of flame hundreds of feet high and a half mile long sprang into the darkening sky. There was explosion after explosion, shaking the entire city.

I ran over to the window and quickly saw what it was. "They're dynamiting the gasoline tanks at Pandacen, on the other side of the Pasig River."

Because of its nearness it was even more spectacular than the destruction of Cavite. Annalee, who used to write scenarios for Mickey Rooney, supplied the adjectives. "Stupendous, terrific, colossal, terrifying, magnificent, overwhelming," she gasped.

The burning gasoline threw up clouds of dense black smoke, on which the flames flickered and danced and threw their light for miles around. For many nights afterward, from Corregidor, we could see the fires still burning.

For some reason the situation seemed to call for farewells. I thought of my wife's cousins, the Fairchilds, and I telephoned them. They sent their car down to the hotel and I took a chance of missing connections with the freighter to go out to their house. They were having a New Year's Eve buffet supper in their big home and they gave me some turkey and three cans of tinned food to take along with me, and a small bottle of New Jersey applejack.

I thought it best to tell them. "The Japs will probably be here tomorrow."

They were incredulous and shocked, since they had been reading the communiques in the newspapers and thought the fighting was going in our favor. I advised them to stay in their homes and perhaps call in some of their neighbors, including some Spaniards if possible, because the Japanese soldiers would be less likely to get out of hand with a number of people around. Spain and Japan were Axis allies, and the Spaniards would probably receive preferential treatment.

We wished each other luck all around and shook hands. As I didn't know what I was heading into I gave them a farewell message for my wife, to be delivered postwar if I failed to come through.

Back at the Bayview, Mel and Annalee were beginning to pace the floor and wonder if the captain would keep his promise to return. Promptly at ten-thirty the captain and another captain drove up. Both their names for the purposes of this account had better be Smith. Both were instrumental in preventing a number of ships from falling into Japanese hands and both were subsequently captured and imprisoned.

We found the dock area a confusion of flames and explosions. Dark figures, overloaded with boxes and cans and anything portable, were struggling away from the fires carrying the stores that couldn't be taken away by the Army.

There were fires down at the end of the docks at Engineer Island, where the Army's ship repair facilities and the oil storage tanks had been dynamited. Burning embers showered on our car as we drove along.

We scrambled onto a tug in the light of the fires and then onto a small freighter about 150 feet long. The central deck was low, with only the bridge and stern elevated. The captain rounded up his engineer who was on the pier watching the fires and explosions, and at eleven-thirty we backed into the bay and headed out westward.

We passed the projecting spars of the two ships which I had seen the Jap bombers sink several days before, and went on past the breakwater and the lighted hospital ship Mactan, which was awaiting orders to get underway for Australia. The Jacobys had tried to get on the ship but had withdrawn their request when they learned that its neutral status would be jeopardized if it carried unwounded civilian passengers. Later, the Japs bombed it anyway, off the coast of Australia.

From the bay Manila seemed a mass of flames. The great gasoline fires at Pandacen threw into relief all the buildings on Dewey Boulevard and along the waterfront. The Manila Hotel was blazing with lights but they were dimmed by the fires in the pier area.

"That's the most spectacular New Year's party that anybody's ever seen," said Annalee.

"A ninety-million-dollar send-off," Mel said.

"I don't want to bore you two with my hunches," I said, "but this one is so strong that you've got to hear it. I feel absolutely certain that sometime within the next few months you two honeymooners and I will sit around a table somewhere south of the equator and drink a Tom Collins. It will be in a hotel lobby and there will be palms around."

We were far out in the bay when the Jacobys' watches said midnight, but we could see the time by the light of the fires on shore. Cavite, off to our left, was still burning and there were two fires in the water off Corregidor.

At midnight we passed the bottle of applejack to all hands and wished "Happy New Year" all around. The Jacobys curled up on the hatch and went to sleep; while I leaned against the rail, watching our bow cut through the dark waters, and reviewed my impressions and recollections from the outbreak of war until the withdrawal into Bataan.

*The '30-30 carbine' was an old Winchester rifle. The .30 carbine produced by Winchester was the cartridge for the war's M1 file.

Following image: Marine with M1 carbine at Guam.

19

At four o'clock on New Year's morning I awakened, cramped and shivering, on the hatch of the freighter that was taking us from Manila to Mariveles. Our motors were stopped and a cold wind was driving across Manila Bay. Captain Smith I and Captain Smith II were seated on the hatch near me arguing over the location of the minefields off Corregidor. Captain Smith I was nursing a bottle of Dewar's.

It was so light that at first I thought the sun was up. Then I saw the illumination came from two ships which were burning a few hundred yards off our port beam. One small fire was eating at the lumber piled on the deck of the Don Josi, which the Captains Smith identified and told me was the second biggest cargo ship in the world. The Don Joss burned for twenty-one days after it was bombed and even then it wouldn't sink. The other, smaller freighter was burning furiously. Flames were eating down into the hull. We could make out the outline of other undamaged ships around us. Behind them loomed Corregidor, dark and forbidding.

Captain Smith II finally won the argument about the minefields. "We can't approach Corregidor any closer before daylight or they will fire on us," he said. "We'd better start the engines and head back into the bay and away from the mines. The minefields are between here and Mariveles and we can't go through them until we get permission from Corregidor. The S.S. Corregidor tried it and got blown to pieces."

They roused the engineer who had gone to sleep, and for the next twenty minutes we headed away from Corregidor. Butte ship was empty and its draft was not more than six feet. The wind promptly blew us back toward the island. We chugged out, and drifted back, and chugged out again for the rest of the night.

I asked the Captains Smith, Where do we go from here? After Mariveles, what?"

They said they had a small seagoing tug anchored off Mariveles with sufficient fuel oil for a two-thousand-mile trip. If the Army didn't need it or them, they would set out for the Dutch East Indies or Australia, trusting to their knowledge of the islands and the smallness of the boat to get through. I woke up Jacoby and we quickly decided that if we weren't allowed ashore at Corregidor or Mariveles we would take a chance on the tugboat.

Except for the burning ships we seemed to have the bay all to ourselves, but we found out later that its waters that night and for the following day and night were filled with small boats of all types making last-minute escapes from Manila, Charles van Landingham of Los Angeles, whose wanderlust had carried him all over the world and who had finally settled down to a job in the Catholic Priests' Bank in Manila, confiscated a small boat from the Manila Yacht Club on New Year's Day and sailed five American sailors safely to Bataan, taking nearly forty-eight hours to cover the thirty miles against adverse winds.

Other nocturnal sailors out that night were Captain Bill Seater and Al Foyt, a former Hollywood promoter and now with the U.S. Engineers. They were bringing out to Corregidor a seventy-five-foot Philippine government customs launch with a string of Japanese Diesel fishing sampans in tow.

In the blackness of Manila Bay on New Year's Eve, Seater and Foyt heard a hail. A voice shouted, "Ship ahoy. We're four Army officers with a ten-cent compass and a bottle of Scotch. Where the hell do we go from here?"

Seater told them to follow the fiery beacon of the burning ships off Corregidor.

Foyt, Seater, van Landingham, and others who made their getaway from Manila even after our own departure, told us that it had been the most unforgettable New Year's Eve in their lives. Nobody knew what the next morning would bring and everyone was bewildered. A handful of people tried to dance at the Manila Hotel but quickly gave it up. The realization finally spread that the Japanese were about to enter the city.

Someone suggested the advisability of destroying all the available liquor stocks in the city and the Americans tackled the job with a will, glad to have something to do to keep their minds off tomorrow. Some of the Army and Navy Club's liquor supply was loaded on a barge and towed out to Corregidor where the barge was sunk by Japanese bombs a few days later.

As dawn broke on New Year's Day the Captains Smith piloted us in close to the north shore of Corregidor and anchored just beside President Quezon's rakish gray yacht, the Casiana. The captains supplied some coffee, the Jacobys brought out a can of corned beef, and we ate breakfast on the hatch. Then we struggled with the rusty tackle of the lifeboat, finally got it launched, and rowed to the nearest of two docks through a welter of small boats and past numerous ships of all sizes which I noticed were all anchored in a row stretching from close to shore far out into the bay.

There were numerous soldiers on the docks, mostly Americans. As they helped us up on the dock the air raid siren cut loose with its reverberating alarm and everybody started running. We scrambled ashore and followed, threading our unfamiliar way between one-story buildings of corrugated iron and wood. We came to an air raid shelter built of concrete and shaped roughly like a subway car. There was room for one more, and Annalee Jacoby went inside. The rest of us raced on, up an embankment and onto a trolley track which we followed in the direction of the disappearing soldiers. The track led into the middle of a hillside and into a long, arched, concrete tunnel.

In the next few weeks we came to know the tunnel well, for it was not only the safest place during air raids but the nerve center of the defenses on

Bataan and Corregidor. It was open at both ends, about a quarter of a mile long, and was jammed with Americans and Filipinos in blue denim, seated four and five deep along each wall for the entire length. Boxes of food and ammunition were piled to a height of six feet along the walls.

The Military Police caught up with Jacoby and myself during the first air alarm, and that day and the next we spent most of our time between the tunnel and the guardhouse, a couple of hundred yards down the trolley track. It seemed that every time we reached the guardhouse to be questioned, the air alarm would sound and everybody would sprint for the tunnel. After the raid we would report dutifully back to the guardhouse.

The M.P.'s asked us, "Where did you come from, what are you doing here, and who are you?"

We produced our press credentials and Mel said, "We were just passing by with two sea captains on our way to Mariveles to catch a tug for the Dutch East Indies. We stopped to get permission to go through the minefields."

The M.P.'s were understandably skeptical. "Oh, yes, of course," they said. "And where are the two captains?" In the rush for shelter we had lost our captains. A trip to the guardhouse was in order. When the all-clear sounded we went back and got Annalee from her shelter down by the waterfront and reported to the guardhouse.

Our interrogator turned out to be Captain Benson of Pittsburgh and we quickly became friends. Benson was big and handsome with high color and a dimpled chin; the type of face they put on recruiting posters. Instead of locking us up, he took care of us for the next few days, getting us something to eat now and then, and blankets and mattresses, and once, miraculously, a bottle of Four Roses. But the M.P. book had no provision for two civilian men and a girl in a military area in wartime and Benson didn't know exactly what our status was.

A friend at court was urgently needed. He appeared in the person of Major Diller (subsequently twice promoted and hereafter Colonel Diller), aide to General MacArthur and public relations officer and censor during the brief USAFFE interval in Manila. Colonel Diller, when we encountered him in the big tunnel during the second air raid alarm of the morning, was astonished to see us, but friendly. He wasn't sure at first whether we could remain on Corregidor but he would be glad to give us transportation to Mariveles.

For some reason Mariveles suddenly became the place where we least wanted to be. We guessed that once we were up in the woods we would be completely out of touch with everything, with no possibility of getting any stories out and with nothing to eat but coconuts—if any grew there. Corregidor was fast becoming a known quantity. Everybody looked well fed and the tunnel seemed a likely place to sit out air raids. During the next few days, whenever an M.P. suddenly threatened us with deportation to Mariveles,

Colonel Diller would come to bat for us with instructions to "give them time to complete their arrangements with the captains."

We never managed to make arrangements with the captains, but the colonel's intervention sufficed until General MacArthur was informed of our presence on the island and regularized our status. MacArthur saw that we got uniforms and had us assigned to the officers' mess, but not even the general would give us permission to send stories.

The first two or three nights we slept on the platform of the "Bottomside" station on Corregidor's electric trolley line. It was very cold, despite the blankets provided by Captain Benson, but we never thought of complaining. Annalee took it all with a smile and the soldiers did everything possible to make us feel at home. One soldier I remember as typical. He was Corporal Lash, a gangling, tow-headed, slow-spoken Regular Army soldier from Texas.

He awakened us in our open-air trolley station boudoir the morning of January 2. "Ma'am and gentlemen," he said. "Our cook passed by this morning and saw you sleeping here and thought you might be hungry. He wishes you would come to our mess for a bite to eat."

The mess was just down the steps from the trolley station in a wooden building next to the Bottomside cinema, and we ate there for many days— when the air raids permitted the serving of food. At first there were three meals, with plenty of canned fruit and jelly and butter. Then, suddenly, two meals a day, with no fruit and fewer and fewer vegetables.

We quickly got acquainted with the Army officers on Corregidor and when the daily bombing was finished they took us to see the island, which the Army called Fort Mills.

From the air Corregidor looked like a tadpole with its thick blunt head planted in the China Sea at the mouth of Manila Bay and its tail curling off to a narrow point in the bay four and a half miles away.

The largest flat area of the island was also the highest. It was called Topside and from it sheer walls of rock dropped down 650 feet to the China Sea in front and on the sides to Manila Bay. The Topside barracks, which ran parallel to the long axis of the island, were said to be the largest in the world. They faced a half-mile square parade ground and athletic field, around which were located the officers' homes, single houses for the higher officers, and double or quadruple quarters for the others. The homes were of white stucco with bougainvillea and hydrangea growing in the gardens.

From their porches there was an incomparable view of the sunsets over the China Sea and of the rough beauty of Bataan. There was a large bamboo cinema, an officers' club, and a big, three-story hospital with the Red Cross painted on its roof. There were machine shops, protected by five feet of reinforced concrete; quartermaster and storage buildings; and the tanks for water which was drawn from wells dug down into the solid rock of the island.

The big guns were there, the 12-inch rifles and the mortars which dominated both the north and south channels into Manila Bay, the Boca Chica and Boca Grande passages. The guns were hidden underground and poked their noses out only to fire.

From Topside you could see the waterfront of Manila, thirty miles away, and also the four other islands stretching in a chain across the southern entrance to the bay. The nearest and largest was Fort Hughes, and beyond it Fort Drum, chiseled out of solid rock in the shape of a battleship, with a battleship mast of rock, and its guns and quarters hidden below deck; then Fort Frank on tiny Caballo Island over near the Cavite shore; and one other small unfortified island called Carabao.

Roads wound down the hills from Topside to the central area, called Middleside, where there were more barracks and shops and quarters for the non-commissioned officers; and a school for the children of Filipino soldiers and another school for the American children. Anti-aircraft guns were spotted here, some 75's.

Then the island dropped off steeply to Bottomside where the ground was level and only a few feet above the surface of the bay. The cove on the northern side was known as the Army Dock Area. There were two concrete piers and behind them mechanical and electrical shops and the bakery. Tucked in a fold in the hills leading up to Middleside were the big cold-storage plant and the shops of the U.S. Engineers.

The southern shore of Bottomside was the Navy Area, with a single L-shaped concrete pier. The beach was low and sandy, and it was guarded by barbed wire and pillboxes manned by U.S. Marines. The trolley line, for both freight and passengers, ran all the way from Bottomside to Topside; when it ran. After the bombing of January 1 and 2 the trolley was no longer usable.

From Bottomside going east toward the tail of the island, rose a mighty hill of rock, roughly cone-shaped, from the water's edge to a height of nearly six hundred feet. This was Malinta Hill and its interior was a network of tunnels. The largest was Malinta tunnel, where we found shelter during the air raids. The main road the length of the island ran through the tunnel and the trolley line extended as far as its easternmost entrance.

From the principal tunnel a dozen laterals branched off on each side. Walking through the tunnel from the Bottomside entrance you came first to the Quartermaster's lateral, then a store which sold cigarettes and chewing gum as long as they lasted, then the Quartermaster's department where supplies were issued, and the Signal Corps offices and so on.

On the left were the ordnance shops, laterals for the storage of food and munitions, then the anti-aircraft listening post headquarters, the USAFFE headquarters, the hospital tunnel, and then a lateral used as an office and dormitory. Laterals running off from the hospital tunnel, which also had an entrance on the northern side of Malinta Hill, contained the various wards—

126

medical, surgical, amputations, dental—and dormitories for the nurses and other women on Corregidor.

In one lateral off the hospital tunnel, Quezon and Sayre and the women members of their parties ate together with the doctors and nurses. In the hospital section the walls were whitewashed and clean and the civilians assigned there slept comfortably in hospital beds or double-decker iron cots. Except during air raids there was enough light and air in the tunnels, perhaps more light than fresh air.

The main Quartermaster's lateral of Malinta tunnel led all the way through the hill to connect with the Navy tunnel, near the southern edge of Corregidor. Here Admiral Rockwell moved the staff of the 16th Naval District after Cavite was evacuated. The Navy tunnel contained radio equipment in an air-conditioned lateral, and shops, desks, beds, a combination mess and reading room. Vicious-looking torpedoes were stored in the rear of the tunnel near an exit which led to the opposite side of Malinta Hill. Between the Bottomside entrance to Malinta tunnel and the Navy tunnel were two other shafts driven straight into the hillside, containing bunks for Navy personnel and civilian workers.

Rows of desks lined each side of the USAFFE tunnel, with MacArthur's at the extreme right-hand side in the rear. General Richard K. Sutherland, chief of MacArthur's staff, pored over papers at a desk in front of the general's. In front of them were the desks of officers of G-3 and G-2, the air liaison officers, the press relations department. Just inside the door sat fatherly Brigadier General Carl Seals, the USAFFE adjutant general. Some distance behind MacArthur's desk were two rows of double-decked beds for his USAFFE staff.

MacArthur stayed in the tunnel as little as possible. He and his family lived about a half mile away toward the inside tip of the island, on a grassy hillside. At times President Quezon occupied the house up the hill from MacArthur, and for a while Jacoby and myself were permitted to stay in the house assigned to Sayre, only fifty feet down the hill from MacArthur's.

A narrow road wound steeply up to the top of Malinta Hill, where there were lookout positions and an anti-aircraft battery consisting of one "pom-pom" type gun which had been taken off the U.S.S. Houston before the war. From the lookout positions atop Malinta Hill you could get a bird's-eye view of most of Corregidor.

Going through Malinta tunnel and on toward the tip of the island the main road ran level and about three hundred feet above the surface of Manila Bay. The hills dropped sharply away from the road to a large cove on the south shore of Corregidor, where there was an unused hangar for naval flying boats. Toward that end of the island there was a cluster of homes and barracks, the naval radio in still another small tunnel, and "Kindley Field," a narrow short runway where slow airplanes could land.

Batteries of guns, mostly 75-mm. and some 37-mm. field pieces, guarded the approaches to the island from the rear and sides. Pillboxes overlooked the few beaches which offered likely landing places. Everything possible was underground and protected.

Everybody called Corregidor the "Rock," and the adjective that seemed to fit it best was "rugged." Corregidor was indeed a mighty fortress. Doubtless it would have been impregnable—if the airplane had never been invented.

20

BUT AIRPLANES HAD BEEN INVENTED, AND DURING JANUARY they were over Corregidor for two or three hours almost every day. There was something hideously obscene about those tiny silver planes buzzing around high up against the blue cloudless sky. They were so small, at above 20,000 feet, that they looked as if you could put them in a matchbox.

In the intervals when the noise of the last load of bombs had died away, and the planes were out of range of the anti-aircraft and circling for their next run, you could hear the motors plainly. The noise of the motors was deadly and vicious. You thought of being tied down to slimy tree roots in a muddy jungle, and having a rattlesnake weave his ugly head two inches from your throat, waiting and picking his place to strike. You thought of all the evil nightmares you had ever had.

Everybody knew when the planes were coming.

First, about seven-thirty in the morning, when the sun was hidden behind the clouds over the mountains in back of Manila, would come the observation plane. It was either "Photograph Joe" in his high-wing monoplane, or the twin-engined, twin-tailed Lockheed monoplane that used to fly right over the island. Joe would circle over the channel between Corregidor and Bataan and the .30- and .50-caliber machine-guns would shoot golden tracers all around him. The 9-inch guns had orders not to open up because Joe had a camera and would photograph their flashes and get their location.

Joe would circle deliberately and then he would release a silver balloon and watch the wind carry it up in the sky. That was to test the wind currents. It filled us with bitter anger to see the deliberate way he got the stage set for the daily murder.

Joe would putt-putt away, flying straight over the middle of Bataan and up to Clark Field, only thirty miles away.

Then Captain Suzuki would call his pilots together out on Clark Field while mechanics loaded the bombs in the silver-winged planes and checked the motors. Suzuki would show the pilots the photographs Joe had taken and give them the weather data and point out their objectives.

At about eleven-thirty the planes would take off and start circling to gain altitude because they had only a short distance to cover and a long way to climb. "Fine weather. Good hunting," Suzuki-san would tell his pilots.

Then the siren would sound on Corregidor and the red lights flash on in Malinta tunnel and the crews would run to their posts on the 3-inch anti-aircraft guns and the .50-caliber machine guns, and everybody else would get under cover.

Then the planes would come over, twenty-seven of them or maybe fifty-four. They would crisscross Corregidor without dropping, taking their time, deliberately getting their targets lined up. The anti-aircraft would open up and burst in them and around them, but if one was shot out they would re-form in their V-formation and keep coming.

Having picked their targets out they would come back flying straight in from over the channels, sometimes from the north and sometimes from the south.

Then would come the noise of the bombs falling. The bombs didn't screech or whistle or whine. They sounded like a pile of planks being whirled around in the air by a terrific wind and driven straight down to the ground. The bombs took thirty years to hit. While they were falling they changed the dimensions of the world. The noise stripped the eagles from the Colonel's shoulders and left him a little boy, naked and afraid. It drove all the intelligence from the nurse's eyes and left them vacant and staring. It wrapped a steel tourniquet of fear around your head, until your skull felt like bursting. It made you realize why man found he needed a God.

The roar of the explosions was a relief from the noise of the falling bombs. You felt the concussion driving against your ears and heard the clatter of collapsing buildings and saw the dust billowing high in the air.

Then would come the fires, and the heroism. Men and women dashing out and picking up the wounded while the bombs were still falling. They would carry the dead and the wounded to the hospital tunnel. You would hear the cars long before they reached the tunnel. The urgency of their horns, blowing all the way down the hill from Topside and then up the slope from Bottomside, told you they were bringing dead and those about to die and those who would be better off dead. The M.P.'s would make the cars slow down as they drove into the big tunnel and they would stop at the hospital tunnel and blood would be dripping down from the cars or the trucks. Then the stretcher bearers would gently lift out the bloody remnants of what had been an American soldier or a Filipino worker a few minutes before. They would lift out the handsome captain whose legs were bloody stumps. They would lift out carefully the 18-year-old American boy who would never again remember his name, or his mother's name, or anything else, but would just look at you blankly when you spoke to him.

When the bombers had finally done their day's murder and gone away there would come the horror, when you went to see the damage they had done. The horror would come when you helped to dig out the bodies of thirty-five young Americans from the "bomb-proof" that had received a direct hit. The bomb explosion didn't kill them, but it blew their mouths and noses and lungs full of dirt and suffocated them.

Then would come the communique: "54 enemy bombers raided Corregidor for three hours today. There was no military damage."

Of course, the communiques had to be worded that way. You couldn't tell the enemy he was hurting you. The wonder was that the bombs didn't do more damage than they did.

The first big raid on Corregidor, on December 29, was one of the worst. The bombs blasted the big barracks on Topside; they tore into the Red Cross painted on the hospital roof, they wrecked the officers' quarters and the cinema, and they knocked out the anti-aircraft control post at Topside. They almost killed MacArthur who was standing in front of his house and refused to be driven to shelter even when the bombs hit near him, and the planes came low and close.

The planes came back on New Year's Day and for the next nine days thereafter. General MacArthur estimated that, considering its size, a greater concentration of bombs dropped on Corregidor than on any other area on earth.

The bombs wrecked the trolley lines and burned out most of the Bottomside shops; they tore down a water tank and repeatedly punctured the water mains, creating a serious problem in sanitation; they burned up fuel supplies; they sank President Quezon's yacht, the ship on which we had escaped from Manila, a half-dozen other ships anchored in a straight-line out in the bay, and nearly all the small boats used for communication with Bataan. They bounced off the roof of the power plant and the cold-storage plant leaving both of them in operation.

When the bombers went away for a while, after the 29th, Corregidor shook itself and found amazingly that it was not too badly wounded. Almost everything above ground had been hit but the damage was quickly patched up, as far as possible, and auxiliary shops were built underground and supplies moved into the tunnels. The trolley line was beyond repair but there were plenty of trucks and gasoline. Not much food had been lost. Only one gun was put out of action and that was quickly repaired. Casualties were relatively low.

The planes came back intermittently until about January 20. Then they moved on south to the airfield which had been prepared on the Island of Jolo, in the southern Philippines, and from which the bombers operated against Borneo and the Dutch East Indies.

Corregidor had had a foretaste of what was to come later.

It was obvious to everybody on the Rock that with enough bombs and enough bombers the island could eventually be pounded into submission. Even the underground areas could not escape. The Japanese evidently reached the same conclusion, for when they next came back in force, from the first of April onward, they came with scores of dive bombers and heavy bombers and attack planes. They blasted the barbed wire guarding Corregidor's beaches, they knocked out the anti-aircraft guns and the big coast defense rifles, they killed our Marines in the trenches along the beaches. Finally, after a month of pounding, they captured Corregidor.

21

WHEN THE PLANES WEREN'T OVERHEAD LIFE ON CORREGIDOR was not too unpleasant. For the first few days there were still some of the minor pleasures of
peacetime life in the big army garrison—a little ice cream or a bottle of Coca-
Cola; but they soon became major luxuries and then disappeared altogether.

I met a lot of old friends from Shanghai in the Fourth Marines, who were
assigned to beach defenses of Corregidor after having been bombed out of
Olangapo. Colonel Samuel Howard, the Marine commander, set up headquarters in the Navy tunnel. Lieutenant Colonel "Duke" Hamilton got me a
pair of marine shoes to replace the China-made oxfords which had stood up
during the hike from Baguio but were now decidedly down at heel. Corporal
"Gabby" Kash of Los Angeles gave the Jacobys and myself a half-dozen cans
of salmon and a big can of tomato juice.

I asked Gabby, who had been a protegee of radio announcer Carroll Alcott in Shanghai, how he accounted for the fine morale of the Marines and
why they seemed to be less bothered by the bombing than the rest of the
forces.

"Well," he said, "it's mostly because we have to live up to our traditions
and reputation. Everybody expects us to be good—just a little bit better than
anybody else—and so we just have to be good."

Sergeant White, star shortstop and rugby player of the Fourth Marines
during their Shanghai days, lost a leg early in the Battle of Corregidor, but he
was one of the most cheerful men on the Rock. I used to chat with him for a
few minutes every day while he was in bed. Within ten days he was getting
around easily on crutches.

I asked him if he wasn't in pain.

"I must have been," he said, "because they tell me I was delirious and
pretty hard to get along with for a week. But I don't remember it at all. I'm
all set now. They'll give me an artificial leg as good as new. I'll get preference
for a civil service job that'll pay me one hundred and thirty dollars a month. In
a couple of weeks our help will be here and we'll chase the Japs out of the islands and they'll take me to Australia in a hospital ship and then send me
home."

It was a little cold sleeping in the trolley station, so Jacoby and I looked
around for a place to live. Cabot Colville, former second secretary of the
American Embassy in Tokyo and now a member of Sayre's staff, told us we
could sleep on cots on the porch in the house assigned to Sayre, next door to
General MacArthur's. Sayre, his wife, and her 12-year old son were sleeping in
the hospital tunnel. Annalee was also assigned a bed in the tunnel, over her
strenuous objections. At Sayre's house we could get an occasional shower,

when the bombs hadn't disrupted the water supply, and it also was high enough above the bay level to provide a good lookout post.

At night we could sit on the grass outside and watch our guns firing in Bataan. In the morning we would see our anti-aircraft firing on the Japanese dive bombers which made almost daily raids on our improvised airfields at Cabcaben, on the southeastern tip of the peninsula. The house was handy to our first mess, which was driven out of Bottomside by the bombings and set up on a slope to the east of Malinta tunnel. We seldom made it for breakfast but the cooks would save us a cup of coffee. Later, after a couple of weeks, General MacArthur transferred us to the officers' mess which was just outside the eastern entrance to the tunnel.

There we ate more frequently but in lesser quantities than at the soldiers' mess. The officers were served a cup of coffee and a piece of toast and sometimes a piece of bacon for breakfast; a cup of soup and a half sandwich at lunch; and for dinner some kind of salmon, canned vegetable, and dessert of rice pudding or something similar. The Chinese chef, Ah Fu, was an artist—but you could only do so many things with salmon and rice.

Social life in the evenings centered around the officers' mess and the mess for convalescent patients and hospital attendants outside the northern entrance to the hospital tunnel. It was cool, and the stars shone brightly above the bay, and we listened to San Francisco on the radio and to Tokyo, and to the puppet station in Manila. Later, USAFFE set up its own "Voice of Freedom" radio in Malinta tunnel with news broadcasts three times daily to the troops.

There was considerable grumbling the night Bing Crosby broadcast to Bataan, because the Japs jammed the music and dialogue—all except the cheese ads. There had been one of the worst bombings that day and nobody had had much more than a piece of bread and a cup of coffee. Our reaction was, "For God's sake, Americans, stop making cheese and make bullets and airplanes, because we need them fast."

Living next to General MacArthur had its disadvantages. If his phone rang in the night it would awaken us and we would know that some serious threat had developed in Bataan. In the mornings the general would walk around his lawn and circle our house with his long, purposeful strides. He never paid any attention to air raid alarms until the planes were actually overhead. To save face, we would have to ignore the warning too and stifle our inclination to dash for the safety of the tunnel. Many mornings we would walk along with him and get the latest news.

Getting news and getting it out was our first concern after our status on Corregidor became established, and for Jacoby and myself it was the toughest battle of the war. As early as the first day we told Colonel Diller, "We want to report this story."

Diller said, "Go ahead and write it." We wrote and wrote and wrote. We wrote of the last night in Manila, the fires and the destruction, we wrote about the bombing of Corregidor. But the censors wouldn't let the stories through. I spent a day with Lieutenant Jennings and some other Marine friends in a concrete trench during a heavy bombing raid and had one eardrum injured and nearly got killed—to get a story. I wrote about how it felt to be nearly killed by bombs, and Diller still said no. There were no facilities for press transmission.

There seemed to be no hope. We decided that unless we could do our jobs it was up to us to move on and stop eating the food needed for someone who was doing a job. So we started investigating the possibilities of getting out by boat. In that way we became intimately acquainted with the water transport setup which was one of the most interesting and important phases of the defense of Bataan.

After most of our ships had been sunk by the bombings early in January only a few small boats remained for transportation between Corregidor and Bataan. There were four or five tugboats, which were used to pull barges from Corregidor to Mariveles or Cabcaben and back with loads of fuel and food and ammunition. Both our friends, the Captains Smith, and their tug had been needed by the Army.

All that remained of President Quezon's yacht, except for the masts still sticking out of the water off the North Dock, was a well-fitted launch. It was used to ferry passengers to Bataan. The Signal Corps operated one small launch, built on whaleboat lines, which ran to Cabcaben just before sunrise and again just after sunset, timing its schedule to avoid the bombings. With the wind blowing, Manila Bay became surprisingly rough, and riding in the Signal Corps launch under these conditions was like riding a rollercoaster.

The Philippine Government customs launch No. 4, which Bill Seater and Al Foyt had brought out from Manila on New Year's Eve, was taken over by the Army Engineers. It soon became known as the "Pirate Boat." Its crew, headed by Seater, included several Norwegian seamen whose ships had been sunk by Jap bombs in Manila Bay. There were also several White Russians, one of them an expert machine gunner, and a Filipino sailor or two. Seater and his crew were commended for their heroic work during the final days of Bataan when they made a number of trips under heavy shellfire to rescue American nurses and troops and convey them safely to Corregidor.

During the early days on Corregidor the Engineers, with their hands in everything and dozens of difficult jobs to do with improvised materials, refused to be bound by Army red tape. When the Engineers heard that some metal or some wire, or something else they needed for vital construction, could be found at such and such a place in Bataan, they would simply send over their launch and bring back the materials. I went on many a night raiding party to Bataan in the Pirate Boat. Some days we would go over and anchor in shallow water off the tip of Bataan and spend the afternoon swimming and washing ourselves and our clothes.

The Engineers knew how to fight a war in the most comfortable possible way. They worked hard and efficiently and when their work was finished they settled back and enjoyed themselves. Their tunnel, just across from the power plant in the Bottomside section, was well lighted and well furnished. For a while they even had cocktail parties. The wherewithal for them was obtained the night of January 1, when the wine supply was brought ashore from President Quezon's yacht. An officer of the Engineers stood on the dock in the darkness and as the soldiers came ashore with cases on their shoulders he directed them, "One here and one there." "Here" was a truck sent to the dock by the president; "there" was an engineer truck.

The boats which were most interesting to the soldiers on Corregidor were not even floating. They were two barges, one loaded with whisky from the Manila Army and Navy Club and the other with dried prunes and raisins. The barges were sunk in shallow water off the North Dock by Japanese bombs. Some soldiers spent hours diving in the oil-coated water, cutting their hands on glass and getting smeared with Diesel fuel from head to foot, to bring up a single bottle. They would be so thirsty from their exertions that they would drink it right there before coming ashore.

Undamaged by the bombs were three inter-island ships: the large and modern Legaspi and two smaller Diesel-engined vessels. With these ships MacArthur organized a blockade-running system. During late January and February the ships slipped out of Manila Bay at night and ran down to Cebu, where they loaded rice and other provisions which were brought back to the Army in Bataan. On their outward trips the ships carried American and Filipino aviators hoping to reach Australia and Navy men who had no warships to fight in.

The remnants of the U.S. Asiatic Fleet could have been counted on two hands. The biggest was the sub tender Canopus which was anchored off Mariveles and used as a repair vessel. There were the three Yangtze River gunboats: the Oahu, Luzon, and Mindanao, and three or four auxiliary minesweepers, minelayers, and tugs. There were one or two ships' boats and a number of private fishing yachts which had been brought out from Manila. And there were Lieutenant John Bulkley's PT boats.

Shortly after we arrived on Corregidor the Engineers' launch broke one of her twin-propeller shafts, making her useless for towing. Someone suggested trying to get through to Australia on the one remaining engine, but the Engineers repaired the boat quickly and put it back in service.

Then we located what seemed to be the ideal getaway boat, a 65-foot schooner belonging to an executive of Jan Marsman's companies. The owner, who was on board with a crew of two Manila businessmen, was anxious to get out. We began working in earnest. Our friends among the Engineers gave us some drums of Diesel oil for the auxiliary engine. We made a special trip to Bataan to get a compass off the Yusang. We pored over charts of the islands, planning various routes to the south through the Japanese blockade. We pestered MacArthur's staff for information as to which islands the Japanese had seized and which were unoccupied.

While we were hard at work on the boat we continued to write stories in the hope that one would get through. Finally, on January 9, Colonel Diller agreed to transmit one short story for me. It was about the abortive tank attack in southeastern Luzon on Christmas Day and it came from Sergeant Robert Mitchell, who had made his way to Corregidor and was undergoing treatment for his wounds. He was convalescent but still weak, and his face was pale beneath his reddish-hair. He was anxious to get back to the tanks and he finally did late in February, when he was permitted to return to active service in Bataan.

The day after I sent through a short account of Mitchell's experiences the censorship clamped down again. There was never any explanation, but I think the situation in Bataan was then so uncertain—with the first big Japanese push in progress—that nobody had much time to bother about our stories.

Mel and I tackled the problem from a new angle. We began haunting the Navy tunnel, calling on Admiral Rockwell and his staff and doing a quiet job of salesmanship. Finally we got Commander Mike Cheek, the Intelligence officer, on our side, and Admiral Rockwell agreed to assist us.

"Since we haven't many ships," he said, "our wireless is not too busy. We can transmit some stories for you." He agreed that the first story could be one thousand words long, and thereafter each correspondent would be permitted five hundred words daily. In addition to Mel and Annalee and myself there were three correspondents in Bataan—Frank Hewlett of the UP, Nat Floyd of the New York Times, and a man from the Reuters (British) news agency.

The transmission problem had been solved but there was still the necessity of writing stories that would meet Diller's approval. He turned thumbs down on most of our efforts. I had noticed that the daily USAFFE News Bulletin, compiled by Major Romulo and Captain Kenneth Saner from intercepted radio broadcasts, had been headlining the deeds of what they called the "world's champion anti-aircraft battery." It was Battery G of the 60th Coast Artillery. Colonel Diller thought it would be all right if I visited them in Bataan and wrote about them, I got the story and it went through.

Meantime, our yacht was ready to sail and the owner came to tell us.

We decided that, inasmuch as we could now do our jobs, we would be earning our keep, so we let the yacht go without us. We learned later that it got through safely to one of the islands in the southern Philippines. There the crew took to the hills to sit out the rest of the war.

22

WHEN I FINALLY LEFT CORREGIDOR, I DESTROYED MY NOTES and diaries on orders of General MacArthur. The Jacobys and I were going to attempt to run through the Japanese blockade and we didn't want any written information to fall into enemy hands if we were killed or captured.

However, on arriving in Australia, I found in my wallet a few torn pages of the diary I kept on Corregidor and Bataan. One page has part of an entry from January 6. It says: "Casiana (President Quezon's yacht) sunk today by bombs through sheer neglect. Quezon bought it from E. L. Doheny who bought it from Prince of Monaco. Quezon had it about four years, got it for song. Its U.S. and Filipino flags flying from masts which still project above water."

The "sheer neglect" of which I accuse some undesignated person or persons evidently reflected Quezon's own indignation at losing his yacht. He felt, and I recall that I did, that the yacht and other ships should not have been left anchored in a straight line off Corregidor's North Dock—an easy target for the bombers—but should have been scattered around the harbor. Since the bombing at Clark Field where our planes were all lined up in neat rows, and in Manila Bay, where the ships were nicely lined up for the bombers, I have an obsession against seeing things in straight lines, especially ships and airplanes.

On the same day I wrote in my diary:

[Ed. Note: All spelling and grammatical errors in the following diary entries are as the author intended]

"Got to tunnel before air alarm and breakfasted at Bottomside. Some sort of meat with cream sauce. Saw Major Hughes of Army Transport who just got back from Cabcaben (at southeastern end of Bataan) where Japanese bombed for seven hours yesterday trying to knock out our two runways. Hughes promised to look out for boat for us and tip us if anything going out.

Been a real friend and a real hard worker, handling transport to and from Corregidor - Brooklyn boy Col. Pierce of 26th Cavalry. I learned USAFFE reorganizing forces in Bataan. Some divisions at one third infantry strength.

USAFFE now trying to shape up front line with trained units. Hard job since so few Scouts or experienced troops. Body washed up on Corregidor taken to hospital. Possibly Jap airman or Filipino officer, probably Jap, judging by the gold teeth.

I was in Navy tunnel during bombing but for some reason it didn't seem as safe as Malinta tunnel so I ducked out and ran over there. Foolish.

I'm on Navy blacklist according to Commander Mike Cheek, Intelligence officer. Said the Navy thought I was a "Bolshevik" for my stories about Manila. Nevertheless, they agreed to send stuff for Mel (Jacoby) and myself starting tomorrow.

Turned in first colorless summary to Diller for censorship hoping it will pass so at least folks back home know I'm living.

Bombs for about three hours. Army's remaining waterfront equipment, launches, fire barge, etc., blitzed. One direct hit on Middleside battery killed 35. Some others dug out okay but badly shaken. I'd rather get a direct hit than be buried that way.

Got some stores, pineapple juice, etc. Also bottle beer. Sergeant Rutherford presented pack of Luckies. Navy radio on Monkey Point also bombed.

Good chow. Mutton, Catsup, beans, peas, bread, rice pudding, coffee."

My diary for January 7-8 reads:

"Only small raids both days. Japanese apparently concentrating Baatan [at the time I didn't even know how to spell Bataan] ground forces. Met Dean Schedler of Quartermaster Corps, a civilian who was friend of Ray Cronin our bureau chief in Manila. Also met Al Foyt, tall, big-eared, mustached Hollywood adventurer type, civilian employee of Engineers, Foyt calls himself "the guy with the ears," and says, "My mother was frightened by a Yellow Taxi with the doors open."

Schedler and Foyt took me to Army Engineer tunnel in devastated North Dock section. Foyt, who came here last year "to get a ringside seat at the war" was blown into sewer in January 6 bombing which wrecked the Bottomside shops containing machinery, tools, garage equipment, etc. There were two direct hits on Engineer tunnel which bounced Engineers around but didn't hurt them as they have six feet of concrete and about thirty feet of rock over their heads.

Engineers hard-boiled bunch, cheerful because they are active, doing everything from repairing water pipes, putting out fires, to digging out bodies from bomb ruins. Lt. Col. Lloyd Milenz in command. They tough and efficient. Even have a gorgeous secretary, Mrs. Helen Grady, wife of an artillery captain. Her freshly pressed blue slacks, clean white shoes, seemed an amazing touch amid so much death and fire and devastation.

Engineers just had showers, due to bomb hit bursting open water pipe outside their tunnel. Served me White Label whisky with ice, and sliced Edam cheese.

Night January 6 went with Engineers on 65-foot, twin Diesel-engine customs launch to Cabcaben, Bataan. Had brawl on dock when somebody hollered son of a peech at our boat for flashing light on dock so we could see to tie up. Engineers drew .45's and so did those on dock and there was some slugging and nearly shooting. Just tense nerves.

Rode 15 miles into hills to field headquarters of Engineers. Three of us dangled feet from the tailboard of station wagon. Dark but able to see big trees, heavy vines, thick vegetation.

Visited Engineer chief, Colonel Stickney, waking him about midnight and remaining until 3 A.M. He comfortable in tent with bed and mosquito netting. Wearing violently striped pajamas. They talked shop while I sat on tent step. After while colonel exclaimed, "Gad, gentlemen, I'm forgetting my hospitality." Pulled out a bottle of Martell Brandy and passed it around twice.

Colonel told us story of a major who was cut off by Japs during our retreat into Bataan. Lay for hours in small bamboo clump and watched helplessly while Japs ravished women of nearby village. Japs poked bayonets into bamboo but failed to see major who later escaped and rejoined us in Bataan.

Also told us that retreat was somewhat disorderly. Of battery of six 8-inch guns, only two reached Bataan. Two were left on railway siding where Japs got them. Two others put out action. Many other stories of grousing, inefficiency.

Colonel said our outlook none too good. Only two regiments of nervous constabulary guarding entire west coast of Bataan. Also said our green troops still running. I argued with him that we had let the Filipinos down badly, failing to provide them proper weapons, or air support, or any direct leadership for small Filipino units. He agreed."

January 7

Good dinner in officers' mess, after which visited wrecked Topside area from where able see Manila buildings, just distinguishable in distance. Saw Battery WAY, formerly our anti-aircraft control post on Corregidor, which knocked out by accurate Jap bombing.

Major McNair (of Red Bank, NJ) of anti-aircraft command, which now located in Malinta tunnel, said Jap bombing over-all is not so hot. All "stick stuff" without precision bombing at single targets. Japs take bearings on high point of Corregidor always fly at 21,000 to 25,000 feet and from same direction. Their routine makes work easier for our AA which is 90 per cent information—plotting course, speed, direction winds, etc. One battery has best record because it is located where can shoot at Japs before bombs start falling.

That's easier on nerves than shooting after bombs already in air. This battery got several direct hits on bombers, causing mid-air explosions.

Jap 97 bomber is a slick plane, twin-engined medium bomber. Also have used some 4-engine bombers. Their low-level strafing by fighters is directed at specific targets, showing they had information about what to attack on Corregidor. It has been effective.

Our P-40's in Bataan now confined solely to observation. Fly in pairs, one observing and other watching for hostile aircraft. They shooting down one Jap plane daily.

Talked with three Air Corps mechanics in morning. Stranded here being part of dive bomber squadron which arrived just before war but whose planes never got here. They casually discussed merits of new American planes, A-20-A, B-17, B-24, B-25, B-26, etcetera, apparently wonderful ships which had been sent to Europe. Heartbreaking to hear about them.

There was only one brief entry for January 8:

No breakfast. Spent most of day riding around harbor looking for possible boat for trip south provided censorship doesn't open up. One prop shaft broken on Engineers' boat. We went aboard inter-island steamer Don Esteban, one of few boats not sunk by Japs. Drunken Scotch engineer in charge, looked like Glencannon, with purple shorts, green undershirt. Wavered in breeze as American Army lieutenant administered some sort of oath whereby he pledged loyalty to American Army. Some trouble on boat between Engineers and Army Water Transport men. Typical of interdepartmental jealousy, rivalry. Believe argument was over who should have jurisdiction over Don Esteban.

January 9 & 10

Worked on boat proposition. Customs launch taken to Mariveles for repairs to broken propeller shaft but seems definitely out for our purposes. Army needs it. Jap fishing sampan Suntay II which seized in Manila is available. Captain Smith II, who brought us out from Manila, will go if he can be convinced there is a 50-50 chance of getting through. He is well acquainted with islands and would be ideal skipper. However, USAFFE now says chances getting through not so good as Japs patrolling Zamboanga-Jolo-Borneo waters through which would have to run to reach Java. Might be able to get to some island in PI from where could work down to Australia.

25 bombers, 9 fighters attacked Mariveles today. Fighters strafed and blew hell out of six old Navy seaplanes which were supposedly hidden from view along beach. Some kind friend no doubt told them where they were.

Asked Major McNair, who other officers say is one of most popular and best young officers on Corregidor, why our planes were caught on ground at Clark Field. He answered, "Policy. Both national and local." That cost us most of our Air Force and may cost us Luzon.

Lt. Col. Reginald Vance, who flies ancient P.I. army biplane to Bataan every morning and evening, has head in bandage. Also Major Wilkinson of British Army who was riding with them. They made crash landing on our small Corregidor airfield and their heads were cut on cockpit.

Had long talk with Quezon. Quezon affectionate with family—wife, two daughters, one son. Wears army field cap, beige jacket, sometimes army pants (jodhpurs) or striped slacks. Slippers. In wheelchair.

Major McNair said many soldiers who didn't fit in well anywhere in Army before the war now are among his best men, notably as watchers who have to sit in exposed positions throughout raids in constant touch by one-way telephone with AA command post. Some men crack up under bombing. Army gives them other jobs. Everybody agrees bombs more terrifying than other weapons because individual has no way of fighting them. Everybody (except MacArthur) seems as scared as the staff captain who said, "I never knew I could or would be so frightened. Wonder if I'll get over it."

Attitude of some Americans out here toward Filipinos is distrustful, somewhat hostile. These Americans claim the Filipinos should have been able and prepared to defend their country without our help, since they were asking for independence. I say this argument is absolutely false and unjust. Our bargain was to free them in 1946, not December 8, 1941. Until 1946, it was our job to defend this American territory.

However there is justification for our officers' contention that even our Army felt disinterested in making thorough defense preparations as long as independence was coming in 1946.

WE STILL NEED PLANES

January 11

Sunday. Chaplain Trump of 4th Marines, old friend from Shanghai, said three services during morning air alarms, which almost continuous. Trump and I used to argue hammer and tongs in Shanghai over U.S. policy. He was a rabid Republican and isolationist.

I played poker with Quezon's aides most of morning, losing $20 to President's physician, a major. We played in the hospital mess tunnel, and halted our game while chaplain read services to doctors and nurses and they all joined in singing hymns.

After game I went out for a smoke and the air alarm sounded while I was talking to Sergeant Domingo Adversario, for 14 years MacArthur's orderly, for 12 years in army and 2 as personal servant. Domingo, 39, and Solomon Bayoneta, ex-Filipino Scout now chauffeur, saved MacArthur's life the other day. Here's the official report: "MacArthur narrowly escaped serious injury during recent bombing raid when a large bomb exploded less than 10 feet from him. General was accompanied by two orderlies, one of whom served him 12 years. During raid the orderlies protected the general to best of their ability providing him with steel helmet and shielding him with their bodies. Piece of rock struck general in shoulder and one faithful orderly was wounded in hand."

This report dated January 1, refers to December 29 bombing, first big Corregidor blitz. Here's the way Domingo tells it.

"We were inside General's house Topside, when air alarm sounded. I told General go down (apparently to air raid shelter) and he ask me if I hear airplane. When I hear he go outside, we all three leaning against embankment. One bomb striking tree in front of us, I holding helmet front General's face, my face, half and half, chauffeur standing behind him.

"Piece shrapnel hit my finger where holding helmet cut it almost one half off but it now recover. After, Japanese planes come very near and machine-gun us but we no time to dodging only lean backward. I feel general's knees shaking."

MacArthur is certainly a hero to his valet, Domingo thinks he's wonderful. Domingo went to Washington with the General and lived at Ft. Myer where he spent his happiest years although Domingo had to leave his bride of three months behind when he went to U.S. Said MacArthur always in tip-top condition, walks, walks, walks constantly, does calisthenics, no drinks. Always leave parties at 11 P.M.

Domingo objects to one part of his job—waiting on table for women. Also doesn't like ironing and household chores which feels un-soldier like.

Scene in tunnel during air raid. Filipino workman with red-haired statue of Virgin carefully guarded and wrapped. Figure over half his size.

Note for story—if can ever send. Corp. William Hamby, Tillamook, Oregon, who fetched wounded to hospital during air raids. Former logger, now chauffeur for a colonel. One of wounded was Hamby's best friend, whose leg was blown off. He died after whispering to Hamby, "Keep 'em flying, fellow."

23

DURING THOSE FIRST DAYS WHEN CORREGIDOR WAS UNDER heavy bombing attacks we were too busy keeping our skins intact to learn much about what was going on in Bataan. It was still terra incognita.

I watched the maps on the walls of the USAFFE tunnel and saw that our lines were holding pretty well. That was encouraging until I made the shocking discovery that the powerful army of more than 150,000 troops which we had imagined was defending Luzon had existed only in our imaginations.

Instead of sixty thousand American soldiers, there was only one regiment of infantry, the 31st, and in its biggest fight its front-line strength was only 636 officers and men.

There were less than thirty tanks in Bataan. There were about ten airplanes. The American forces, including tanks, Air Corps personnel. Signal Corps, and Engineers, did not exceed five thousand on Bataan with another seven or eight thousand on Corregidor.

The remaining soldiers on Bataan were some thirty thousand Filipinos, of whom approximately half were well-trained Scouts and the remainder virtually untrained recruits.

Our original front line on Bataan, which was designated as the MLR or Main Line of Resistance, extended from Moron on the China Sea side to Abucay on the east coast. On the USAFFE maps the original MLR was indicated in blue pencil with the Japanese positions penciled in red.

General MacArthur did not have even enough troops to hold an unbroken line across the fifteen-mile-wide peninsula, and he had to leave part of the mountainous area in the center undefended. The Japs quickly found that out.

After January 15 the blue pencil lines on the maps began to be pierced by little red arrows, indicating where Jap infiltration parties had come through the undefended portion of the slopes of Mt. Natib.

Then more and more red lines appeared until finally about January 26 the whole former MLR was indicated in red and our second line of resistance had suddenly become the mainline.

The second front line which our forces held until the fall of Bataan extended from below Bagac on the west to the town of Pilar on the bay side. That meant that only about eighteen miles of the entire Bataan Peninsula was in our hands.

The front line crisscrossed the only east-west road on the peninsula, so that neither side could use it. Our communications and transport of supplies were confined to a horseshoe-shaped portion of the road around the southern end of the peninsula, extending from the front lines on the west back to

Mariveles and Cabcaben, and then up to the front lines on the east. Communications with Corregidor were maintained from Mariveles and Cabcaben.

Mt. Bataan and Mt. Mariveles, the latter 4,600 feet high, were within our lines. Both mountains ran from northeast to southwest and both were so rugged and jungle-covered that no roads could be built across them. General Wainwright commanded the western sector, and General Parker was in command of the eastern sector on the Manila side of Bataan.

After the censors decided to let us tell some of the story of the war in the Philippines, I began to commute between Bataan and Corregidor, spending two days with the troops getting stories and then two days back at Corregidor writing them and getting them past the censorship. I found that by personally chaperoning the stories to General Sutherland's desk and by haunting the USAFFE tunnel until he finally read the copy, the stories moved much faster.

Starting out from Corregidor to make a circuit of Bataan, I would ride over in one of the PT boats, or with Ensign George Petritz in his launch, and get off at Mariveles. Going into the calm waters of Mariveles Bay we would pass the submarine tender Canopus aground at the entrance and the Dewey floating dry dock. The dock was kept submerged during most of the day while the Jap bombers were overhead and then floated late in the afternoon. It was used to repair the PT boats and other small craft which maintained communication between Corregidor and Bataan.

Landing at the Mariveles quarantine station I would walk a few hundred yards to the road and hitchhike a ride on the first passing vehicle. The road ran straight and level for about two miles north from Mariveles. A mile of the level stretch was being widened as a runway for the bombers which we all expected would fly in any day.

For the first few weeks, until the gasoline situation suddenly became alarming and strict rationing was enforced, the road was always thick with traffic. Dust coated the leaves and vines and bushes, hung thickly over the roadway. It was so blinding that when two vehicles met, one had to pull up alongside the road and let the dust from the other subside before proceeding.

General Wainwright's field headquarters were an hour-and-a-half drive from Mariveles through the thick dust and under the heavy canopy of foliage which nearly blacked out the sun. You turned off the main road, into a single-track road leading up the mountainside and toward the middle of the peninsula. As you went higher the underbrush grew less thick, but the great trees, with their enormous bases, seemed to grow even taller and the vines extending from the tree tops to the ground thicker.

Because of the trees and hilly country it was impossible to make much use of our artillery on the west coast of Bataan. Some big guns were spotted on points of land projecting into the China Sea, including some 155's and an old 6-inch naval gun which MacArthur's artillerymen had dug up from somewhere. The 155's in this area could fire into the Moron-Bagac area and time after time they inflicted terrible slaughter on Japanese forces trying to attack our lines.

There were also some smaller, more mobile 75-mm, guns on the west side of our line, right in the front-line foxholes and trenches with our troops. Many of the artillerymen were friends of Mel Jacoby, who had served in the same ROTC unit at Stanford, and Jacoby and I tried many times to locate them in the field but never succeeded.

A couple of miles from Mariveles by airline, but some five or six miles by road, was a level place in the hills known as Little Baguio. In this area of giant trees were concentrated behind-the-line headquarters for Bataan.

At Little Baguio food, munitions, clothes, and supplies were distributed to the front-line units. The anti-aircraft control post for guns sprinkled around Bataan was located there and the headquarters of General George and his midget Air Force were nearby.

The main road ran from Little Baguio to the small town of Cabcaben, at the southeastern tip of Bataan. Behind Cabcaben were Base Hospital No. 2, with three thousand beds in the open air, and a refugee camp for some twenty thousand Filipino civilians who had fled from their homes.

Cabcaben consisted of two palm-lined dusty streets leading down to the bayfront and to the stone jetty at which the supply barges from Corregidor were tied up to load and unload. Driving through the town you turned north along the Manila Bay side of Bataan and came to our airfields, two wide, brown, and dusty runways. Anti-aircraft batteries, including New Mexico's 200th, were hidden in camouflaged positions around the turnways.

This side of the peninsula was much more level and open than the west coast, and the beaches were low and smooth. Barbed-wire entanglements were stretched out into the shallow water to guard the beaches. The handful of tanks and mounted 75's still in action maintained a patrol along the road, which ran through two small bayside villages and up to the city of Balanga, smashed flat by Japanese dive bombers and artillery. The area of rice fields extended about four miles inland from Manila Bay and this open terrain was dominated by our artillery. The front lines consisted of foxholes, trenches, and machine-gun strong points, protected by barbed wire.

This was the setting in which the Battle of Bataan was fought, from January 1 to April 8. The battle developed in three stages. We won the first round; the second was a stalemate; and the third was a black and bitter and crushing defeat.

The first phase of the battle extended from January 1 until February 10. After preliminary skirmishing while our advance units were still fighting delaying actions, the Japanese hit our main line of resistance on January 6 at Moron on the western flank. Having taken most of Luzon almost without a struggle they pushed on, recklessly and confidently, and captured Moron. The weary

26th Cavalry, which had borne the brunt of fighting in the Lingayen area, was ordered to counterattack. They recaptured Moron.

Then the Japanese hit our right flank along the shore of Manila Bay and pushed back the lines of the 41st Division, Philippine Army. The Japanese suffered heavy losses for every foot they gained, for they were under fire from our big 155 artillery. Then came a momentous day in the history of the Philippines. MacArthur ordered the 41st Division to attack and restore their lines. Up to then no unit of green Filipino soldiers had done anything except retreat, under orders, as we withdrew into Bataan.

The 41st went forward under a blasting barrage. They restored their positions. They routed the Japs out of the fox-holes and trenches from which the 41st had withdrawn. They found they could defeat the Japs and they pressed their attacks far beyond their original positions—so far that they had to be recalled in order to straighten our lines.

The Japs thrust at another place, a few miles inland up the slopes of Mt. Natib. Their agile soldiers found that part of the mountain was undefended and slithered through and into the rear of our lines. They climbed trees and began sniping, picking off our officers and the men carrying supplies to the front. Simultaneously they made a headlong attack against the 51st Division of the Philippine Army, which was holding positions inland and adjacent to the 41st. The 51st was driven back for a half mile.

MacArthur called on his lone American infantry regiment, the 31st, to restore the gap. In five days of dogged, foot-by-foot fighting, the 31st regained all but 150 yards of the salient. But by that time hundreds and hundreds of Japs had infiltrated over Mt. Natib and our positions were becoming untenable. On January 26, MacArthur had to withdraw his forces back to the second and final main line of resistance, extending from Pilar to Bagac. There could be no further retreat.

The Japs thought it was all over. They pushed forward, confidently marching down the east coast road in groups of five and six hundred. Our 155's blasted them off the road and the Jap drive was stopped cold. By the end of January the Japs had failed in their attempt to crack our line in frontal assaults. Lieutenant General Masaharu Homma, the Japanese commander, gave up and withdrew his forces for a few miles.

Homma tried new tactics. He attacked MacArthur's flanks from the China Sea side. This was a serious, almost a fatal threat to Bataan. The Japanese landed on five points of land along the west coast. MacArthur couldn't withdraw troops from his front line to face them. That would have left the front wide open. But somewhere MacArthur found the men he needed, half a company here, ten men there, a squad from somewhere else.

These makeshift forces penned the Japs on the points and prevented them from cutting the west road and coming in the rear of our front lines. Part of the 57th under Colonel George Clarke, and 45th Filipino Scouts, after aiding the 31st U.S. Infantry in fighting on the east coast, were rushed over to fight against the landings. The naval battalion of Marines and sailors, commanded by Commander Frank Bridget, pitched in. The PT boats broke up one attempt by the Japanese to reinforce their landings. Three P-40's took the air one night and bombed and strafed another landing group.

Through the thick jungle our forces inched their way forward to mop up the Japanese on the points. The fighting was slow and hard and costly. But finally, about February 10, the last Japanese was killed. Altogether about 2,500 of them died in the futile attempts to crack our flanks.

Homma made one final effort. A Japanese regiment drove a wedge into the western side of our front lines. That sector was held by Igorots from the mountains of Baguio. The Igorots did not crack. They fought until they were killed and finally piled up so many enemy bodies in front of their positions that the Japanese drive lost its momentum. The Japs dug into their salient, determined to fight to the last man. The Igorots led an attack by our infantry and tanks which wiped them out to the last man. Our front was restored.

That was the last gasp of the first Japanese offensive. Homma's original landing force had been cut to pieces. MacArthur estimated "the Jap" had lost thirty thousand men killed or wounded in six weeks of fighting in Bataan. The Japs were short of ammunition, of medicine and guns. They pulled back all along the line.

MacArthur's spies, coming out from Manila, reported the Jap officers were having trouble getting troops to go to the Bataan front. Some of the younger Japanese threw away their uniforms and tried to disguise themselves as Filipinos. The Jap officers rounded up every Filipino with a short haircut, suspecting him of being a Jap soldier.

Then came the second phase, the lull while the Japs waited for reinforcements. They might have won in the first phase if they had not moved their Air Force to the south, to Malaya and the Netherlands East Indies. From the end of January until nearly the end of March the Japs had only a handful of planes, possibly less than thirty, flying in the Philippines at any one time. That was the reason Bataan held so long.

The Japanese were waiting for reinforcements and MacArthur, too, was awaiting reinforcements. His soldiers were full of confidence. They had the feeling of victory. They had licked the Japs and thought they deserved reinforcement. Wainwright wanted help. General Parker wanted help. So did Jones and Lim and Capinpin.

They knew they could win with the proper tools. They believed the Philippines had to be held, now that Singapore and Java were going. They thought help was coming. The Japs, apparently, knew that it wasn't.

So the Japs took their time and brought in their reinforcements and brought their planes back, about the end of March. Meantime, our forces, which a few weeks before had been confident of final victory, were running out of food, medicine, and bullets, and out of hope too.

The Japs called in General Yamashita, who had blitzed Malaya and Singapore. On April 1, with his reinforced troops, Yamashita struck. His planes hit everywhere at once. His troops smashed against our front all along the line. They landed on the cliffs on the China Sea coast and simultaneously on the level east coast of Manila Bay. They attacked everywhere in that final terrible assault.

For eight days our forces held: the young Filipinos, the veteran Scouts, the survivors of the 31st Infantry, the aviators without airplanes.

Then the Battle of Bataan was ended.

24

BUT BEFORE IT ENDED, THERE WAS A LOT OF EXCITEMENT. One part of the Battle of Bataan I enjoyed was riding in the PT boats. They offered an opportunity to strike at the enemy instead of just sitting and taking it during bombings. They went fast and hit hard, and they gave you a good chance to get away and come back to hit again later. They were one weapon that we had that could hold its own. Unless you were very unlucky, riding them wasn't especially dangerous. They were so small and fast that they were difficult to hit. During the Philippine campaign only one was lost due to enemy action.

For sheer pleasure of movement, the PT boats are hard to beat. They cut cleanly and powerfully through the water. Of all the moving vehicles I have ridden in this war, the greatest thrill has been the take-offs in big four-engined naval patrol bombers when they get up on the step and tear across the water at 100 miles an hour before lifting into the air. Then come the dive bombers in a dive, and then the PT boats.

There was some trouble coordinating the work of the PT's with that of the Army in the Philippines. The Army men, including those manning the artillery on the west coast of Bataan, thought that the entire Asiatic Fleet had left for Java in the early days of the Luzon campaign. In addition, the Navy sometimes neglected to inform the artillery batteries when the PT's were going out on a mission. Consequently the PT's were sometimes fired on by our own artillery from the Bataan shore. But the PT men got even in an ironic way. They, in turn, thought that our entire Air Force had been destroyed. And one day when one of our few precious last P-40's flew low over Sisimen Cove, where the PT's were based, the PT's cut loose with their .50-caliber machine guns and put a lot of holes in the plane.

I could never write about the PT boats from Corregidor, even after riding on them and getting first-hand stories from Lieutenant John Bulkeley and the rest of the crews. Admiral Rockwell refused to permit any mention of torpedo boats in my dispatches, even though Washington announced, and every paper in America headlined, the successful attacks. The admiral argued that the Japs might think they had been hit by a destroyer, a submarine, or even a cruiser.

On Corregidor we first heard about the PT's on January 19. The previous night Lieutenant Bulkeley had made his first attack on Jap shipping in Subic Bay with two boats. Bulkeley and PT-34 got back safely after creeping to within 1,000 yards of an enemy transport or cargo vessel of 2,000 tons and putting a pair of torpedoes in it. PT-31, commanded by Lieutenant Edward DeLong, ran aground in Subic and was lost. DeLong and ten of his men finally reached our lines in two Filipino bancas. His second in command. Ensign

William H. Plant of Long Beach, California, and two more of the crew disappeared in the night.

Two days after Bulkeley's first attack, I asked Commander Cheek if I could go out on a raid with the PT's.

Cheek said, "Are you crazy?"

"Probably," I said. "But I'm tired of sitting here taking it. I want to see us hand out something for a change." Mike took me to Admiral Rockwell who gave his permission.

Bulkeley came over to Corregidor later that afternoon and I met him in the Navy tunnel. He was of medium height with cold greenish eyes, and thinning hair. He impressed me as cool, competent, and calculating. He was very much on his toes and he ran his show in his own way.

I told Buck that I'd like to go out with him.

"Our job is essentially suicide missions," he said.

"Well," I said, "I've been around Bataan quite a bit lately and those fellows over there aren't on any picnic. It's the same medicine here on Corregidor. Your boats are at least on the move, and if you do get bumped off it will be quick and practically painless, and you'll be shooting when you go down."

"You can come out tonight if you want to," Bulkeley said, "but you better wait until tomorrow. I'm taking some Army men up and landing them behind the Jap lines where they are going to do some demolition work. It should be interesting," I said okay, that sounded fine.

I went over the next night to go out on the "routine patrol." The PT base in Sisimen Cove was a quiet beautiful harbor on the southern shore of Bataan. I met Bulkeley's senior officers. Lieutenants Kelly, DeLong, and Schumacher and Ensigns Akers, Cox, and Richardson, and the members of the crews.

Buck and the senior officers lived in a native village at the shore end of their wooden pier. They had taken over a nipa shack on the waterfront and put in their beds and pictures of their families. "Mat," a Packard engineer who did wonders in keeping the boats running, shared their quarters. The other officers had another house and the crews shared a larger building.

The PT crews messed on board their ships which were fully equipped with galleys and sleeping quarters despite their small size. Sometimes they went out to dinner on the Mary Ann, the luxurious steam fishing yacht owned by Jan Marsman. The Mary Ann was flagship of the inshore patrol commanded by Lieutenant Ted Raymond of Amesbury, Massachusetts. Her officers were mostly young naval reservists who had been in business in Manila and had been called into the Navy when war broke out. Usually an ex-fishing boat or a big Philippine Fisheries Department boat would go out at night with one of the PT's for offshore patrol, while smaller fishing yachts would assist the

Philippine Army Q-boats and the ex-Yangtze River gunboats in patrolling Manila Bay and the inner coast of Bataan.

Those youngsters who manned the fishing boats for offshore patrol were real heroes. If any enemy ship sighted them they were dead ducks. The PT's could put on speed and runaway, or could stay there and fight, but the fishing boats could only make 18 knots wide open on a calm sea. Their few machine guns were not much protection.

One fishing boat, or one of the PT's, tied up each night at a buoy at the outside end of the minefields. It kept a lookout for hostile craft and also served as a guide for our incoming patrol boats and for the submarines which came into Corregidor from the end of January up until Bataan fell, and even afterward.

Before we shoved off for my first patrol, I made a list of the boys on board, fourteen in all. Then Ensign Richardson came along and took my name, "Just in case, you know." The crews were superstitious about the number thirteen and would either take twelve or fourteen men along.

Unfortunately, from the news point of view, that patrol turned out to be routine. We went up the coast and saw the huge fires behind the Jap lines where the bodies of men killed by our artillery were being cremated. We went into the mouth of Subic Bay and failed to sight anything. I found the bunks down below too stuffy and slept on deck, curled up by the forward torpedo tube with my padded life jacket for a pillow.

Any number of times I arranged to go out in the hope of seeing some action, only to have the mission called off at the last minute. One other night I did go out with Lieutenant Vince Schumacher and we thought we sighted a ship. For a long time we crept up on it, with the torpedoes ready to fire. Then we discovered it was a big rocky island off the upper entrance to Subic Bay. At any rate, riding the PT boats was a pleasant way to get a good sleep—though it was a little wet sometimes on deck—and we had such good meals on the Mary Ann before taking off that the trips were a pleasure.

Bulkeley and PT-41 boat got their second big catch exactly a week after the first. It was Sunday night, January 85. Buck had warned me that it would be routine and so I stayed ashore.

With George Cox at the throttle, PT-41 went into Subic Bay and made an attack at full speed on what Buck told me was a vessel of about 4,000 tons, with a single slanting funnel. They were under heavy fire, and on their way out they luckily dodged a boom of wire and lumber that the Japs had spread across the bay.

Shells from the damaged ship and from shore guns chased them all the way out of the bay. That made them mad and two nights later they took two boats, sneaked up inside the bay, and gave the shore batteries a thorough peppering with machine-gun bullets. I always got a kick out of Buck's description of the sinking of that second vessel.

"It was a classic torpedo attack," he said, "delivered at full throttle in the face of enemy fire." I investigated further and found that Buck called the attack "classic" because that was the way he and his crews had practiced in training. Actually, it was the first attack of its kind in history.

About the second week in February the high-test gasoline needed to run the PT's began to give out. I used to see Bulkley and DeLong and the others on most of my trips around Bataan and one day Buck told me about a plan they were working out.

"We've got only about enough gasoline for one good operation and we have only a few torpedoes left. Then we'll be tied up here. I have suggested that we fill up our boats with the gas that's left and go out and raid Jap shipping along the China coast. After firing all our torpedoes we'll land along the coast, destroy the boats, and hike overland to Chungking."

Buck had served with the Asiatic Fleet and done valuable intelligence work which had won him the nickname of "Charlie Chan" in the Navy. He was well acquainted with the China coast.

I liked his idea and included myself in. "While we're at it," I said, "why not capture some seaport along the China coast like Swatow. I have some recent dope on the Jap garrisons there and on the positions they hold. It ought to be a cinch to take over one of those places provided arrangements can be made for the Chinese Army to cooperate. The Japs don't hold the coast solidly and their garrisons are small in most places."

Buck liked my idea and asked me to go to work on it.

"I have made friends with a Chinese officer, Lieutenant Colonel Chiwang, who is stationed at headquarters of the Philippine Army in Bataan," I told Buck. "I'll bring him down here and introduce you two and ask him to send a message to Chungking getting approval for your landing."

I went up into the woods of Bataan and talked to the colonel. Wang had been sent to the Philippines as an observer for Chiang Kai-shek and when war broke out was attached to the American forces as liaison officer. He was a West Point graduate and had led his troops in the Shanghai battle in 1937. He was under orders to report to his regiment in Burma as soon as possible. I told him I knew how he could get to China, and then took him down to meet Bulkeley.

The colonel agreed to send a wire to Chungking asking permission for us to land and requesting facilities to get us to Chungking. In a few days, an answer came back. Chungking approved the plan and all arrangements were being made. Meanwhile Admiral Rockwell okayed Bulkeley's plan—without the Swatow feature. Nat Floyd of the New York Times heard about the project and decided to go along, one way or another.

Through ways known in both Army and Navy, Dean Schedler and I helped Bulkeley obtain equipment for the expedition: packs and kits and gear of various kinds not needed by the troops in Bataan.

Bulkeley and his officers originally figured on taking seventy-eight men in three boats. Then Nat managed to get the fourth boat in operating condition. We estimated that with the element of surprise and with the firepower furnished by the four boats, we would have a good chance to overcome the Jap garrison on the Swatow waterfront.

With everything all set, the plan was called off. The boats had a more important mission: taking MacArthur out to the new command he was ordered to assume in Australia. When 41 boat left Sisimen Cove, with General MacArthur aboard, there was one hitchhiking reporter along. Nat Floyd had concealed himself in the lazaret. Lieutenant Colonel Wang was taken out by submarine to the southern Philippines and then flown to Australia.

After landing MacArthur in Mindanao, Bulkeley and Kelly in PT-41 and PT-35 attacked and possibly sank a Japanese cruiser off the island of Cebu. Kelly's boat was bombed and strafed by Japanese planes the following day and finally beached, with all but three of the crew either killed or wounded. Bulkeley, Kelly, Akers, Cox, and one or two others reached Australia by airplane, but their crews and the remaining officers stayed behind in the Philippines where they were either captured or killed, or managed to escape to the hills to live as best possible until the war ends.

The PT boats more than proved their worth, in bringing out MacArthur if for no other reason. But in a way I shall always regret that we didn't get a chance to capture Swatow. Bulkeley's wife was born there and it would have been a nice, sentimental gesture.

25

SOON AFTER I STARTED GOING OVER TO BATAAN TO get stories I began hearing about a Captain Wermuth, who, it seemed, was a terror to the Japs. Everywhere soldiers and officers advised me, "See Wermuth if you want some good stories."

The first time I heard about him was when I went over to visit the field artillery. By that time I had visited the anti-aircraft and seen it in action, and I wanted to see how the artillery units were fighting.

I thought it would be a real quiet trip. In my ignorance I believed that the work of the artillery was entirely impersonal: our guns sat some distance behind our lines and fired at the Jap front lines, while the Jap artillery concentrated on our front lines. And nobody fired at the artillery.

I went over one night with Colonel Pete Irwin, Operations officer on General MacArthur's staff, and spent the night at USAFFE field headquarters high up on the slope of Mt. Mariveles. Cars could go only part way up the mountainside and then you transferred to a jeep that negotiated the rest of the climb over a steep path winding between the trees.

Colonel Bill Marquat fixed me up with a bed and four blankets—three underneath to keep the cold wind from blowing up through the canvas, and one on top. I met an M.P., a New York City boy who had just been transferred from Corregidor and who admitted he was scared to death of the woods. Monkeys were chattering in the dark treetops and the M.P. jumped every time the wind rustled the bushes. The officers were kidding him about the woods being full of pythons, but actually nobody I met in Bataan had seen a python or a crocodile or anything very wild except small monkeys.

Next morning we had breakfast in the open with Brigadier General Marshall and then I went on with Colonel George Williams and Major Wade Cothrane who were also en route to inspect the artillery. During the night, reports had been received of a large concentration of Japanese ships off the west coast of Bataan. As we reached a clear spot along the road overlooking Bagac and the China Sea, we could see the smoke of two ships over the horizon. They were apparently standing out to sea and waiting until nighttime to unload their troops or supplies.

The sight was far from reassuring. For several nights previously we had heard on Corregidor that a large Japanese armada was hovering off the coast and each time we took a deep breath and said, "Well, it looks like this is it." But the ships went past, just out of range of Corregidor's guns, and probably on down to Borneo and Java.

About four miles from the Manila Bay side we emerged into a flat area and turned left along a trail through the rice fields toward the front lines.

Cothrane knew the way and he took us to the commander of the 313th Filipino Scout Field Artillery, Lieutenant Colonel Alexander Quintard. Colonel Quintard's headquarters were in an open cut about thirty yards long which was being used as a trench. There were one or two trees near the trench and another clump a few hundred feet up ahead, but except for that the country was stretched out open and level to Mt. Natib, up to the north, and to Manila Bay on the east.

I couldn't see any guns but Colonel Quintard said they were in the tree clump up ahead. Only part of the trees were real, he said, and the rest were camouflage. All around us the rice fields were partially burned away and the ground pitted with shell holes and bomb craters.

"You've come just in time," the colonel said. "At twelve-ten we are going to fire a mission against some Japs across the way. About five or six hundred of them gather there at noon every day in a bivouac area, probably to eat. We've got the position plotted and will give them a surprise."

"How did you get the information?" I asked.

"An officer named Wermuth, captain in the 57th, has been doing some scouting over there. He and a couple of Scout sergeants are there watching the firing for us.

"Wermuth," the colonel went on, "has been spotting a lot of targets for us. Couple of weeks ago he volunteered to set fire to the town of Samal, on the other side of the lines, so that we could see to fire into it and wipe out some batteries the Japs had planted there. He set the fires all right but I'm afraid we didn't give him very much time to get out before we opened up."

The colonel told us that as a rule his guns fired mostly at night while the Japs fired mostly in the daytime, taking advantage of their aerial observation. Our gunners were forced to depend on scouts and on their knowledge of the country which enabled them to fire at open areas where the Japs would be most likely to establish camps and set up guns. We had one last observation post on Mt. Natib. A few days later that observation point was in Jap hands and from then on our artillery was nearly blind.

Colonel Quintard told us about it. "Mr. Moto is over us here in his observation plane just about from sunup to sundown. When we have to fire, as we will in a few minutes, he spots our positions and radios back to his own guns. Then we catch hell. The dive bombers were on us for three hours yesterday. So we try to fire mostly at night, or when Mr. Moto's back is turned."

Maybe Mr. Moto heard the colonel mention his name. In any case, while the colonel was still speaking, he appeared overhead. He putt-putted past from east to west, did a lazy circle, and then kept going west. We hoped he would keep on going.

A young Filipino, perched on the wall of the trench, with a telephone headset over his ears, said to the colonel: "Batteries all set to fire in ten minutes, sir."

"Lee," the colonel said, "if you want to go up and watch the guns shoot, Lieutenant Filemon here will show you the way." As I climbed out of the trench. Major Cothrane said: "That firing will last only about ten minutes. That will make it twelve-twenty. Be sure you are back here by twelve-twenty-five." He pulled out his watch and pointed to twenty-five minutes past twelve. Then he handed me his watch.

"Sure, but what's the rush?" I asked.

"We're having lunch at that time and we don't like anybody to be late," he said. "Don't forget, no matter what happens in the meantime, be here at twelve-twenty-five."

It was only about five hundred feet to the guns, which were big 155's, but for some reason Lieutenant Filemon wanted to ride over. He backed a car out from under some camouflage and lost a few minutes doing it, so that we were still some fifty feet from the clump of trees where the guns were hidden when they suddenly opened fire. We got out of the car and went up close and watched the Filipino Scouts running up to feed the guns, jamming home the big shells and then the powder charges.

After a few rounds one of the guns coughed out a big ring of white smoke. It swirled upward in the still air, spreading but still holding its circular shape, to a height of several hundred feet. I looked up nervously over to the west. Sure enough, there was Mr. Moto high tailing back in our direction. He couldn't have missed seeing that smoke ring. The Scouts kept feeding the guns, and one after another the guns roared with deep-throated, earth-shaking "whurrumphs."

Major Cothrane's watch said twelve-twenty-five, so Lieutenant Filemon and I climbed in the car and drove back over to the battery control trench.

The trench was about eight feet wide but only three feet deep. Over at one end a table was set. Captain Lawrence Meade and a young lieutenant joined us. I still didn't understand why Cothrane was in such a hurry.

We were eating corned beef and bread and, I remember especially, peanut butter and some canned pears. I had out my notebook and was getting some information from Captain Meade. He told me the Filipino artillerymen, both the Scouts and the recruits, were all proving to be fine soldiers. They had toughened up quickly and were standing up well despite the frequent dive-bombing attacks by Jap planes.

While he was talking I heard a distant whistling. It seemed to be three separate whistles. They grew into a scream and rushed toward us at alarming speed, getting louder and louder until they burst, directly overhead. It was my first taste of shellfire and I determined not to show any emotion. I looked around and saw that I was all alone at the table. The others were crouched against the forward wall of the trench, which was really only a dry creek bed which had been widened and deepened by a little pick-and-shovel work.

Colonel Quintard got to his feet and finished the rest of his coffee. He, Colonel Williams, Cothrane, and the young lieutenant walked over to the other end of the trench where it was deeper. Meade came back and sat down and since I was talking to him I couldn't leave, much as I wanted to.

The next salvo came over, bursting up ahead of us about where our 155's were emplaced. Meade hit the dirt and there I was sitting alone again. But when the next shells came I got into the spirit of the thing. As soon as we heard them whistling we'd do a headlong dive to the bottom of the trench. I must have flopped flat ten times and each time my fountain pen slid out of my pocket into the dust. Finally, Meade finished and we went over to where the others were crouched against the forward wall of the deepest part of the trench.

"Now you see why I wanted you to get back," Cothrane said.

"Yes," I said. "And one other thing. Unless I'm mistaken, those Japs mean us. They're not just shooting at anybody over on this side of the line. They're trying to hit us."

Colonel Quintard laughed. "That's it. You've got the idea. It's a good sign that they are shooting back. Means we probably raised hell with those fellows in the bivouac. When Wermuth comes back we'll find out." Sometime later, I learned from Wermuth himself that our salvos had burst squarely among the Japs.

"What about our men at the guns?" I asked the colonel. "Those shells seem to be hitting among them."

"They have slit trenches and foxholes right alongside the guns. There's nothing they can do but drop into them and take it. The shells the Japs are sending over are antipersonnel ammunition which is set to explode over the position where the Japs estimate our guns to be. Thanks to their airplanes, their estimates are pretty accurate and our boys are getting a terrific pounding. In artillery parlance, they have temporarily neutralized our batteries."

All this time the shells were coming over. I was sweating and shivering at the same time, and, as usual, wishing I had a tin hat. Pieces of shrapnel whirred into our trench and I got my fingers burned picking one up for a souvenir. Colonel Williams examined it professionally and said it was a fragment from a Jap 105-mm. field gun.

When the Japs ceased firing that day, after sending over twice as many rounds as we had shot, I rode on down to the town of Balanga and made arrangements to go up to the front lines the following night to visit the 31st Infantry. I wanted to be able to dateline one of my stories "With the 31st United States Infantry at the Bataan Front." My other dispatches had been "With Anti-Aircraft in Bataan," "With Field Artillery in Bataan," and so on. Now I wanted to write one "Bataan FRONT."

My desire to do that had grown out of an encounter with my old friend and recent rival, Frank Hewlett of the United Press. By the fortunes of journalistic war I had managed to get the first dispatches transmitted out of Corregidor and Bataan. Frank's office heard about it and sent him a wireless through the Army. He came over to Corregidor to investigate and I met him on the docks. He told me that he had answered the wire: "Associated Press unrepresented in Bataan."

I went over the next night, again with Colonel Irwin. It was rough crossing the bay and it was already dark when our launch tied up at the dock in Cabcaben.

Stumbling through the dusty street at the end of the dock, Colonel Irwin found the khaki-painted sedan that had been sent to meet him and we climbed in.

We had driven only a half mile up the east road when we discovered we were in for a really rough trip. Our tiny Filipino chauffeur apparently suffered from night blindness; someone had done an over-enthusiastic job of blacking out his lights and with the headlights dimmed he couldn't see a thing. When he turned on his bright lights sentries threatened to shoot us because the road was within range of Japanese artillery beyond the front.

We zigzagged from one side of the road to the other, narrowly missing the ditches in which many cars had already been wrecked. Drivers going in the other direction cursed at us and jammed on their brakes as we almost rammed them headlong.

By the time we got to Pilar, some five miles from the front, Colonel Irwin decided it would be suicidal for him to continue his trip around the peninsula. He bunked for the night in a nipa shack.

I found my way to the advance headquarters, located in a sandbagged dugout on one of the side streets of Pilar. The commander was a major in the army reserve, who told me he had been a Houston, Texas, schoolteacher before he was called to active duty some months before the war started.

"Are you sure you want to go to the front tonight?" he asked. "The 31st is in rather a tough spot, attempting to restore a salient driven in our lines on the east coast of Mt. Natib. And there's a heavy Jap attack in progress just now."

By that time I wasn't exactly sure I wanted to go, but I said, "That's okay. I want to see those Americans in action."

"You won't see much at night time," he said, "but go if you want. We have automobiles going up every hour to carry messages. There is one due back any minute now."

While we waited for the car the major and two American lieutenants told me that they had been catching hell from the Jap artillery all afternoon. The provincial capital of Balanga a few miles further back had been shelled even worse. The east coast road had been under fire most of the day.

About 10 P.M. a young Filipino officer pushed aside the burlap bags at the entrance and came down the steps into the dugout. He was rubbing the sleep from his eyes.

"Third Lieutenant Gonzales reporting for duty, sir," he said.

The major told him he was to drive up to Abucay Hacienda and was to take a passenger along. "You probably won't get any shells," he said, "but watch out. Their snipers have been working around here this afternoon and all the way up the road to the front. They are shooting from the treetops."

Gonzales stumbled out into the darkness and I went after him, tripping several times on the roots of the big trees under which the dugout was located. The lieutenant found his car parked in an open space between two nipa huts across the street. He awakened the driver, who was in civilian clothes. Gonzales explained to me that the driver spoke a few words of English, a few sentences of Spanish, and for the rest talked to himself in some obscure dialect that Gonzales did not understand.

We had trouble starting the ancient Chevrolet sedan. Finally, it kicked over on three of its four cylinders, stuttering like an erratic machine gun. It had no muffler and the sound could be heard for miles around. The windows would not close. I had no jacket over my shirt and was shivering in the cold air.

We chug-chugged out onto the main road and headed north toward the front. We had no lights, but this driver could see perfectly in the dark. He pulled up at the side of the road to let some big trucks pass us in the opposite direction. They were towing five or six 155 guns on trailers. The country was flat and we could see the guns outlined against Manila Bay, which was a lighter expanse against the darkness of the night. Off in the distance between us and the front we could see the flicker of numerous fires alongside the road.

"Hey. What's up here?" I asked Gonzales. "Why are those guns going away from the front?"

"They move every night," the lieutenant answered, "to trick the Japs who have spotted their positions the previous day. I have never seen them back this far before. Maybe our front line is moving back, or the Japanese have broken through."

I could see that my companion was not the optimistic sort. I asked him how long he had been in the Army.

"About three months, sir," he answered. "I was a law student at the University of the Philippines. I never wanted to be a soldier, but it seemed to be my duty so I got a commission. Frankly, I never wanted this courier job either. But again it is my duty."

As we talked, the Chevrolet kept chugging surely and steadily through the darkness. We came to a bridge and the lieutenant ordered the chauffeur to halt.

He leaned out the window and shouted, "Guardias! Sentineles!"

There was no answer. "That is funny," the lieutenant said. "There should be sentries here."

I thought to myself, "Oh-oh. This is going to be like Baguio all over again. We are going to drive past our lines. But this time there won't be any way to walk out."

"Drive on," Gonzales told the chauffeur. He turned to me. "One of our couriers was killed last night just about this time and in this spot. A sniper fired through the windshield, wounding the driver. The courier got out to investigate and was killed. Also we have to be very careful on this road because several times the Japanese have broken through and captured one of our cars or jeeps. One of them was driving up the road last night and shot some of our sentries. Then the Japs took the sentries' uniforms and assumed their posts. When another of our cars drove up they stopped it and killed everybody in it."

If the lieutenant was trying to scare hell out of me he was doing a very thorough job. We passed another bridge and again there were no sentries. By this time we had driven past the fires, which we saw were eating at the remains of nipa huts in small bay shore villages which the Japs had shelled that afternoon. I knew that we were supposed to drive straight up the coast to the town of Abucay, about a half mile short of our front lines, and then turn left into a side road leading to headquarters of the 31st on the slope of Mt. Natib. We drove through several villages which I had never seen on the map, and I wondered if we had passed Abucay.

Finally we crossed a bridge and were challenged by a pair of sentries. The chauffeur jammed on the brakes. It was impossible to see much in the darkness, but the sentries' helmets looked—to me—like Jap helmets. One of them stood three feet from the car, covering us with a rifle, and the other about five feet behind his companion. I whispered to the lieutenant, "Hold your pistol ready!"

After stopping us, the sentries didn't seem to know what to do next.

"Come over here!" Gonzales ordered the nearest one. He stood still. Gonzales tried it in Spanish. No answer. He switched to Tagalog. The soldier just stared at us, waving his rifle. I started to talk to him in Japanese, and immediately thought better of it.

Just at this minute there was a tremendous, sharp boom, which seemed to break right over our heads. It was followed by another and another. We realized it was shells going over us, but we didn't know if they were ours or Jap.

Gonzales leaned over me and stuck his head out of the window, holding his pistol down below the opening.

"I am Third Lieutenant Gonzales," he said. "I am en route to the advance command post of the 31st Regiment at Abucay Hacienda. I order you to give me the password." The sentry just stood.

The chauffeur came to our rescue. He chattered off a string of words in some dialect. The sentries grinned and relaxed. The chauffeur turned around, "It's okay." He pulled the gear into low and we drove on. The big guns were still firing.

We drove past the shadowy buildings of Abucay to a point beyond the schoolhouse and then turned off into a narrow sideroad through the fields. A short distance over to our right the sky was full of tracer fire from machine guns. Some of them seemed to be hitting around us. "That is the front, sir," Gonzales said.

There was a line of low trees—ideal for snipers—along the road, which climbed gently uphill toward the distant, dim slope of Mt. Natib. It was pitch black but the driver only slowed down a little, shifting to second, and kept on. We drove for about three miles up the slope and came to a spot where the road leveled off.

"We are almost there," said Gonzales.

Just as he said it there was a sudden outburst of shellfire from somewhere nearby. After my baptism of shelling the day before I didn't like the sound of it. We stopped the car and got out, ready to drop beside an embankment along the roadside. The shells seemed to be bursting over a ridge just up ahead of us. Finally we decided they weren't aimed at the road, and drove on up for a few hundred yards.

"This is where we start to walk," the lieutenant told me. "Too bad you haven't got a steel helmet."

We stumbled on up the road, not daring to use even the lieutenant's blacked out flashlight, and felt our way along a path which circled down through a clump of trees. I kept my hand on Gonzales' shoulder so as not to lose him. After we had inched our way along for a couple of hundred yards we heard a challenge:

"Halt! Who goes there?"

We identified ourselves and the sentry led us across a wooden bridge, through a grassy clearing and to a tent pitched against the hillside. I introduced myself to General Lough, U.S. Army, and to General Lim, the first Filipino to graduate from West Point. Tracers were streaking across the sky above the hollow in the hills which sheltered us, and the shells were still cracking nearby.

"You picked a hell of a time to come up," General Lough said. "I knew you AP reporters got around, but I never expected to meet one here." I could see that he was wearing a bathrobe over his uniform. He explained that the 31st had been attempting for five days to regain a half-mile gap in our front lines. With heavy losses they had finally recovered all but 150 yards. Two hours before my arrival the Japs had made their first night attack, hitting the 31st's lines after creeping undetected to within thirty yards of our outposts.

"We finally stopped them with machine guns. The pressure seems to be off just now," General Lim interposed. "That is our artillery you hear, firing just ahead of our front-line positions."

I asked General Lough if I could go up to the actual firing line, which was about a quarter of a mile away over the hill. "I can't send you now," he said. "These trees are lousy with snipers."

I stayed there for a couple of hours, getting the story of the 31st Infantry, the first and only American infantry regiment to fight the Japanese in the Philippines. A field telephone connected headquarters with the front lines, and twice while I was there the outposts reported new Japanese attacks. On the second thrust a party estimated at fifty to one hundred Japs broke through our front line and circled around onto the road behind us.

Just after we received that news, Lieutenant Gonzales said to General Lough, "Sir, I must return now to headquarters to report the situation here."

"Okay," the general said, "but keep your eyes open going down that road. The Japs that broke through have probably taken to the trees or dug in along the embankment. Don't stop for anything."

I shook hands with Lough and with Lim, who despite the presence of snipers had been puffing on a thin black cigar, shielding the light with his hand; and with the young American lieutenants operating the field telephone.

Gonzales led me back to the car, which we were able to see only when we came to within a few feet of it. The chauffeur wasn't at the wheel. "By God, the snipers got him," Gonzales said. We looked again and found the chauffeur curled up on the front seat. He was snoring almost loudly enough to drown out the sound of the shells cracking overhead.

We drove on down the road through the inky blackness and after a short distance we heard a challenge. It was from a tank parked by the roadside—an American tank.

One of the tank crew shouted a warning: "Some Jap snipers broke through and are on this road. We are looking for them but haven't found them yet. Don't stop for anything until you hit the main road."

We went on down the road fairly fast and finally came to the level portion. The main road was only about a half mile ahead. Suddenly the driver stepped on the brakes so hard that we were thrown against the front seat.

Our front wheels were within a few inches of a tree which had fallen squarely across the road. There were trees on both sides and it was impossible to go around.

"By Santa Maria and all the saints," Gonzales said, "it looks like we have run into an ambush!"

I was wishing to Heaven that I'd brought a tommy gun along instead of a notebook.

We told the chauffeur to try to run over the tree. The bumper scraped and jammed and we saw we couldn't make it. There was nothing to do but climb out of the car and move it.

"Wait until I count three," I said, "then all jump out, swing the tree off to the left, hop back in, and get the hell out of here."

It couldn't have taken us more than twenty seconds to jump out, shove the tree aside, and run back to the car. Every minute I expected a flock of bullets in my back, but not a shot was fired. I still don't know how that tree got on the road. It might have been knocked flat by shellfire, or the Japs who placed it there may have been driven away before we arrived. We rode on back to headquarters at Pilar and pulled up outside the dugout.

Gonzales said to the chauffeur, "That's all for tonight. You can park here."

By the first light of dawn I could see the chauffeur's white teeth glistening in a grin. "Thank you, sir." Almost before we could shut the rear doors he had stretched out on the front seat and was sound asleep. For him it was all in a night's work.

26

BATAAN'S NAVAL BATTALION WAS CALLED THAT PARTLY because its members included some one hundred sailors, and partly because it was led by a naval officer, Commander Francis J. Bridget, a veteran aviator and former air attaché in the American Embassy in Tokyo. Frank came to the Philippines a short time before the war started and was cited for heroism during the bombing of Cavite.

The Naval Battalion was born of urgent necessity late in January when the Japanese landed troops from barges on five points of land on the western coast of Bataan. There were about five hundred men in each of the five landing parties, and they were under orders to cut the main road along the western side of the peninsula and thus sever our communications with the front lines.

The most dangerous Japanese landing, because it was nearest to the main road, was at Langoscawayan Point, only a mile from Mariveles. To stop the Japs there, MacArthur called on the men who were nearest. They were one hundred sailors stranded at Mariveles when their ships had been sent to the bottom or departed for Java without them; some three hundred Marines from Cavite Navy Yard who were camped in the woods behind Mariveles; and about three hundred Army Air Corps troops—pilots and bombardiers and gunners and mechanics—whose planes had been destroyed on the ground or had never arrived. That was the Naval Battalion.

All of these men were novices in jungle fighting. Many of the sailors had never fired rifles and the aviators had never tossed grenades. Frank Bridget had never commanded ground troops. But they pitched into the Japs and pinned them to the point and fought them for eight, bitter, sleepless days and nights.

Frank set up his field headquarters a mile from Mariveles. For a mile north of Mariveles the road had been widened for a runway for airplanes, and just beyond the wide part it crossed a small stream and turned away and started to climb between two low hills. Frank got a couple of sandbags, an empty box, and a half-dozen field telephones, and set them up just over the bridge and a few yards off the road on the left.

The Japs were on the seaward edge of a 300-foot hill which rose out of the rice fields about three hundred yards away.

Frank fanned out his sailors and Marines and aviator troops, and sent them crawling into the jungle underbrush covering the hill. In a few hours they ran into the Japs, advancing slowly up from the sea and cutting their way through the underbrush.

Slowly the sailors, aviators, and Marines pushed forward, losing a good many men unnecessarily because they did not know how to take advantage of cover and didn't know how to cope with the Japs' tricks. The Japanese gave way, back toward the end of the point, and toward sundown Frank called his men back a ways and held a line across the hill.

Then somebody realized that the Japs were well within range of Corregidor's big guns. That night the 12-inch mortars opened up against an enemy for the first time since they had been installed on the Rock. They dropped shell after shell onto the point, just far enough from our own troops to keep from doing them any damage.

Frank thought that in the morning all the Japs would be dead or wounded. But in the morning a startled sentry came running down from another hill nearby and announced that it was covered with Japs. During the night—and probably before the bombardment started—the Japs had swum from Langoscawayan to another nearby point. Frank didn't have enough troops to check the advance from this new direction, so he had to withdraw his men and rush them to the new front.

The next few nights the Japs kept up that game of leap-frog, swimming from point to point during the night. They were obviously awaiting reinforcements, and if they had arrived the fight would have been over, because we did not have the forces to check simultaneous advances from both points.

About the fourth night Frank outguessed them. He called for shelling from Corregidor against one of the points. When the Japs vacated it and swam over to Langoscawayan, Frank sent a handful of his men with machine guns down onto the point which the Japs had just left. The next night, when the Japs tried to swim back again, they ran into machine-gun fire and were forced back. So they were finally held on Langoscawayan. Frank's men moved in to mop them up and clean them out before reinforcements could arrive.

The Japs employed all the tricks that they used later in the war. One of them called "me surrender," and came out from a tree a few feet ahead of our Marines. When four or five Marines went over to grab him a hidden machine gun opened fire and cut them down. Our sailors and aviators were fooled, and killed, in the same way. But they kept going forward and killing a few more Japs every day.

When the fighting had been underway for about eight days I happened to pass by en route to General Wainwright's headquarters. I recognized Frank by the roadside, the first time I'd seen him since Tokyo. He seemed to be talking into six phones at once. During a lull I asked him a foolish question, "What would you give to be in an airplane right now?" He shrugged his shoulders and said, "Oh, Lord..."

He looked terrible. His faded khaki was caked with dust, his face lined and strained. From his conversation on the phones I could tell I'd arrived at a crucial time in the fighting.

"What's that, Hogey?" Frank said excitedly into one telephone. "They've all gathered in one place and are pushing through the center of your line? You can't hold them? You've got to hold them, Hogey old boy!"

He talked into another phone: "Perez," he shouted, "Perez! Perez! You've got to lay a few shells in there in front of Lieutenant Hogaboom. His center is under heavy machine-gun and rifle fire. He can't hold out long."

Then to Hogey. "Hold on, kid. I'll give you some help in a minute!"

He grabbed another phone. "Miranda. Lieutenant Miranda. How many rounds have you got left for that mortar? Only five? Okay. Stand by to fire. We may need them."

"Perez! You have nine rounds, right? Look, you've got to make every one count. You can't miss. Load your howitzer!"

Frank took a second to explain that on a hill over to the right he had a 75-mm. howitzer and on another hill a small mortar. There were also some 75-mm. mountain pieces, but these couldn't be brought to bear. In some way, Frank seemed able to listen to all six phones at once and to make the proper answer into each of them without getting his orders scrambled. They were field telephones, in little brown canvas cases stamped Western Electric. Frank spoke into one of them.

"Hogey. How are you doing? That's tough. But hold it."

"Perez. All set now. When I give you the word, fire!"

"Hogey. Watch this now. Perez is going to throw one over for you. Tell me where it lands."

"Perez. Okay. Let the first one go."

Up on the hill to the right the howitzer boomed and a few seconds later the shell burst over the hill just in front of us.

Frank said, "Hogey. How was that? A little off? Okay. Hold everything."

"Perez. Look, son, give me just ten yards more elevation this time, please. Let her go right now."

The howitzer boomed again, lobbing the shell into the air, and the burst seemed a little bit farther away.

"Hogey, How was that? On the nose. Swell, kid. Are they still coming?"

"Perez. That was just right. Fire the rest of them." Perez lobbed over his seven remaining shells, as fast as he could fire them. But the Japs kept coming. Hogey reported a dozen of his men were killed and the pressure was still on the center of his line.

Frank said, "Hold em!" Then he gasped. "What's that? Your center has already had to give way? Well, hold the flanks."

Frank made a sudden decision. He twirled the black handle on one of the phones he hadn't been using. "Rock (Corregidor)," he said. "Bat. Boston," giving the code names until he got USAFFE headquarters. The phone wires led to Corregidor through cables under Manila Bay.

"Colonel," he said, when the connection was made, "I'm afraid you'll have to give us a hand here. My guns are out of ammunition and my boys are exhausted. They've been eight days without sleep and we're having a devil of a time to get food to them. We'll hold on as long as possible, but if you have any spare troops around, we'd appreciate your sending them down." Then, elatedly, "Thank you, sir. I'll do that." He rang off.

Frank shouted at two Marines standing near us. "Hey, Johnny! Hey, Smitty, boy! You two grab that truck and burn up the road up to kilometer one-seven-six (four miles to the north). Tell the commander of the Fifty-Seventh Filipino Scouts that Corregidor says for him to send some men down here and give us a hand."

Johnny and Smitty jumped into the truck, backed around, and raced up the road. Frank yelled to some other Marines.

"Hey, fellows, grab a few boxes of those grenades and hurry on up the path and get them to Lieutenant Hogaboom. He needs them."

Frank rang one of the phones. "How's it look now, Hogey? Hey, that's swell. Your center has reformed and the pressure has eased off. Nice going. We'll have some help in there shortly."

Frank remembered to thank Perez. "Perez. That shooting of yours did the trick. Our line is holding now. Swell work."

That was one time the Army functioned swiftly. It seemed like less than twenty minutes after Johnny and Smitty left when they were back, followed by one of the familiar, red, open-sided buses which provided most of the transport for MacArthur's Army.

A heavy-set man, with a thick black beard and a helmet tilted jauntily over one eye, walked over and saluted. He was carrying a tommy gun, as were the twenty Filipinos with him. He said, "Commander. I'm a captain of the Fifty-Seventh Filipino Scouts. Our colonel sent me here with these men. What is the situation, sir?"

Quickly Frank told him. His men were tired out, hungry, under heavy pressure.

The captain saluted again. "Thank you, sir," he said. "Please give me a runner to show me the path over the hill to the center of your lines. Some more of our men will be down later and we'll relieve all of your force by midnight, at the latest."

He turned to his Scouts, grinned at them, and waved his arm. "Come on, boys," he said. "This is our meat." The Scouts marched off, single file, with the captain leading them.

When the Scouts got up to the front lines they slapped the exhausted Americans on the back and said, "We'll take over now, Joe."

Frank looked like a man who had been saved from a firing squad just as the executioners' fingers were tightening on their triggers. He let all his breath out in one big sigh and collapsed on the ground.

"If that captain ever has any trouble about getting into heaven," he said, "I hope St. Peter calls me and all my men as witnesses for him."

Neither Frank nor I knew it, but that captain was Arthur Wermuth. Within five days he and the Scouts killed the last Japs on Langoscawayan Point.

27

IN ADDITION TO THEIR LANDING AT LANGOSCAWAYAN POINT, the Japs had succeeded in putting men ashore at four other places on the west coast of Bataan behind our front lines. The Japs fought to the bitter end, and it took our troops almost two weeks of slow, costly jungle warfare to wipe out the last of the landing parties.

On February 5, I went over to Bataan with Lieutenant Bulkeley and hitchhiked up the dusty west coast road on a variety of vehicles including trucks, ambulances, jeeps, and buses. On those trips I usually took my gas mask out of its canvas case and used the case to carry toothbrush, razor, towel, soap, cigarettes, and Life Savers. Those last two items were a guarantee of immediate friendship with the troops in Bataan and a passport to lots of newspaper stories.

That afternoon I stopped along the roadside to talk with Brigadier General Clinton Pierce, who had been promoted since the Lingayen fighting and was now directing operations against the Japanese landing parties. Pierce was as full of fight as ever, although he was limping around with one foot in a bedroom slipper. He told me the caliber of the enemy troops had changed.

"These fellows fighting us on the west coast aren't the scared kids they threw against us at Lingayen," he said. "These are real, seasoned fighters. But they are still lousy marksmen. A sniper took three shots at me before knocking off my toe the other day." Pierce had won the DSC and he still insisted as he did at Lingayen he wasn't a hero. "Hell, I'm just doing my job."

A few miles up the road I jumped off a bus and went over to chat with the crew of a tank control car. They were listening by shortwave radio to the tanks which were mopping up the Japs on Saysain Point down in the woods below us. They were all Wisconsin boys. Over the radio we could follow the course of the fighting as the tanks plunged through the trees to knock out the Japs who had dug into foxholes and trenches.

"There's a couple of Japs hiding behind that tree over there. Can you get them?"

"No. I can't get through here. Tell Charley to hit them with his machine guns." After the tanks had cleaned up, the infantry was to go in the following morning.

The tank troops hadn't known that there were any reporters in Bataan and they asked eagerly for news of our reinforcements. "Where the devil are those planes that Henry Ford is turning out, and the rest of them?"

I drove on up to General Wainwright's headquarters which were deep in the woods about four miles behind our front lines. The general was deaf in his right ear and so was I, and we had trouble arranging ourselves to sit and talk at a bamboo table outside of his tent.

Wainwright was tall, gray and wiry. He gave an impression of quiet strength, both physical and spiritual. His troops loved him, for he would never order them to do anything he himself would not undertake. He made almost daily trips to the front and had fought the Japs with rifles and hand grenades. He and his Filipino driver had charged and knocked out a Japanese automatic rifle which was inflicting heavy damage on one of our front-line positions. Wainwright, like Pierce and the other outstanding front-line American officers in Bataan, thought that his feats were nothing extraordinary. His job was to fight.

At that time Wainwright was optimistic. "Right now we have got the Japs stopped and our position is more favorable than it has been since December 8. If the United States will send me two divisions of American troops, or provide me with two trained Filipino divisions, and just enough airplanes to keep the Jap planes off our heads, I will guarantee to drive the Japs off Luzon in short order." There was no doubt in his mind that the Japs could be defeated and the Philippines held.

We talked until late that night and went to sleep under several blankets and under the comforting, protective roar of our 155's which were firing over our heads against the Japanese front lines.

In the morning Colonel Frank Nelson and Major Johnny Pugh of Wainwright's staff gave me a command car to ride down to Saysain Point and watch the final mopping up of the Japs. When we turned off the main road and down the narrow path leading through the woods to the sea, the driver put on his steel helmet, placed a hand grenade on the seat beside him, and cocked his rifle. The woods were still full of Jap snipers, and for the hundredth time I wished I owned a steel helmet.

In the woods beside the path were many Filipino soldiers, eating their breakfast of rice and waiting orders to go into action. Big branches and vines slapped us in the face as we wound down the road for nearly five miles. The China Sea was only a short distance away but the underbrush was so thick that visibility in places was less than a yard.

We found Captain Horace Greeley's command post deep in the woods in an area where the underbrush had been cut and trampled into a semblance of a clearing. Greeley had dug a foxhole between two flange-like roots of a giant tree, and a few feet away a tiny Filipino was seated in a shallow foxhole, which looked like a bathtub, talking over a field telephone. Against the tree were stacked scores of Jap rifles, grenades, light machine guns, helmets, and gas masks.

Greeley was a pilot and had been attached to the American Embassy in Chungking until shortly before the war. He and his squadron had lost their planes in the early Japanese raids on Luzon and had been given rifles and sent to Bataan to fight as infantry.

Greeley was near exhaustion. He had a heavy beard and his face was deeply lined. He described the situation. "The Japs landed at the end of the point about two weeks ago. Sentries discovered them when they had come about a half mile up this path. We were rushed down here to meet them. Our troops spread out across the point, which is about two miles wide. Filipinos are in the center and Air Force units, pilots and mechanics, on the flanks. It has been slow, tough going. You have to crawl through the underbrush, and some days we have advanced less than five yards. Each Jap has to be killed individually and that takes time. The last two days it has been going faster and now their survivors are penned in an area where the trees and brush have been cleared by mortar fire and by our tanks. They have dug in and the tanks are working on them now."

We could hear the tank machine guns and 37-mm. cannon firing, and frequently the high-pitched crack of a Jap rifle.

The tiny Filipino at the field telephone let out a shout: "Hooray, sir," he said to Greeley. "The tanks report that they can see the water." That meant that our forces were nearing the seaward edge of the point. The fight should be almost over. A jeep drove down the path and General Pierce got out and limped over. Two soldiers with tommy guns went ahead to watch the trees for snipers and Greeley led us three hundred yards farther down the winding road to the front-line command post of Captain C. A. Crome.

Crome's left hand was tied in a blood-soaked bandage, but he grinned with satisfaction as he addressed the general. "By God, sir," he said, "we've got them on the run. The so-and-sos didn't want to surrender. I hollered to them to quit and they answered back, 'Nuts to you, Joe,' so I sent in the tanks this morning. They're coming out now."

Three tanks clattered from around a bend in the road and stopped by the tree which was Crome's command post. All around us sharpshooting Filipino Scouts were lying on their backs with their rifles ready to pick off any Jap snipers still tied in the surrounding trees. The tank crews climbed out, covered with sweat and dust. They pulled cigarettes from the pockets of their green dungarees and smoked greedily. Others took big gulps of water from their canteens. Constantly interrupting each other, they reported to Crome. "We got almost all of them."

"There are still a couple left but they won't do much damage."

"Joe here shot thirty-five in one trench alone. They ran around the corner to escape my tank and ran into his fire."

"Two of them took off their shoes and threw them at my tank. We shouted to them to surrender but they wouldn't give up. We had to run over them."

"Now we're starting to get even with those bastards."

I questioned the tank man who made that last remark and he explained.

"Two days ago, in an operation like this a few miles up the coast, one of our tanks hit a landmine planted in the road. The tread was blown off and it was stalled. We couldn't get down there to get the crew out because the Japs had machine guns planted all around the road. Our infantry tried and a lot of them died trying. Yesterday we fought our way down to the tank. We found that the Japs had covered it completely with dirt. Our friends had suffocated inside. It was a hell of a way to die."

With General Pierce we walked twenty-five yards down the road and came out onto the battlefield. It was about as big as a football gridiron. All the trees had been smashed and crushed to pieces, the undergrowth burned and flattened. The entire area was pitted with foxholes six or eight feet long and trenches thirty or forty feet in length. The Japanese had dug in to fight to a finish and had died there. A few survivors had fled into the brush and retreated down rocky cliffs to the beach where they continued to fight for nearly a week longer, hiding in caves in which they were finally killed by dynamite and grenades. Altogether some five hundred Japs died there.

In describing the fighting in a dispatch for The AP, I wrote that I remained on the battlefield until the stench of death drove me away. In New York, the words "horror of the scene" were substituted for "stench of death." That was a serious mistake on the part of the editor who made the change. There was nothing horrible about the scene. Those Japs looked absolutely beautiful: they were so quiet and so perfectly harmless.

28

IN THE HISTORY BOOKS THE BATTLE OF LUZON WILL PROBABLY be told in a couple of sentences: "The outnumbered Filipino and American defenders of Luzon withdrew to the jungle-covered peninsula of Bataan and to the fortress of Corregidor, where they held out against large Japanese forces for more than three months. The defending troops were short of food, medicine, and ammunition. When the end came all of them were undernourished and as high as two-thirds of their total numbers were suffering from wounds, malaria, dysentery, and other diseases."

History may also note that the delaying action fought in Bataan may have given the United States sufficient time to recover from the Pearl Harbor disaster and to build up its Pacific forces to an extent that the Jap advance was finally stopped—at Coral Sea and Midway.

In itself, Bataan wasn't an important battle, as history-making battles go. But to the men who fought there it was highly important. I learned in Bataan that there is no such thing as "unimportant patrol activity" or "minor skirmishes." To the men involved in those skirmishes they are all-important. You don't have to be killed in one of the world's great battles to make your death important to you, your family, and your friends.

To the people who read about Bataan in the future, the words "Filipino and American troops" will have an anonymous quality. "Troops" is an impersonal word. It suggests a lot of anonymous men in uniform. The troops in Bataan were neither anonymous nor impersonal, for Bataan was a very intimate and personal war. It was fought in such a small, confined area that thousands of people got to know each other very well. They shared each other's successes, the minor victories like shooting down a plane or knocking a sniper out of a tree. Together they shared the horrors of final defeat as they are now sharing the hell of life as helpless prisoners of brutal, vicious little men with big bayonets.

Sharing things was a big part of the Battle of Bataan. At first, when there was plenty of everything, it didn't mean much. Everybody had enough food, enough cigarettes, enough quinine. The change from "enough" to starvation rations came with startling suddenness. It seemed almost overnight that there was a severe shortage of gasoline; a complete absence of canned fruits and vegetables; and only a pack of cigarettes a week per soldier; if the soldier was lucky. But the sharing continued. There was no "mine" and "yours." Everything was "ours." It was a big event when a company got a case of canned corn, or maybe some coffee or a few pieces of candy. Traveling around Bataan I would occasionally share those big events and be able to share some of the cigarettes I had brought from Corregidor.

I got to know the men themselves: The M.P.'s who would stop cars and give me a lift; the civilians who ran the motor pools where cars and trucks were concentrated; the lieutenant from Denver on guard at the enclosure where the Jap prisoners were confined; the nurses and doctors and their Sunday night "parties" at Base Hospital No. 2 in the Bataan woods, where they somehow manufactured some ice cream and made good cookies, and sat around listening to the radio broadcasts from home; General Weaver, the tank commander, at his camp in the woods, where he proudly served a "roast beef" dinner of carabao meat and a bottle of sherry that had gone sour; the Filipino Scout sergeant at the bakery, who sat up night after night keeping the records of his men up to date, and who showed you his own record of more than twenty years of honorable service. Even the little things, the little happenings of a day, were important.

I remember as if it were yesterday my first visit to Battery G of the 60th Coast Artillery. They had shot down twelve planes with their anti-aircraft guns. It was strictly sharpshooting, for they had to conserve their ammunition, and they claimed a world's record for the number of planes shot down to the ratio of rounds fired. I spent a day with them at their position on a hill overlooking the channel between Bataan and distant Corregidor and saw them shoot.

They were proud of their commander. Captain A. A. Abston, and he was proud of them, of Lieutenant J. D. Kwiatowski, who came from Pittsburgh; of Lieutenant L. E. McDaniel, who had flown a P-40 until it was shot down with another pilot at the controls; of Privates Edward R. Wright, Ernest E. Wheeler, Louis Rio; of Corporal Clarence Graham and Sergeant Verdi, who came from Netcong, New Jersey. Whenever Battery G was mentioned in the USAFFE News Bulletin after that I thought not of "Battery G" as an anonymous entity, but of the men who made it up.

Months later, after my return to the United States, I received letters from the families of two of the men of Battery G, people for whom the men of Bataan were anything but anonymous.

Remembering Bataan, I think of Joaquin Miranda of the U.S. Engineers. I remembered meeting him in the lobby of the Manila Hotel the night before Pearl Harbor. He had said then that "this waiting is becoming intolerable."

When war came he went to Corregidor with the Engineers, for he was a master draftsman. Then he volunteered for a dangerous assignment: to go into Manila and get badly needed information for MacArthur. By night he left Corregidor in a small banca and disembarked on the north shore of Cavite province. In the morning he walked over to the nearest road and hid under a pile of fish in the cart of a Filipino. He rode past the Japanese sentries and got into Manila without being detected. He dressed himself in a white suit and lounged around the streets, watching how the Japs acted and how his fellow Filipinos reacted to Jap rule. He delivered scores of messages from distracted officers on Corregidor to their families in Manila. He was in the home of one officer's wife when a Jap car drove up and an English-speaking captain came into the house.

Joaquin slipped off his white coat and went into the kitchen. He busied himself at the stove. The Jap captain browbeat the American woman, until she was sobbing and the three-month-old baby in her arms was crying. Then the Jap walked into the kitchen. "Who are you?" he demanded of Joaquin.

"I am the cook, sir."

"You don't look like the cook to me!"

"I am sorry, sir, but that is my occupation." Finally the Jap went away and Joaquin slipped out to Corregidor with his information. He brought us word that the Japanese were mistreating the Filipinos, confiscating food, and enforcing repressive measures. Filipinos who worked with the American Army or Navy were being tortured and killed. Three or four more times Joaquin slipped into Manila and came safely back again, each time bringing reports of vital importance to MacArthur.

The Battle of Bataan was especially intimate and personal for young American officers like the tall dark lieutenant and his blond companion whom I had met at Baguio. I never saw those two again but I did meet scores just like them, young Americans who had been lawyers and reporters and insurance salesmen a few months before.

When our troops backed into Bataan there came a time when they had to stop retreating and had to hold their positions. The young Americans had to go to every Filipino kid in their outfits and pat them on the back.

"Hold everything, Joe," they'd say. "Those Japs aren't too tough. Our help will be here any day now. You know me and you can trust me when I tell you that. Let's lick hell out of them."

Many of the noncoms in the U.S. 31st Infantry were given commissions and assigned to duty with the young Filipino troops. Under their steadying influence the youngsters not only stopped retreating, but they learned to stand and hold and finally they learned to attack. Give a Filipino a little edge, just the slimmest chance of winning, and he is a tough soldier.

There was no doubt the Scouts were tough soldiers. There was the Scout private you saw on the operating table in Base Hospital No. 2 in the woods near Little Baguio. He was horribly shot up but he was grinning, smoking a cigarette out of the corner of his lips, and asking the doctor how soon he could get back and fight "those damn' Japs." The doctors and nurses told us they could always tell when their patient was a Scout. He would never show any signs of suffering or pain, never whimper; never complain because he would be crippled or blind for life.

Then there was General MacArthur, as he strode through the woods of Bataan or paced tirelessly about on Corregidor. MacArthur never allowed himself the luxury of letting down. He always kept his shoulders back and his chin thrust forward at a fighting angle. He always looked serenely confident, even in the blackest moments. He spoke to privates, always with a word of praise or cheer, as readily as he spoke to the members of his staff. His hair grew long but his trousers retained their crease and his shoes their polish. It was part of his personal code to keep them that way.

There was MacArthur, a soldier and a man of culture, whom some men hated because he was both prophet and poet and a master of the English language; who could tell you the details of every great battle in history; whose incisive brain and great military knowledge should have been occupied in planning great battles, massing hundreds of thousands of men and thousands of tanks and planes to attack, not to defend, for MacArthur knew that wars are not won by defense.

MacArthur always thought in terms of offense. He would say, "I will take this company of men, and those three tanks and that torpedo boat, and hit the Jap there." He never thought, as some commanders did, in terms of what he might lose.

Back on Corregidor there was Mrs. MacArthur, the general's wife, and their son, Arthur. Mrs. MacArthur wore cotton-print dresses and a crocheted turban. She and the general had decided to die together, when the end came, and of Arthur, they said, "He is a soldier's son." During the daytime Mrs. MacArthur sat under a canvas shelter in the officers' mess at the entrance to Malinta tunnel. She knitted and read and chatted with the officers and men. The nurses came out to sit and talk with her, and Mrs. Quezon, Mrs. Bewley, old Mrs. Seals, the wife of General Seals, and the other women civilians on Corregidor. Like the general, Mrs. MacArthur never let down. She always had a word of cheer and encouragement. She was one of MacArthur's finest soldiers.

I remember one day on Corregidor when I was caught far from shelter when the siren screamed. Bombs were already shaking the island as I ran down the long road to Malinta tunnel. A car overtook me and stopped. Mrs. MacArthur opened the door and invited me to ride with her to the tunnel. By stopping, she had spent the precious couple of minutes that might have meant the difference between her being killed on the road, and reaching a place of safety.

I remember, especially, Captain Arthur Wermuth of the 57th Filipino Scouts and Corporal "Jock" Yacob, who was Wermuth's partner. Wermuth was already a legend among our forces by the time in early February when I tracked him down during those mopping-up operations against the Japanese landings on the west coast. A few days before, in similar fighting, he had been shot through the chest, the bullet just missing his lung and coming out through his back. Jock had been shot at the same time, but the 6-foot 2-inch corporal had put Wermuth on his back and carried him out of range of the Jap machine guns.

Wermuth was tough and competent, a veteran of life outdoors. All his life he had spurned conventions and looked for adventure. Many times his dislike of stifling forms and customs had got him into trouble, but now, in war, he had come into his own. I had difficulty getting him to tell me his story but when he finally did, checking his diary as he went along and occasionally calling over one of his Scouts to refresh his memory, I remarked, "Art, I'm going to call you our one-man army!"

His Scouts served us dinner of carabao steak, and we sat afterward for hours and talked. It was obvious from their tone of voice and their quick response to his orders that the Scouts worshiped this heavy-set man with the black Vandyke beard which he had grown since the war started.

The Scouts had followed Wermuth on a score of epic feats of reconnaissance: the burning of Samal; an anti-sniper "suicide" detail in which the Scouts cleaned out three hundred Japs who had infiltrated our lines and tied themselves in trees; a scouting trip on which Wermuth alone killed thirty Japs with his tommy gun and the Scouts killed forty or fifty more; several daring patrols behind Jap lines where Wermuth captured prisoners and brought them back alive; an attack with hand grenades on a hidden Jap machine gun which had cut down three Marines who went to the front lines with Wermuth in search of excitement.

To the Scouts, Wermuth was a symbol of American boldness and resourcefulness. He told them repeatedly, and he believed himself, that help was coming; help in sufficient quantities to turn the tide and enable them to drive the Japs from their homeland and return to the families which, of necessity, they had left behind in Manila or in their native villages, at the mercy of the Japs.

As we sat in the woods that night and talked Wermuth told me: "You know, I've been lucky. Three wounds and still walking around. I wouldn't mind being killed, but the one thing I hate to think about is capture. If there is any way to avoid it I will never be taken prisoner as long as I can shoot."

Ten months later the name of Captain Arthur Wermuth was on a list of prisoners published by the Japs. Apparently, when the end came in Bataan, he had nothing left with which to shoot. Every minute of imprisonment must be a lifetime of torture for him.

Another fighter like Wermuth, another one-man army, was Lieutenant Roland G. Saulnier of New Bedford, Massachusetts. Everybody along his sector of the western Bataan front knew "Lieutenant Frenchy." Frenchy's parents were French-Canadians and he spoke English like a character in a play on French-Canadians.

When the war started he was a private in the Army at Manila, in charge of pigeons. In the early fighting in Bataan he suddenly found himself the only American with a battalion of Filipino troops and he took command. For a few days he was scared stiff, but then he discovered that he enjoyed fighting, had a talent for it. He nursed his Filipino youngsters along as a mother pigeon would her flock, slapping them on the back, running to help in response to their frantic cries of, "Frenchy! Those damn' Japs are attacking!" He stopped the Japs cold along his sector of the front, fighting with machine guns, hand grenades, pistol, rifle and bayonet. And Frenchy, too, assured his young Filipinos that help was on the way.

There were the boys of New Mexico's 200th, whom I met the second night of the war and whom I visited on Bataan whenever possible to swap yarns and stories of our experiences. They quickly changed from green youngsters to experienced, resourceful, anti-aircraft experts. Their physical appearance also changed, shockingly, from the husky, healthy youngsters of Manila to thin, sickly men with deep-lined faces. Just before I left Bataan I went over to see Sergeant Joe Smith and the Davis brothers and the other boys of Battery F. I wrote a story about them and months later, through an editorial in their hometown paper, I learned that to many people in the United States, also, the Battle of Bataan was not remote but highly intimate and personal.

The editorial in the Carlsbad Current-Argus, written by Managing Editor Kenneth L. Dixon and entitled "Letter to Lee," said in part: "Yesterday, we carried your story about your visit to the Carlsbad boys of 'first in spite of hell' Battery F. You said all of them were alive and well. You said they were having a tough time of it, but were cheery about the whole thing.

"Things are plenty bad on Bataan, and those boys' parents here in this little Pecos River valley city know it. They aren't kidding themselves. But you'll never know how much that story pepped them up. It gave the whole town a shot in the arm that won't quit.

"Now they know that their boys—our boys—were all right a short time ago, anyway.

"You remember mentioning talking to Sergeant Joe Smith. Well, his mother called up the office and she was so happy she was nearly crying over the phone... You remember speaking of the Davis brothers. Well, their dad, who is a photographer here, came running over to read the story before the paper was on the press... He's still worried about the boys but he knows they're still together and still okay—and man alive, but that helps!

"There's dozens of other cases all over town. It's all the same story."

The nurses on Bataan were great guys. They dressed in Regular Army khaki pants and shirts and lived under shelter tents. They washed their underclothes and bathed in a muddy stream that ran through Base Hospital No. 2. With the bombers overhead, they walked about the wards of their open-air hospital, carrying out their duties and cheering up the Filipino and American wounded. When the bombs fell near they helped the shell-shocked patients crawl into foxholes dug right under their beds. Twice, in the final horror-filled days, the bombs fell—not near—but squarely on the hospital.

Some of the nurses who survived were taken to Corregidor. There they lived for a month longer in the tunnel, while bombs and shells rocked the whole island and frequently blew out the electric lights while a pain-racked soldier was on the operating table.

Since the fall of Corregidor, nothing has been heard of the nurses...

On Corregidor there was President Quezon, small and intense. Most of the time he was in a wheelchair, gravely ill of a tubercular condition that was aggravated by the dusty air in Malinta tunnel. While his aides pushed his wheelchair along, President Quezon would talk warmly and spiritedly of the fight that the young Filipino soldiers were making. Frequently, he had to cover his face with a handkerchief, while his slight body was shaken by coughs. He had told his people that they would have to learn to fight and die, and he was proud of the way they were learning.

Perhaps the man I shall remember longest, of those I knew on Bataan, was a Filipino. He was dead when I saw him, with a straight line of machine-gun holes across his chest. It was the same day that I met Wermuth, and some of Wermuth's Scouts had escorted me down to Saysain Point to watch the final mopping up of the Japs there. Alongside the path through the jungle we saw the body of a Filipino in constabulary uniform. He had been killed while fighting off a score of Japs. Other Filipinos were digging a grave a few feet away. The face of the dead man looked familiar, and I asked his name.

"That is Sergeant Hilario Francisco, sir," one of the others answered. "Perhaps you knew him in Manila. He was frequently on duty at the Manila Hotel."

Then I remembered the night shortly before the war when an American woman had slapped the face of Sergeant Hilario Francisco and shouted at him, "You Filipinos are dirt."

I wished that she could have been there that afternoon, in Bataan, when his fellow Filipinos shoveled the dirt into Sergeant Hilario Francisco's newly dug grave.

29

RIGHT UP TO THE DAY THAT BATAAN SURRENDERED, thousands of our troops clung to the hope that help was on the way.

Even when the Japs broke through on the east coast and their airplanes and artillery were pounding the main road and the airfields, and General King was going forward under a white flag to surrender, most of our troops didn't give up. They walked back along the dusty road to Mariveles, now jammed with wrecked or fuel-less trucks and jeeps and artillery mounts.

They still hoped that by some miracle our planes would dive out of the sky and check the advancing Japs and give us a chance to reorganize at the last minute and start to win. Failing that, they hoped to get to Corregidor and hold there until help came. For most of them Mariveles was the end of the road.

On Corregidor, too, they held on to their hope to the last day. All they knew, when the end came, was that help had not reached them. They did not know, and would not have believed, that no help was going to be sent. Someone thought it couldn't be done.

Sometime shortly after December 8, perhaps immediately, the decision was reached in Washington that the Philippines could not be reinforced, even with airplanes, and that MacArthur and his men would have to do the best they could with whatever they had on hand.

Sometime in January it was decided that even though the Philippines were lost some effort should be made to send medical supplies and ammunition to the forces holding out in Bataan. Maybe if we had been in Washington we would have seen the reasons for that decision.

Anyway, the decision was made and Brigadier General Patrick J. Hurley, former Secretary of War, was called to Washington. The President told Hurley he had a job for him.

Pat said, "Mr. President, I thank you, sir, but no thanks. I'm getting on in years and I did my part in the last war."

The President told Pat that he needed him.

Pat said: "Mr. President, I've got my plans all made for this war. Way out in Arizona, in the mountains, I've found a narrow canyon between two rocks. And when I say narrow, I mean narrow. It's so narrow that when I call my hound dogs from up in that canyon and they come out to meet me, they have to wag their tails up and down. There isn't space for them to wag them sideways. Mr. President, I'm going to crawl up in that canyon and stay there until this war is over."

The President told Pat that the job he had in mind wasn't one that just anyone could do. What was needed was an adventurer, a man who loved to take chances.

Pat said: "Mr. President, why didn't you say so in the first place? Of course, I'll take the job."

So Pat took the job and also the funds that the President gave him and got in an airplane and flew across the Pacific. He went to Australia and flew up north to Port Darwin and then over to Java.

Hurley chartered five ships and loaded them with .50-caliber ammunition, hand grenades, 3-inch anti-aircraft shells, aspirin, bandages, quinine and sulfanilimide, and some canned goods. Two of the ships were lost near Darwin Harbor when the Japs staged their first big raid of the war there, catching us by surprise and inflicting heavy damage on a big convoy.

The other three all got through to the Philippines. That meant that all three ships that started, made it. There may have been other ships too, because Secretary Stimson, on the basis of information given to him, announced after the fall of Bataan that for every ship that got through two ships were sunk.

Hurley mounted some .50-caliber guns on his three ships for protection against dive bombers and got American soldiers to man the guns. The ships' crews were given bonuses, but it would be unfair to believe that they made the trip in order to make money. Nobody who saw the ships sail northward thought the crews would live to spend their bonuses.

One of the three ships was the Anhwei, an old China coaster which had brought British women and children to Manila after the war started. It was commanded by British officers whose families were in China, and the crew was Chinese. All of them had personal reasons for wanting to do anything they could to strike a blow at the Japs.

Another ship was the Dona Nati of the Philippine-owned De La Rama line. Its officers and crew, with the exception of the Swiss chief engineer, were all Filipinos, and they too had a decided personal interest in trying to hold the Philippines. I was told the third ship was the California Farmer.

The California Farmer ran through Macassar Straits, and made it. The Dona Nati sailed from Brisbane and ran right through the Japanese Mandated Islands, and got there and back safely. The Anhwei steamed up through Molucca Straits, and reached the Philippines.

Those ships made the trip just at the time when huge Japanese expeditionary forces in transports and warships were coming south through Macassar and Molucca Straits. Looking at a map, you would say it couldn't be done. But it could be done, and those three ships proved it. They proved that in war, as in peace, the way to get things done is to go ahead and do them, and not to say they are impossible.

While those ships were on their way running north to the Philippines, MacArthur had already set up a "blockade-running" organization of his own. That organization functioned because in the first three months of the war there was not any fixed Japanese blockade of the Philippines. Occasionally, the Japs sent a warship into Philippine waters.

MacArthur had about a dozen ships which had been engaged in inter-island trade before the war and which had survived the bombings. None of them was armed. The largest was the Legaspi, a modern 3,000-ton passenger and freight ship. The others ranged in size down to 70- and 80-foot motor launches, but most of them were fairly roomy with three or four decks.

MacArthur sent one of the ships out through Corregidor's minefields one night late in January. It was the Don Esteban. Two weeks later, with the Philippine Army's three Q-boats guiding it, it came back into Manila Bay. It had been to Iloilo and it brought back sorely needed supplies; rice and a little fruit and some medicine.

Then MacArthur sent the Legaspi and it got through. Then the Princesa made it.

When the first boats came back it was a tremendous uplift to the morale of the men in Corregidor and Bataan. The reports of what they brought were exaggerated. The arrival of one small ship was enough to cause rumors that our convoy, at last, had arrived. Soldiers at the Bataan front refused to believe that only one ship had come in.

Captain Arthur Wermuth got mad as hell at me one night when I told him the truth: that a group of small ships which had suddenly appeared in the bay between Corregidor and Bataan was not a convoy but some vessels which had been moved from the south side of Corregidor to escape shelling by the Jap guns at Cavite.

When the Filipinos asked me about reports that the convoy had come, I'd either evade the question or say, "Sure, help is coming." I thought Wermuth should know the truth, and could stand knowing it. But he didn't want to hear it.

MacArthur's blockade-running was getting results, so he sent Major Bird of the Quartermaster Corps down to Cebu to arrange for transshipment of the supplies that he knew were en route from Australia. Bird squeezed himself into the fuselage of a P-40, which is strictly a one-man airplane, and the pilot pulled it off the Cabcaben runway one night and set it down in Cebu two hours later. Bird worked with Colonel Thomas Cook at Cebu.

The supplies from Hurley's ships reached Cebu but they never got to Corregidor. The Japs sent a warship into the Inland Sea and it sank all but about six of MacArthur's small ships that they had missed on their previous raids, including one carrying President Quezon's baggage. The Japs almost got Quezon too, but he slipped through their hands on a PT boat and got to

Mindanao where he boarded an airplane for Australia. One or two of our small ships were captured intact by the Japs while their crews were ashore.

Later, two submarines went to Cebu to try to take some of the supplies to Corregidor, but again it was too late. The Japs by that time had finished their campaigns in Java and Malaya and had come back to mop up the Philippines. The submarines, however, had previously performed several valuable missions in running into Corregidor. In all, at least seven submarines made the trip between late January and early May, when Corregidor finally fell. I'll never forget the arrival of the first sub. Its trip was supposedly secret, but word quickly spread with electrifying effect. It meant that we still had contact with the outside world! The sub tied up at the south dock on Corregidor and I went down to talk to the sailors. They had been at Pearl Harbor and the reports they gave us were far grimmer than the official announcements of damage. But they had good news too.

"Darwin is lousy with American soldiers," they said. "The harbor is chock-full of ships and they should be heading up this way soon. There are so many troops there that they have to ration beer. Only five thousand bottles are sold every day and our soldiers stand in line for hours to get one. We've got plenty of planes there too."

That sub brought in ammunition for the anti-aircraft guns. Unfortunately, it wasn't exactly what our gunners wanted.

They had requested a device to enable them to cut the fuses on their 3-inch shells so that the guns would shoot high enough to hit the Jap bombers. The old fuse cutters wouldn't do the trick. Somewhere along the line the request got garbled and the submarine brought not fuse cutters but more 3-inch shells. It also brought .50-caliber ammunition, of which there was plenty at that time.

Other subs came in from time to time. They brought supplies and they took out a few fortunate people: Quezon and his family and staff; Sayre and his group, some Navy officers, and a number of Army pilots. One of them also took out $2,000,000 in gold bars belonging to the Philippine Government. The paper money on Corregidor was burned, several million dollars of it, while soldiers and sailors looked on enviously.

Hurley's three ships and those submarines represented the only efforts that the United States made to get aid to the Philippines, except for the bombing raid that MacArthur arranged after he reached Australia. That raid was really a salute to the dead of Bataan who would have still been living if the United States had not decided that the Pacific was a secondary front.

Even months after that last raid MacArthur still did not have the men or planes or ships in Australia to take the offensive against the Japs. Those materials, as it turned out much later, were going to North Africa.

30

AFTER THE HEAVY BOMBING ENDED, Sayre decided to move back to his house on Corregidor and Mel and Annalee Jacoby found another house nearby. They invited me to share it with them.

We would sit there at night in the darkness, watching the flashes of our artillery up the east coast of Bataan and getting ready to duck if the Jap guns on the south shore of Manila Bay should open up against Corregidor.

From about the middle of February we had begun to discuss plans for leaving the Philippines. I had made my arrangements with Bulkeley while Jacoby was keeping in touch with the Army officers operating the small ships running to the southern islands and coming back with supplies.

We had two motives for wanting to leave. None of us wanted to fall into Japanese hands there or anywhere else. We had heard that Don Bell, the American radio announcer in Manila, had been tortured and killed after failing to escape from the capital. We had strong reasons to suspect that we would face the same fate.

Our second reason was less selfish. By mid-February we had learned that there was very little likelihood of reinforcements being sent to Bataan. We began to suspect that Bataan was becoming an embarrassment to the military leaders in Washington: the longer it held the louder the American people were clamoring that help be sent. And the government had no intention of taking the risks involved in a major relief expedition. MacArthur's messages, when they were answered, informed him of that fact.

We believed that if we could escape from the Philippines and get to Australia and then fly to the United States, we might be able to persuade the authorities that the battle was not yet lost. We might be able to convince them that MacArthur's Army had become a veteran, tough outfit, full of fight and confidence; and tell them that a few airplanes could make all the difference in the world, and that given a little encouragement the people of the Philippines would fight with us to the death.

We wanted to convince them that, unless we proved to the native populations of the Orient that the United States was not buying time at their expense, there was grave danger that those populations would turn against us and join the Japanese.

When the inter-island ships came in from the south we would go down and look at them longingly, and watch the soldiers unload sacks of rice and big bunches of bananas. It was ticklish work, since the Jap guns at Cavite would shell the dock unexpectedly at almost any time of the day or night. Jacoby and I were caught on the dock during a severe shelling on February 15.

I spent a very unhappy hour in the water under the concrete pier while shells thudded down overhead or screamed into the bay just beyond.

On the morning of February 22, Jacoby met me at the mouth of Malinta tunnel. "Annalee and I are going out tonight," he said. "You'd better come along."

"I'm supposed to go with Bulkeley," I reminded him.

"Yes," he said, "but you better check up on it. I hear there is a possibility his trip will be called off."

I went over to the Navy tunnel and found Captain Ray, the chief of staff. He was standing outside the southeastern exit and watching an exciting artillery duel between the Jap guns at Cavite and our guns on Fort Drum, the rocky "battleship" fortress which lay a few miles to the south across the sparkling waters of the bay. We saw salvo after salvo burst in the waters around Fort Drum and sometimes hit on the "deck" of the battleship. The shells hit before we heard the sound of the guns. When the splashes had already subsided we would hear the noise of the bursts.

With the morning sun behind them it was almost impossible to spot the flashes of the Jap artillery, but Drum's own guns were firing back. It was a favorite pastime on Corregidor to watch those duels between Fort Drum, Fort Hughes, or Fort Frank and the Jap guns. We thought we were out of range. But one day the Japs fired at Corregidor and from then on you were always ready to hit the dirt when you walked or rode around the Rock.

"Captain," I said. "Bulkeley has told me I could go along with him on his trip to China. Now there is a chance for me to leave by another way. What is your advice?"

"You better go the other way," Captain Ray said. "Bulkeley's orders may be changed, or the boats may be sunk or breakdown, or they may be required for some other purpose."

I thanked him and found Jacoby, and together we made arrangements to see MacArthur after noon. He received us at his desk in the USAFFE tunnel.

"Do you want to go?" the general asked.

We told him that it depended on whether we could do more good by staying than by going. The general refused to make our decision for us, but as a result of what he said we decided to take a chance on getting through.

MacArthur talked to us for more than an hour, as eloquently and stirringly as ever. He discussed not only his own desperate situation but the entire world picture. His heart was in the Philippines, but his brilliant mind grasped the whole strategy of the world struggle. He felt that there was not sufficient understanding in Allied councils of the time element in the Pacific or of the fact that we did not have unlimited time to defeat Japan.

He pointed out the futility of trying to defeat Japan by "blockade" and "attrition," now that Singapore had fallen and Java was about to go. With the capture of those places Japan would have all the raw materials and the bases needed for a war of blockade and attrition against us. He was disturbed but he was not bitter. He was ready to face his fate like a soldier; but, like an American soldier, he wanted to win—not to lose.

"Go armed while you are in the Philippines," the general advised. "When you board a ship to leave the islands, if you are fortunate enough to make connections, throw away your khaki, your guns, passports, and all diaries and identification papers. When you get to Cebu look up the names of some businessmen and learn enough about them so as to enable you to assume their identity, if you are captured."

When he shook hands with us he said, "I hope you'll make it. Say goodbye to Annalee for me."

As we walked out of the tunnel we met an old friend, Captain Smith, who had brought us out to Corregidor from Manila. He asked us to shake hands with two Filipinos, one very short with a barrel belly and stiff gray hair, and the other younger and slimmer. "They are waiting to get a glimpse of MacArthur," the captain said.

In a few minutes, the general walked out of the tunnel. Captain Smith was about to speak to him, but just then Mrs. MacArthur came through the tunnel and the general took her arm and walked away.

The two Filipinos were elated. "I was so close that I could have reached out my hand and touched him," the fat one said in Spanish.

"Maybe, if the senora had not arrived just then we would have had the opportunity to shake his hand."

"Don't be selfish," the elder replied. "We have been closer to him than almost any of our countrymen."

I called the captain aside and asked him the identity of the two men. "They are the captain and chief officer of the Princesa de Cebu, a small freighter that had made two trips through the blockade." The Princesa de Cebu was the ship on which we were to sail.

MacArthur had given me credentials which read:

HEADQUARTERS. UNITED STATES ARMY FORCES IN THE FAR EAST.
Office of the Commanding General. Manila, PI.
To whom it may concern:
This will identify Mr. Clark Lee. Mr. Lee is a representative of The Associated
Press and has been accredited by this headquarters.
He is now traveling on a special mission with military approval. All military organizations are directed to render every assistance to aid him to his destination.
(sgd) DOUGLAS MacARTHUR.
Commanding General.

We spent the afternoon making final preparations. I wrote some last dispatches and arranged for Dean Schedler to be relieved from his duties in the

Quartermaster Corps and to act as our correspondent, which he did magnificently until his exciting escape by airplane some six weeks later.

I took my typewriter and packed my razor and toothbrush and the slack suit I had worn out from Manila in my little canvas bag. Regretfully I gave away the souvenirs I had taken from dead Japs in Bataan: the neat little .25-caliber "suicide pistol" with a single bullet in its magazine; the .38 Luger; the rifles, gas masks, fatigue caps, hand grenades, 37-mm. shell, and the rest.

We were not supposed to tell anyone we were going, but it was a difficult secret to keep. The Sayres had left in the past few days and President Quezon and his party. We said goodbye to only a few people. Colonel Diller and Colonel Sid Huff took us into a tunnel lateral where quarters had been fixed up for Mrs. MacArthur and young Arthur. We drank a farewell toast and pledged that we would all drink another one someday, someplace. Mrs. MacArthur came in and wished us luck. So did Major Romulo and a few others.

I went down to the North Dock at six-thirty ready to go aboard the launch which was to take us out to the Princesa, anchored midway between Corregidor and the southern shore of Bataan. The Jacobys weren't there and nobody had seen them. I hadn't liked that dock since the afternoon I was caught in the shelling there, and I kept jumping from one foot to the other, expecting to hear more shells coming over at any moment.

The Jacobys finally arrived and we piled into the launch and headed out into the bay in the deepening shadows. The sun was already down but the sky behind Mariveles was flaming with color. I pointed out to the Jacobys one huge cloud that looked for all the world like a gigantic four-engined bomber, heading in from the China Sea over the southern shore of Bataan. "Let's hope it's one of ours," Mel said. While we watched, the winds scattered the cloud.

The Princesa de Cebu had already weighed anchor and was steaming toward Corregidor at slow speed, keeping well clear of the minefields. We tied up alongside and clambered aboard over the low railing onto an open deck. The ship was about two hundred feet long with three decks in the forward superstructure. The first-class cabins were under the bridge. Pigs and chickens were penned on the long main deck, which was open at the sides. With both her twin Diesels going wide open the Princesa could make about ten knots.

As soon as we were aboard the captain directed the helmsman to change course. "Follow that torpedo boat," he ordered. One of the PT's was waiting to lead us through the channel in the minefields, a course which was now thoroughly familiar to me. The torpedo boat chugged slowly ahead, cutting her speed to accommodate ours. She was too far ahead for me to recognize the helmsman.

We found several other passengers standing on the side of the bridge. One of them was Lew Carson of Shanghai. Lew introduced us to the others who, like himself, had been working in motor pools in Bataan after volunteering to drive supply trucks out from Manila. They were all English, with the exception of Charles van Landingham.

As we left the channel, there was a sudden spurt of firing from the black slope of Mt. Mariveles. Red tracers shot out from the shore and there was an answering line of tracers from the sea. That was a bad sign. It looked as if our shore defenders had spotted a Jap boat out there, only a few miles from us. But maybe they were shooting at one of our own torpedo boats. There were no guns on the Princesa de Cebu.

The Jacobys and I decided to sleep on deck and the boys rigged up three cots for us, complete with sheets and blankets. We put our life preservers by the side of the cots and went over to sit by the rail. Corregidor's big searchlights were probing the darkness behind us, keeping well away from our course.

"Well, here we go again," said Annalee.

We remembered then to tell Annalee one more thing that General MacArthur had told us. When he shook hands with us he had said, "If you don't make it, don't feel badly about having tried. I will fight as long as I can hurt the Jap, but unless we get reinforcements the end here will be brutal and bloody."

What he said had confirmed our own conviction that even if we were dive-bombed and sunk, or machine-gunned in lifeboats, or died of thirst on a raft, we would not regret having tried to get through.

31

THE PRINCESA HEADED STRAIGHT OUT INTO THE CHINA SEA for about ten miles and then turned south along the coast of Luzon. The last we saw of Corregidor was its giant searchlights illuminating the waters north of us and shining on the jungle-covered south shore of Bataan.

We had been underway for an hour when the sea around us and the deck suddenly lighted up. We damned the searchlight crews on Corregidor, thinking at first that they had turned a light on us. Then we saw that the light came from the new moon sinking into the sea to the west of us, silhouetting our ship for any watchers on the coast. The Japs held several towns along the shore in that area, and we had heard that they maintained nightly small boat patrols well out to sea.

We steamed outside of Fortune Island, with its circular beacon still flashing. Since the war no one had been able to get out to the island to turn off the automatic beacon and we understood the Japs were using it for navigation up and down the coast. We had also heard that Jap troops were occupying the island.

About twenty miles down the coast there was a sudden brilliant flare of light from high up on the Batangas Hills. It was directly opposite us.

"Holy horrors!" Annalee exclaimed.

"Well, I guess that does it," said Jacoby.

We thought that the light must be a signal to a Jap warship standing somewhere off the coast. The Japs had watchers on the mountains of Cavite province overlooking Corregidor and Manila Bay, and we guessed that we had been spotted.

I went up on the bridge and asked the captain. "That's nothing to get excited about," he said. "Just some farmers burning off the rubbish from their land."

The most ticklish part of the trip that first night was passing through the Verde Island passage between Luzon and the Island of Mindoro, which lay to the south. The straits were only eight miles wide, with an island in the middle. We knew that the Japs had stationed garrisons on both the Mindoro and Luzon shores of the straits and probably on the island. For all we knew there were torpedo boats or destroyers in the straits. Even an armed launch would have meant curtains for us. Our hull was so thin that a stream of .50-caliber bullets would have sunk the ship.

When I awakened it was full daylight and we were heading into the bay of Pola on the eastern coast of Mindoro. Tiny one-man bancas skimmed the calm bay like water bugs, most of them keeping well away from the ship. Finally, one or two got up enough nerve to approach and then the constabulary chief, carrying a shotgun, came aboard. We ate breakfast on the ship, enjoying fruit and eggs and bacon, things that we had not seen in seven weeks in Bataan and Corregidor.

Ashore at Pola we went to the municipal headquarters and paid our respects and then walked up to the schoolhouse on a hill overlooking the tiny fishing village. We spent the day trying to encourage the villagers, and to answer their embarrassing questions about American help for Bataan.

We went back aboard the ship just before sunset and set our course southwestward. A few miles out a bright light suddenly loomed up about two miles in front of us, and then another and another. We were all speechless except Van Landingham, who sputtered, "Jesus, we're surrounded by Jap ships!"

I felt my way up to the bridge and found the captain. "Just fishing boats," he explained. "They fish with torches, using the light to blind the fishes." We ghosted by the boats without altering course. The fishermen must have been thoroughly startled if they saw the outline of our vessel, for no large boats had been in those waters since war started.

We landed next day at the port of Looc on the island of Tablas and the following day at Estancia on the northeastern tip of Panay. There Jap planes spotted us.

Van, Lew, and I had engaged a car to take us to the big town of Capiz, some forty miles to the west, and while we were waiting for the driver to change a tire, a couple of planes flew over. We took cover in a ditch. The planes flew straight on.

When we got up and dusted off our uniforms we saw the townspeople laughing at us.

"Why did you do that?" they asked. "Do you not know that those are American airplanes?" We thought it kinder not to disillusion them.

Driving inland a few miles we were amazed to see a tremendous airplane runway at the side of the road. Several thousand Filipino men and women were at work, putting the finishing touches on bunkers along the sides of the runway and in the nearby woods. We drove out on the runway and found it all but completed.

The town of Capiz seemed like another world to us. Along the road we had given a lift to two girls, one of whom told us she had won the title of "Miss Panay" in a beauty contest. They were on their way to the hairdressers. We had forgotten there were such things as beauty contests and beauty parlors. In Capiz we bought newspapers from Cebu and Iloilo, chewing gum, Coca-Colas, and even had our shoes shined. There were plenty of automobiles on the streets and American signs everywhere. We went to a hotel and ordered an excellent five-course luncheon. Some American naval officers in khaki came in and we recognized each other from Corregidor.

The Navy officers had arrived a few days before on the inter-island ship Legaspi. They were under orders to proceed to various parts of the Philippines to inspect docking and shore facilities for the ships of our convoy, when and if it arrived.

Next morning we anchored off Barilli, on the west coast of Cebu. Husky young Filipinos from the crew of the Princesa carried us the last few feet to shore on their shoulders. We thanked the Princesa's portly captain and the other officers and said goodbye. The mayor of Barilli met us in the palm-lined, paved streets of the town. He began an enthusiastic speech of welcome to the "reinforcements" for Bataan. One of the Englishmen interrupted him: "I say! We're not reinforcements. We've escaped from Bataan." The mayor's face dropped a foot.

On smooth-paved roads we drove forty miles across the island to the city of Cebu, on the east shore. With its sugar plantations and fruit trees and homes with bright-colored roofs, the island looked like the most beautiful place we had ever seen, and the most peaceful. Cebu City seemed as big as New York, even though it had only one five-story "skyscraper" and most of the stores were boarded up from 10 A.M. to 3 P.M.—the likely times of day for bombing.

We found Major Bird of the Quartermaster Corps in an air-conditioned office down by the waterfront. He was young, handsome, and efficient. He looked at the credentials MacArthur had given us and said, "Too bad you didn't get here three hours ago."

"What's cooking?"

"An American freighter arrived at Mindanao three days ago and is going out tonight to Australia. I just sent my launch over this morning with a few people who are going aboard. If you had been here I'd have sent you along."

"Is anything else coming in?" we asked.

"There should be another ship along sooner or later. I'll keep an eye out for you. If it doesn't show up we'll try to get you to Mindanao and maybe you can catch a plane from Del Monte to Australia."

Major Bird invited the Jacobys to share his penthouse apartment atop the skyscraper. A member of his staff, Major Clelland, told Carson, Van, and me that we could stay at the Liloan Beach Club, fourteen miles north of the city. Bird furnished us an automobile and driver. In a few days the Jacobys also moved out with us, living in the clubhouse which was also our dining room while the three of us slept on the porch of a larger building. Liloan was a beautiful, palm-guarded beach, its white sand stretching for more than three miles. It was also a likely landing place for the Japs if they came to Cebu...

We decided to stand watches at night, each of us taking two hours. We reminded Annalee that it was still her honeymoon and told her she didn't have to stand guard, but she insisted on taking her turn. She and Mel sat up for four hours together almost every night, whispering to each other while the moon shone on the waters and the waving palm leaves. The moon was coming up later and later every night and several times we had real scares.

Three times, before the moon was up, we heard boats approaching across the bay. We dressed quickly and got ready to leave in a hurry. We had plotted several ways across the islands in case the Japs came and had driven over the roads to familiarize ourselves with them. We hoped to dodge them when they landed and get to some other island in a banca. Each time, however, the boats turned out to be friendly fishing vessels.

In Cebu we met Colonel Irvine C. Scudder, commander of the armed forces on the island, and his second in command, Lieutenant Colonel Edmunds. Scudder was a sunburned, white-haired southerner. He told us he intended to put up a fight against the Japs when they landed, although his troops had only fifteen hundred rifles and three machine guns.

A month later, Scudder and his men and their three machine guns did put up a terrific fight when the Japs landed. The Japs themselves admitted that, while bitterly complaining that the American and Filipino forces had dynamited the stores in Cebu and set fire to the city before retiring to the hills.

As day after day passed with no sign of any ship we began to look around again for a small boat that looked capable of floating long enough to reach Australia. Major Bird offered to send us over to Mindanao in a launch to wait there, but we decided against it.

We passed the time swimming out at the beach, playing golf at the Cebu Country Club, and sending wireless messages through the RCA station that was still operating.

We had brought scores of messages from officers and soldiers on Bataan and Corregidor to be sent to their families at home. The Cebu stamp on those messages led to some misunderstandings among the relatives of our troops in America, many of them believing that the soldiers themselves had escaped from the beleaguered peninsula and reached Cebu. In almost every case the messages were taken to Cebu by some third party such as ourselves, Major Bird, or the PT-boat officers.

One night we heard a rebroadcast of President Roosevelt's February 22 speech in which he said the American Navy could not operate in the southwestern Pacific because the Japanese controlled those waters from their Mandated Island bases. That worried us.

"If our Navy can't go there," I asked, "how in hell is a ship going to get in from Australia?"

"And if it gets here," added Mel, "how will it get back?"

We estimated that the chances of a single ship getting through were somewhat in the neighborhood of fifty to one. Its chances of getting back again—of making the trip twice—would be about one hundred to one.

Next morning, we drove into Cebu to ask for news. As we entered the city we detected an unusual amount of excitement. We guessed that perhaps a Jap destroyer, which had shelled the docks and oil tanks a few days before, had come back. Then, across the park from Bird's building, we saw a big ship tied up at the dock.

"By God," I said, "Look at the Queen Mary!" Jacoby was equally enthusiastic. "Whoopee," he exclaimed. "That's it. I'm sure that's it. It has to be!"

"Sure enough, that's old one hundred to one," said Lew Carson.

We drove over, parked, and walked out onto the dock. The ship was painted gray, with the top of the masts a light blue. We could make out the name, Dona Nati. All the American officers in Cebu were standing on the dock. A couple of American soldiers were leaning over the railing of the ship, a 9,000-ton motor vessel built in Italy for the New York-Los Angeles-Manila run of the De La Rama line. We wanted to jump up on the deck and shake hands with those soldiers. Instead we called out, "Hi, Joe, what's cooking?"

The sergeant answered, "Nothing much. What's cooking here?"

"All quiet. You see any planes on the way in?"

"Not a one. We had a quiet trip."

We asked for magazines and newspapers. They threw us down some old American magazines and some Australian papers. We saw by the dates on the papers that they had been in Sydney, and more recently in Brisbane. So we knew they had come from Australia.

"Many Americans down where you come from?" Mel asked.

"They're to hell and gone all over the place," the sergeant answered. "Plenty of soldiers and plenty of planes—"

One of the American officers joined in. "Well, if you see any planes around here, take a shot at them. All the planes hereabouts are Japs."

Three days later, while Lew Carson was on watch at four o'clock in the morning, a car pulled up in front of the Liloan Beach Club. Lew challenged the approaching figures and ordered them to halt. But they kept coming. It was Lieutenant Colonel Edmunds and his aide.

"Pack up your things and get going," Edmunds said. "Bird sent me out here to tell you to come on into Cebu as fast as you can."

We were on our way in fifteen minutes. We went up to Bird's apartment and he gave us some breakfast. "I thought it best to get you down here," he said. "The Dona Nati may be pulling out this morning. I don't know yet. Anyway, stick around the apartment here until you hear from me." We surmised that he was not telling us all he knew. Lew and I went up to the RCA to send a couple of last messages and then went back to the apartment.

Bird returned about ten-fifteen in the morning. He looked grim. "Here's the score," he said. "A Jap cruiser is coming up the coast, headed for Cebu. It is due here at noon at the speed it is making. The Dona Nati is going. If you want to go, you can. I'm going down to the dock."

At the dock we held a last minute consultation. Mel, Annalee, and I couldn't make up our minds. It seemed highly likely that the cruiser would catch the Dona Nati a few miles out of Cebu and our voyage would end abruptly. But while we were talking we walked up the gangplank. The last boxes of ammunition and canned food were being taken out of the Dona Nati's holds.

A naval officer, a friend from Corregidor, shouted at us from the dock. "Don't be damn fools," he said. "Come down off of there!" Then Bird shouted, "This may be your last chance." We walked inside the ship and put our luggage in a cabin. It looked wonderfully clean and comfortable. Then we went back on deck, still undecided.

Bird yelled to us that he would send his Chris-Craft to follow the ship. "Jump overboard in case they shell you," he said. "The Chris-Craft will pick you up." We hollered at him to put some life preservers in the small boat. There were no extra ones on board.

The crew began battening down the holds but still the Dona Nati did not cast off. We saw that Bird and the captain of the ship were holding a long-distance bridge-to-dock argument.

"Where are my orders?" the captain yelled. "I will not sail without my orders." "You already have your orders," Bird shouted back. "Orders, bah. These are not orders." We found out later that the captain's anxiety was justified. Bird had been unable to get any definite orders regarding course and destination from the Army at Corregidor, so he had just reversed the orders under which the Dona Nati had sailed from Brisbane to Cebu. The captain was worried about being sunk by our own submarines unless they were notified in advance of his course.

By this time the forward lines had been cast off. The ship started to drift away from the dock, turning on the stern line. Another Navy officer rushed out onto the dock and yelled at us across the widening space between ship and shore. "Hey, you dopes, you better get off! The cruiser is only an hour away. If you stay aboard you'll be shark bait by this afternoon."

Even then we considered going ashore, but it was too late. The gangplank had already been pulled up.

32

THERE ARE TWO ENTRANCES TO CEBU HARBOR, divided by a mile-long island. The Jap cruiser was coming up from the south, so the captain of the Dona Nati wanted to run out through the north channel. At 10:50 A.M. he signaled with the bridge telegraph for full speed astern on the starboard engine. The stern line was still tied to the pier, but they cast it off when we backed into the channel.

Colonel Scudder, Major Bird, and the other Army and Navy officers on the dock waved a hasty farewell and then ran for their cars to head for the hills behind Cebu. They knew that the Jap warship would shell the dock area, as well as the Dona Nati.

There was no doubt in our minds that the Dona Nati had priority on the Jap's target list. An observation plane had flown over Cebu two days before and spent a long time making photographs of the docks. The promenade deck of the Dona Nati seemed to be higher than the Empire State Building. From it we could see cars and pedestrians in the streets of Cebu, all of them going back up toward the hills.

Captain Pons tried to swing the Dona Nati around so it would be headed out the north channel, but the wind caught the empty ship and turned it back again each time. Pons maneuvered backward and forward for more than thirty minutes. Then he gave up and dropped the anchor. With the hook down, the wind brought the stem around. Pons ordered the anchor up and we steamed out through the north channel at our full speed of thirteen and a half knots. With a normal load the Dona Nati would make fifteen knots, but there was nothing in the cargo hatches now and there hadn't even been time to pump in salt water ballast.

Jacoby looked at his watch as we headed out of the harbor, "It's just eleven-thirty," he said. "That cruiser is due here at noon. At this rate it should catch us just about as we pass that island at the entrance to the harbor."

I had already made a mental measurement of the distance from the deck to the water. It was about forty-five feet from the lower stem deck and about fifteen feet more from the open deck space behind the first-class cabins. "If it catches us," I said, "let's hop over and take our chances on getting ashore. It will be better than getting blown up on board." The Chris-Craft that Major Bird was sending as our "escort" vessel was just pulling out from the dock about a half mile behind us. There was not a sign of a cloud in the noonday sky, and no hope of any fog to hide behind. The mountains of Bohol and Leyte, far across the inland sea, were clearly visible.

We steamed out through the north channel, passing two smaller and slower inter-island ships. Both of them were sunk by the Jap cruiser that afternoon. We hardly dared look to the south across the calm blue waters. The ship's crew went about their jobs as if nothing was up. At noon they announced lunch and we went down to the comfortable dining salon. There was a large table in the center with eight places where the American machine gunners sat and two smaller tables at each side. The Englishmen who had come out of Corregidor with us were already eating.

We turned east after leaving the harbor and within a couple of hours the northwestern corner of Bohol was between us and Cebu. There was no sign of the cruiser. We listened to the Cebu radio station. At two-fifteen it went off the air and a half-hour later it came back on.

"News flash!" said the announcer. "A Japanese cruiser shelled the docks and waterfront section of Cebu from 2:25 P.M. until two-forty this afternoon. It has just left the harbor and is speeding away to the southeast." The cruiser wasn't following us. That meant that we had at least a breathing spell.

A half hour later the engines suddenly stopped. I ran up to the bridge and found the captain, the chief officer, and the American Army sergeant peering through glasses and conferring anxiously. Someone loaned me a pair of binoculars and through them I made out a camouflaged ship, lying motionless against the coast of Leyte. It was a big ship, its hull painted in blotches of light and dark gray. Its masts were a lighter color.

"That's no Jap warship," I told the captain.

"It might be a submarine tender," he said. Then he studied it further. "Whatever it is, it has run aground between Bohol and Leyte. The channel there is only a few hundred feet wide."

The captain decided that whatever kind of ship it was, it certainly wasn't friendly. He rang for full speed ahead and swung our course sharply to the northeast. "It looks like they've got us," the captain said, "but we'll at least make a try at fooling them. If they see us heading this way they will think we are going to try to run through the San Bernardino Strait up north of here. Possibly they will call off the cruiser."

At nightfall we dropped anchor off the tiny town of Inopacan, on the east coast of the island of Leyte and about sixty miles from Cebu. By that time we had hoped to be well on our way through Surigao Strait. The captain sent a small boat ashore in command of his chief officer, a wiry, handsome Filipino who always wore a smile on his face and a shiny .38-caliber pistol at his hip. In an hour the chief was back aboard with good news.

"That is one of our own ships," he reported. "The British freighter Anhwei which came up from Darwin with a cargo like ours. It has been aground since yesterday."

We spent the next two days anchored off the coast of Leyte. Each day Jap planes spotted us and all day we waited for them to come back with dive bombers or to bring in a cruiser or destroyer to finish us off. There were only two ways we could get out of the islands—either through San Bernardino or

Surigao Straits—both of them so narrow that a single warship could patrol them effectively.

Shortly after noon on the third day Captain Pons turned the Dona Nati south again and just before nightfall we came abreast of the grounded Anhwei. We passed so close we could see the Chinese crew on deck. A tiny launch flying the American flag chugged over to our ship and an Army officer climbed up the swaying rope ladder. We recognized Lieutenant Tom Jurika from Cebu.

"How about towing that ship off the reef?" he asked our captain. Pons was willing to do everything possible, but after a conference it was decided that it couldn't be done until morning, so we dropped anchor for the night. At dawn Jurika came aboard again and told the captain that lighters were coming over from Cebu to unload the Anhwei's cargo, and that after that she would be refloated by launches.

Just as we were pulling up our anchor a wobbly banca came alongside. Its passenger was a reserve lieutenant in the American Navy, a Manila businessman named Green. Lieutenant Green had a bad leg and he had the devil of a job climbing the ladder to our deck. On his own initiative he had sent a wireless message to Corregidor reporting that the Dona Nati was leaving the Philippines and giving its course.

"That information will be communicated to all our fleet units," Green said. "At least you won't be sunk by one of our own subs or planes." Captain Pons thanked him sincerely. That was one worry off his mind. Green probably saved us from getting sunk a few days later.

We anchored that morning off the eastern coast of Bohol and shortly after noon headed east again to run through the Surigao Strait. That was the most dangerous part of the trip up to then. The Japs held the northeastern tip of Mindanao Island, on the southern side of the strait. We strongly suspected that the cruiser that had shelled Cebu was lurking behind one of the islands in the narrow waters.

For luck, I sat on deck for a while with my fingers, elbows, and knees all crossed. The Jacobys did the same. Up until then Mel had always been able to crack a joke—no matter how bad—in tight spots. But that afternoon he was wordless. At four-thirty in the afternoon the captain pointed out to me the tiny island where Magellan had first landed in the Philippines. Shortly after we passed the island it suddenly began to rain. That was the second time I had seen rain in nearly four months in the Philippines. The first time, when I was trying to get out of Baguio just before Christmas, it had been a decided handicap. Now it was a godsend. Out of a clear sky dark clouds rolled off the mountaintops on each side of the strait and soon we were running through storms and heavy mists.

I stayed up until nearly midnight when I felt our bow begin to bite into the slow Pacific swells. The days that followed were not eventful, but they were not monotonous. Captain Pons wouldn't tell us exactly where we were going, but we knew it was Brisbane and we knew that we would have to run east between Japan's Caroline and Marshall Islands and the points in New Guinea and New Britain where the Japs had landed. Van Landingham had a compass, and Jacoby had a map, and we were able to work out our course and daily position pretty well.

At dinner the night we were passing through Surigao Strait, Jacoby and I got into an argument. I don't remember what it was about, but it certainly wasn't anything important. We had been together constantly for more than eight weeks without ever a difference of opinion.

The argument got hotter, and one of us invited the other outside into the passageway.

"You hit me first!" I commanded.

"I don't want to hit you."

"Go ahead. I can lick you even with one broken hand."

"Okay. If you insist."

He swung a left which caught me a good shot on the jaw. We mixed it for about five minutes without doing any major damage. Then we stopped and shook hands. Neither of us ever mentioned it again and I never thought of it until after I got back to Honolulu. There, time after time, I saw a pair of sailors—just in from a long task force assignment at sea—pound the devil out of each other, without anger, and then suddenly shake hands. Those fights were an effective way of relaxing tense nerves and expressing joy at being alive.

That first night out of Surigao, Captain Pons told me, "The eighteenth will be the most dangerous day. If we can get past that and the next two days, we should be fairly safe." We had left Cebu on March 8. Studying our map, we figured that on the 18th we would pass the converging point for all the Japanese shipping lanes from Truk and the other Mandated Island bases to the Dutch East Indies and to New Guinea. On the 20th we would pass within sixty miles of the furthest south of the Mandated Islands, and between it and Rabaul, where the Japs had set up headquarters on New Britain.

Hearing the captain talk about trouble on the 18th, we all began to expect it. When the 18th finally came we stayed on deck all day, watching the sea and sky. The unbroken circle of sea around us had come to be all-important. As long as nothing appeared we were reasonably certain to stay alive. Toward afternoon we began to encounter scattered rain squalls. There was a neat sign posted in the dining room informing us that one alarm meant torpedoes, two, airplanes, and three, "surface raiders." At four-thirty, the klaxon blared sharply three times. I grabbed my life jacket and ran up to the bridge. The ship was already swinging northward from our course, running for a nearby rain squall.

"There are eight ships over there," Captain Pons said with an air of finality. "One seems to be an aircraft carrier, and the others smaller warships." Within two or three minutes after we sighted them a black squall hid the ships from us and we ducked into another squall, hiding until dark and then going back on course again.

For four months I congratulated myself that we had given a Jap task force the slip that day. In July, when I was traveling on an American aircraft carrier to the Solomon Islands attack, I told Admiral Frank Jack Fletcher the story. "I know all about it," he grinned. "That was my ship, the Lexington. We had been in to attack Rabaul. We knew you were there all the time." Thanks to Lieutenant Green, I thought.

Over the radio we also heard the startling news that General MacArthur had reached Australia. We were stunned and delighted. Captain Pons put it into words for us: "That's the best possible news for my country. If anybody can save the Philippines, MacArthur can and will. These American soldiers on board tell us there are many planes and men in Australia. MacArthur will lead them back to the Philippines."

We discussed the possible adverse effect on morale in Bataan, and decided that the soldiers' love and trust of MacArthur was such that they would interpret his leaving as Pons had done.

The next morning we ran into more trouble. About eleven-thirty the lookout sighted three ships. They appeared to be a tanker refueling two submarines. We put on our life jackets and stood around on deck. I remember saying a prayer for the second time since the war started. It wasn't much of a prayer, something like, "Oh, Lord, I know I've got to die sometime, but please don't make this be it. It's too nice a day to die."

When we saw the ships, Captain Pons immediately swung his course from southeast to southwest. The Dona Nati was making her full thirteen and a half knots so he couldn't speed up. We lost sight of the ships. Cautiously Pons edged back on course again. Again we saw the ships. The captain sent every available man in the crew up into the masts and rigging. They perched there tirelessly, clinging to the wires. We changed course and lost the ships again. Pons steamed west for two hours, then north, then northeast and gradually back onto our southeasterly course. By that time it was dark and we finally lost sight of the vessels. Probably they were a couple of American destroyers and a tanker from the Lexington's task force.

By going off course we had lost so much time that on the following day we had to pass between Rabaul and the Jap Mandated Island in daytime, instead of at night as Pons had originally planned. We watched intently all day without sighting anything. From then on we began to relax. After the 20th it was smooth sailing. We steamed east almost to Fiji, turned south around New Caledonia, and then west through the Coral Sea to Brisbane. We arrived there on March 30 after a trip of twenty-two days from Cebu. As we sailed up the narrow river to the port we passed many American ships and saw American jeeps and trucks on the shore. We shook hands with each other and exulted, "By God! The United States is moving. Now to get started back to the Philippines."

We got a taxi at the dock and drove through wide streets of what looked like an American city. We went to several hotels and found them all filled. "American aviators," the clerks told us.

Finally, we went to a small hotel, and while Lew Carson went to the desk the Jacobys and I sat down in the lobby. I noticed there were potted palms in the room and I suddenly remembered something.

"You two have probably forgotten the hunch I told you about on New Year's Eve," I said to the Jacobys. "I'm going to test your memory. I'll buy a drink. What'll you have?"

"I'll take a Tom Collins," Annalee smiled.

"Make mine the same," said Mel.

33

THE AMERICAN OFFICERS IN BRISBANE WANTED TO KNOW something about the Japs, and I tried to tell what I had learned.

A few days before we sailed away from Bataan, MacArthur had talked to Jacoby and myself about the Japanese soldier.

"The Jap," he said, "is a first-class fighting man. These troops facing me on Bataan may not be as good as the best troops in the World War, but it would take the best troops to beat them.

"Their officers spend lives heedlessly, even for unimportant objectives. The individual Jap is a fanatic. He will throw himself on a landmine to explode it and clear the way for others. Or he will fling himself on my barbed wire and let those following him climb over his body."

I recalled to the general an interview which I had two years before Pearl Harbor with Lieutenant General Masaharu Homma, then commander of Japanese forces at Tientsin, whose troops had blockaded the British Concession in the North China port and stripped British men and women and slapped their faces. I told Homma that the blockade appeared to me part of a deliberate plan to drive the white man out of the Orient; but he disclaimed any such purpose on the part of Japan and denied responsibility for the inexcusable assaults on Britons—blaming them on "gendarmes whom I am unable to control."

Our talk touched Japanese-American problems and drifted to the Philippines, where two years later Homma was to turn up as commander of the invasion forces opposing MacArthur. Homma said he hoped the United States would recognize Japan's "true mission" in the Orient and would not cut off Japan's sources of needed materials. If the United States tried to oppose Japan, then war was inevitable. Many Japanese, he said, had considered it inevitable for years.

"I think I understand your American psychology very well," he said. think that every American believes he can handle any two Japanese soldiers. Is that not true?"

I replied, "'Well, we have our own ideas."

Homma went on, "I think I am right in my analysis. At any rate, we are proceeding with this in mind and are prepared to Jose ten million men in our war with America. How many are you prepared to lose?"

MacArthur, at the time, and later Admiral William Halsey as commander of our southwest Pacific naval forces, both gave the only possible answer to Japan's willingness to fight to the death for victory. They said, "There is only one way for America to win the war, and that is to kill Japs, kill more Japs, and kill still more Japs."

I also recounted to MacArthur on Corregidor an interview with Rear Admiral Kanazawa, whom I knew first as Japanese Navy spokesman in Tokyo and later as naval attaché in occupied China. Ten months to the day before Pearl Harbor, Kanazawa had received Russell Brines and myself at his headquarters in Shanghai. After some preliminary pleasantries Kanazawa pointed to a large map on the wall and outlined in startling detail just what Japan intended to do if it became "necessary" to fight the United States.

"America has a triangular defense system based on a line from Alaska to Hawaii to Panama," he said. "It is generally overlooked that Japan has a similar triangle running from Yokohama to here—" he pointed—"and here." The last two places were New Caledonia and Singapore; which were then respectively French and British territory. That didn't bother the admiral.

"If the United States attempts to take back one inch of territory which we have already taken or which we may be forced to take in the future," he said slowly and seriously, "we will put up an impregnable defense with airplanes, ships, and soldiers.

"We will fight inch by inch. We will fight to the last man. We will make the cost in blood, ships, and planes so frighteningly great that, we believe, America will eventually become discouraged. The American people will decide that the cost is not worth the gains. They will say that, after all, the Orient is a long way off and perhaps Japan is the logical nation to govern it. Then our war will be won."

The Japanese won the first part of their war in exactly five months from the attack on Pearl Harbor to the surrender of Corregidor. At a cost of certainly not more than 100,000 men, a score of ships, and a few hundred airplanes, they smashed three of the world's great fortresses, drove the United States, Great Britain, and the Netherlands out of the Far East, and conquered a vast and rich empire containing all the natural resources needed to make Japan the world's most powerful nation.

The Japanese won partly because they planned well and struck boldly and fearlessly. Mostly they won because of the indecision and slowness of the United States and our failure to send more than token forces to the Far East. While they were fighting on many fronts in the first months of 1942, and moving troops and supplies over lengthy and unconsolidated lines, the Japanese were wide open to attack at a score of points. But we reacted too slowly after Pearl Harbor. Planes alone could have held the Philippines, Singapore, Hong Kong, Wake Island, and the Aleutians, just as later they were to drive back the Japs at Midway and to hold Guadalcanal and Port Moresby.

Without planes the Japanese drives could not be stopped. The Japanese Air Force was the decisive factor everywhere. It turned the tide in the Philippines on the first day of war. The sinking of the Repulse and Prince of Wales opened the way for Malaya's conquest. Hong Kong and Wake Island were battered into submission by planes. The gallant Dutch Air Force, with its antiquated planes, was shot out of the air in a few days.

With air control established, the Japanese Air Force operated like a smooth, first-class machine. Aerial co-ordination with ground troops, the result of long practice in China, was extremely effective. Their Zero fighters flew circles around our P-40-B's, our old Brewsters, and even British Hurricanes at Singapore.

Their Army and Navy worked perfectly together. A few months before they went to war the Army and Navy had been at loggerheads as a result of their long-standing dispute over whether they should strike first to the north, against Russia, or to the south. In Shanghai just before the war this bitter feeling exhibited itself in the form of bloody fighting between elements of the Imperial Army and Navy, and in the exchange of open insults between Army and Navy officers, even in the presence of foreigners. But when the crucial moment came, when the final decision was made, the bitterness was forgotten and the Army and Navy worked perfectly together as a single team.

From the technical point of view the really amazing feature of Japan's campaigns was the thoroughness and perfection of their preparations. They worked out their logistics problem, the problem of supply, perfectly. Every foot of space in every ship must have been utilized in the most effective way possible. When their troops reached an invasion point their reserve ammunition and trucks, gasoline and oil, food and spare clothes were right there with them. As the Air Force moved southward from base to base, cargo ships brought along the bombs, fuel, ammunition, spare parts, and portable mechanical shops needed to put the planes into instant operation. Of course, there was very little opposition to any of the Japanese landing operations, but even so the planning was remarkable.

The entire Japanese plan was a desperate gamble but everything, everywhere, broke right for them. Their audaciousness paid great dividends. They were gambling that their attack on Pearl Harbor would paralyze the U.S. Navy long enough to give them time to conquer Southeastern Asia, and their calculations proved correct. They gambled that they could knock out our Air Force in the Philippines, and in Malaya, and they won. They believed that we would be too slow in sending planes to reinforce the Netherlands Indies and Singapore, and they were right. They caught our planes on the ground again and again, in the Philippines and Malaya and even in the Indies. They used the element of surprise to the utmost.

In addition they knew every foot of ground they were to fight over. Through the years their spies had laboriously gathered all the information they needed. They knew what type of clothes and what arms and equipment to use in the jungles of Malaya and the mountains of southeastern Luzon. They knew what tactics to use to confuse our troops and terrorize the civilian population.

Soldier for soldier, our troops proved themselves better than the Japanese. In Bataan our Filipino and American troops killed an average of five Japs for every fatality in our forces, and sometimes as many as seventeen or twenty to one. These figures were later equaled by our Marines on Guadalcanal. What made the Japanese tough foes was their refusal to surrender.

It was costly and difficult to rout them out when they dug themselves into the jungle; and in headlong assaults on our front-line positions they would keep coming and coming, disregarding losses, until they overwhelmed our defenses.

The twenty-five hundred Japanese who died in January and February in the unsuccessful effort to crack our Bataan flank were perhaps typical of the first soldiers that Japan sent to the Philippines. They were members of a regiment recruited in the Kansai district of Japan, the industrial cities of Kobe and Osaka, and the nearby ancient capital of Kyoto. Their ages ranged from 21 to 24 years—compulsory military service in Japan starts at the age of 21. They had never been on duty in China and when they came to the Philippines they had been told they would have a quick, easy victory and would not meet any American troops. They had been trained thoroughly as both infantry and artillery units.

We took some ninety prisoners out of the whole twenty-five hundred, and most of those were too seriously wounded to go on fighting. Perhaps that number is too small to permit any conclusions regarding the health of the whole regiment. But in any case four out of five of the prisoners were suffering from some chronic disease, usually venereal. When captured their physical condition was poor, due to lack of food and water, but most of them were husky and well built, approximately 5 feet 3 inches tall and weighing around 115 pounds.

Many of the first Japanese troops to land in the Philippines were reported to be youngsters in their teens, but in this connection it must be remembered that it is extremely difficult for a non-Japanese to tell the age of a Japanese. There were also reports of women among the Japanese. There is no doubt that there were some girls with the Japanese forces and that on occasion they were seen carrying rifles and machine guns, possibly to give the men a rest or possibly to preserve the weapons of soldiers who had been killed.

In China, as I had personally seen on many occasions, women camp followers traveled with the Japanese forces. A certain number of women were assigned to each company. In making provisions for accommodation and travel, arrangements were always made for the women, many of whom were Koreans. On occasion, the women had been known to fight but their main role was that of prostitutes. It is not unlikely that the women seen with the Japanese troops in the Philippines were there for a similar purpose. However, some of the women may have been nurses.

I talked to one American, formerly a member of a tank crew, who told me that he had seen many women soldiers in the Lingayen Gulf area. He said that one afternoon, when he was in one of six tanks defending a bridge, large forces of Japanese charged down the road and at the tanks. The road was quickly heaped with bodies, and still the enemy kept coming. When he was changing ammunition in his machine guns, a large group succeeded in approaching close to the tank, "They suddenly threw down their rifles and tore open their blouses. I discovered that they were women. I was so horrified at the thought that we had been slaughtering women that I passed out there in the tank." Subsequently, he was transferred to other duties and he was serving as an M.P. in Bataan when I met him and heard his story.

With some exceptions, the Japanese equipment was not as good in quality as ours. Their chief infantry weapon was the .25-caliber (7.7-mm.) rifle, which had a higher muzzle velocity than the American Springfield or Enfield, but was about seven inches longer and more clumsy to handle. Snipers had a finely made, short carbine. Many of the Japanese carried a sub-machine gun of .25-caliber which fired a clip of twenty shots and was effective at short range. The heavy Japanese machine-gun, slightly larger than our .50-caliber, was operated by a crew of three. One soldier carried the gun lashed to his back. In action he would fall on his face and the second man would aim and fire the gun while the third fed the clips. This gun had one feature which none of our officers had seen before, a device which dripped a drop of grease onto each bullet before it was fired.

The Japanese made effective use of a finely manufactured grenade thrower which the soldier carried with ease and which fired projectiles for distances up to seven hundred yards. The projectile could also be used as a hand grenade. Some of their infantry carried flamethrowers, while anti-tank units were equipped with a discus-shaped grenade which was hidden on the dust-covered roads of Bataan or thrown against our tanks. They also used gasoline-filled beer bottles, with a short fuse, as an anti-tank weapon. Some of the beer bottles had been taken from the Japanese brewery in Manila.

From the equipment which I took from the bodies of Jap snipers, and which some of our soldiers picked up, I compiled a list of the gear which these "one-man supply trains" carried on their missions behind our lines. We estimated that each sniper could fight for two weeks or longer, provided he could get water from the countryside.

The equipment included: a rifle and ammunition, a gas mask, a green combination mosquito net-camouflage hood covering helmet and shoulders, a green, corded net to camouflage the rest of his body, a black wire eye screen to protect him from sun glare; a coil of rope for climbing trees and tying himself to branches. There were also a sack of rice, a small bag of hardtack, a half-pound of hard candy, a package of concentrated food, a can of field rations, small can of coffee, vitamin pills, quinine, stomach pills, a can of chlorine to purify water, a mess kit and canteen. Also an antidote for mustard gas, roll and triangular bandages, toothbrush, spare socks, gloves, and a flashlight with varicolored lenses. All this was neatly stowed away in a small pack carried on the back.

Spare lenses for the eyeholes of the gas mask included some especially made for use in subzero weather, which indicated that the equipment was originally intended for use in North China or Manchukuo. Some of the Japs wore heavy woolen shirts and leggings, and many carried fur-lined packs which were never made for use in the subtropics, but the majority had clothing and equipment suitable for the climate.

The smallest Jap field artillery piece was a 37-mm. gun. They also had 88-mm. and 105-mm. guns in Bataan, most of them apparently mounted on wheels and drawn either by horses or by the soldiers themselves. The Japanese supposedly got both the 88 and 105-mm. guns from the Germans. The artillery work was excellent, partly because of the advantage of aerial observation. Their 105 had as great range as our own 155.

The Japs were well drilled in the tricks of jungle fighting. One of their favorite stunts was to toss firecrackers into the trees some yards from one of their machine-gun nests. The exploding firecrackers resembled the crack of Jap rifles. When our soldiers went over to investigate, the hidden machine gun would cut them down. The Japs also threw firecrackers in night attacks to confuse our troops and create the illusion of strong forces. Some of the Japs wore pads on their hands and knees to enable them to creep stealthily through the underbrush.

In charging our positions the Japs would shriek what they imagined to be blood-curdling yells, interspersed with such English words as "ASSAULT!" and "ATTACK!" They infiltrated our lines wherever possible and then split up into groups of two or three men who climbed trees and sniped at our officers, or attempted to approach our behind-the-line camps where they threw grenades and tried to create confusion. They took the uniforms from our dead soldiers, especially the Filipinos, and tried to pass our sentries at night. They were very clever at lying quietly in the brush until they learned our password and then imitating it. This trick worked until our officers discovered that the Japanese could not pronounce the letter L. After that our passwords were liquid with L's—words such as "Hula-hula." The Japs invariably pronounced that as "Hura-hura." It was a dead giveaway.

In fighting at close quarters the Japs would quickly learn the names of some of our officers, and also attempt to imitate the voices of those they heard most frequently. They tried this on Commander Frank Bridget during the fighting at Langoscawayan Point. He was coming down a path alone and he called out to Colonel Fry, commander of the 57th Filipino Scouts, who was somewhere up ahead. "Where are you. Colonel?"

"Down here, Frank. Come down here!"

Bridget had just seen the colonel going in the opposite direction so he refused to be fooled. The Jap who shouted was killed a few minutes later by the Scouts.

The Japs were vicious and cruel when they had the upper hand. I saw the body of one American officer. He had been suspended from a tree limb and bayoneted repeatedly in the back and buttocks. Then his arms and legs had been hacked off. One group of thirty-five Filipino Scouts were found lying face down in a stream. Their hands were tied behind them and then they had been bayoneted in the back and left to drown. Other Scouts were hung from trees while still alive and then bayoneted.

When they were captured the Japs became meek and docile. They seemed small and ineffectual without their rifles and sometimes without their clothes, which they had removed in the hope of swimming to the safety of their own lines. Talking to the prisoners I became more than ever convinced that the Japs are not supermen. The prisoners admitted they were glad to be alive and did not regret their failure to die as heroes. They admitted that they had been terribly frightened when they first came under artillery fire—so frightened that at Langoscawayan many of them jumped off a cliff to their deaths rather than stand up under the fire of Corregidor's 12-inch mortars. They told us that when a Japanese unit was cut off, the officers would almost always commit suicide. They wanted to die quickly rather than fire their last bullet at their enemies and then await the suspense of being killed.

Japanese army units, as I had learned in China, are designated by the name of their commanding officer: the Kawasaki regiment, the Tada company and so on.

In action and under fire, the discipline of the Japanese Army is generally good. But when Japanese troops are not fighting they are hard to control; especially if they have been drinking. They drink badly, and after one or two glasses of beer they frequently become surly and unmanageable. While traveling with the Japanese Army, Harry Brundidge, then of the St. Louis Star-Times, and I narrowly escaped death twice in one day at the hands of Japanese soldiers.

A drunken private grabbed an officer's sword in a restaurant in Taiyuanfu, capital of Shansi province in North China, and threatened to cut our heads off. Captain "Baroness" Takada, who was our escort, managed to disarm him only at the risk of his own life. Later that evening, while we were returning to our hotel, a Japanese soldier thrust his bayonet at Brundidge's stomach and when I objected pointed it at me. I still don't know how we got out of that situation.

On another occasion, at a party given by Japanese Army officers for foreign correspondents, I saw a major draw his sword and swing wickedly at the head of a British newspaperman. The reporter saved himself by grabbing a chair and thrusting it in front of him. The sword cut cleanly through two legs of the chair.

The outstanding example of Japanese indiscipline—or at least that was the official explanation given by the Japanese Army—was the rape of Nanking. For more than two weeks after they captured the Chinese capital in December, 1937, Japanese troops roamed unchecked through the city, raping, murdering, and burning. In China acts of brutality by Japanese soldiers were commonplace, and when protests were made the Japanese officers always replied that they were unable to control their troops. Apparently for the sheer love of brutality Japanese soldiers would club unarmed Chinese, kick a basket of food out of the arms of an aged Chinese woman, or slap faces without provocation.

In the case of the Occidental, Japanese cruelty was more deeply rooted. The Japanese have been taught that Americans and Englishmen are enemies who threaten the existence of their country, and that it is their sacred duty to drive them out of the Orient. The Japanese humiliate the white man wherever possible, by every means from small annoyances before the war to the outright murder of unarmed Canadian troops in Hong Kong after the capture of that British stronghold. This is part of a deliberate program to impress their fellow Orientals with Japan's strength. Until it is completely disproved, I believe every tale of Japanese brutality that is told. The Japanese with a rifle and bayonet is a vicious, dangerous animal.

In discussing the bravery, fighting prowess, and morale of the Japanese a distinction must be made between the armed members of the military forces and the average civilian at home.

I do not believe every Japanese is a hero. Their politeness is a form of cowardice. It is a throwback to the days when the Samurai warlords roamed the highways of feudal Japan and any commoner who failed to bow his head would have it cut off.

The Japanese lack a sense of humor. They also lack imagination, and in war that is to their advantage since they deal only with immediate problems and do not worry about what may happen to them individually in the future. I have flown with Japanese Army pilots in many tight places. Once we were trapped in a storm in the mountains of North China. The clouds were down below the summits of the mountains and we were forced to fly down a narrow river canyon, banking frequently to keep from crashing against the sides. Every foreigner on the plane was worried sick, but the pilots simply kept going until we flew through the storm and out over the plains of Hopei province. They had not sufficient imagination to be worried.

Despite their love of children and their superficial culture—their art, their neat homes, cleanliness, imitation of Western living—the Japanese are primitive people, with the strength and weakness of primitive people. One of their weaknesses—and this applies to the civilian populace—is their tendency to panic, their blind dependence on superior authority, and their confusion when confronted by a calamitous situation such as an earthquake or tidal wave, or even by some minor upset in their routine of life.

I believe that when our big bombers can cruise over the Japanese islands night after night, spreading death and fire and bringing the horror of war home to the islands themselves, there will be such widespread terror and panic as to seriously disrupt the life of the country, now devoted almost exclusively to feeding the Imperial war machine. Soldiers may have to drive civilians to work at bayonet point.

There is no reason to believe as yet, however, that even a series of serious defeats will break down the morale of Japan's armed forces. Possibly one crushing blow after another might produce such an effect; but from all the evidence in the first year of war it seems more likely that the Japanese will fight vigorously and unflinchingly until an overwhelming weight of steel and explosives smashes their ships, shipyards, and munitions factories, and completely destroys their power to resist.

34

We learned soon after our arrival in Brisbane that the United States was fighting the Pacific war with only one hand, and that the day of the final destruction of Japan's power was still far off.

In reaching Australia we had achieved one of our two purposes in leaving the Philippines. We had come through without getting killed or captured. The other reason, our unofficial mission to try to get help for the defenders of Bataan, was no longer valid. Mac Arthur was in Australia and we knew if it were humanly possible he would organize a counteroffensive and strike back. I thought of going home, but The AP cabled: "Desire Lee join Australia staff."

We flew from Brisbane down to Melbourne to see MacArthur. Mel and Annalee slept most of the way, but for me that trip was the beginning of a nightmarish series of airplane rides. I developed a severe case of altitude phobia. I had first experienced it several months before when flying in a Japanese Army airplane from Hankow down to Shanghai. Suddenly I felt conscious of the distance from the plane to the ground, and it seemed every second that the bottom of the plane was going to drop out or the wings fall off. At any altitude above five thousand feet I had that feeling.

Now, flying over friendly territory in Australia in a sturdy twin-engined Douglas, the sensation came back in aggravated form. Perhaps it had been heightened by my experience in the Philippines. Perhaps I was slightly "bomb-happy" from near misses on Corregidor. At any rate, the feeling has persisted ever since and the scores of hours that I have ridden at high altitudes in transport planes have all been unpleasant. Strangely, when flying in combat planes with a parachute attached to me, I have had no sensation of uneasiness.

I thought that trip to Melbourne would never end. But it finally did and General MacArthur received us at his headquarters. He shook hands cordially. "I am glad you made it," he said. Then he told me about his own trip with Lieutenant Johnny Bulkeley, "that bold buckaroo with the cold green eyes," who had brought the general and his party safely to Mindanao, where they boarded bombers and reached Australia. He also told us Captain Pons of the Dona Nati had been awarded the D.S.C.

MacArthur talked about the chances of defending Australia if the Japanese continued their victorious surge farther south, past the Netherlands East Indies and New Guinea. The chances didn't look too good.

He advised me to remain in Australia for at least a month—until April 30. "By that time," he said, "either I'll hit the Jap up in New Guinea, or he will hit me, or there will be a stalemate." As events turned out MacArthur didn't have anything to hit the Japs with. The Japs attempted to hit him early in

May when they sent a vast invasion force down into the Coral Sea, heading for either New Guinea, northern Australia, New Caledonia, or New Zealand. They ran into the Battle of the Coral Sea.

MacArthur confided that he was going to make one last effort—with the limited forces at his command—to give help to his troops in the Philippines. He told us that he was planning an air raid against the Japanese besieging Bataan and Corregidor.

I asked permission to go along with the ten B-25's and the three B-17's which were to make the flight, but my request was turned down. All the space on the planes would be needed to bring out Army fliers, Navy torpedo officers, and others stranded at the Del Monte field in Mindanao.

A week after I reached Australia the news came through that Bataan had fallen. With shoulders back, but with an ache in his heart, MacArthur issued his memorable statement:

"The Bataan force went out as it wished—fighting to the end of its flickering, forlorn hope. No army has ever done so much with so little. Nothing became it like its last hour of trial and agony...

MacArthur went ahead with his plans to raid the Japs. Brigadier General Ralph Royce led the bombers up to Mindanao, from where they pounded Jap shipping at Davao and Cebu.

Three of the bombers raided Nichols and then flew over Corregidor, which was still holding out although Bataan had fallen less than a week before. Many an American and Filipino on Corregidor said a prayer of thanksgiving as he saw the blue and white stars on the wings of those big planes. The soldiers ran out of their foxholes and tunnels, ignoring the Jap shells, and cheered. "This is it," they exulted, clapping each other on the back. "Help is here at last."

But help wasn't there. That raid was actually the last gasp in our efforts to save Bataan. I believe that when MacArthur left Corregidor in mid-March he thought that in Australia he would find men and guns and planes, and the ships needed to take them across water to counterattack the Philippines or at least to hit the Japs somewhere in the southwest Pacific.

Twice MacArthur was ordered to leave the Philippines to take over as supreme commander in the southwest Pacific, which sounds like an all-inclusive command but actually included only limited areas west of a certain meridian. The third time MacArthur could not, as a soldier, ignore his orders. When he left Corregidor he said to General George Moore, commander of the fortress: "Hold the fort, George. I'll be back!"

When he got to Australia the first thing he said was, "I have left the Philippines and I shall return... I shall keep the soldier's faith."

The vast army of men and ships that MacArthur expected to find in Australia wasn't there. The best he could do was to get back together those ten B-25's and three B-17's and send them up to the Philippines to make that last raid. The very presence of those B-25's in Australia was the tip-off regarding our policy in the Pacific, Those bombers had been bought and paid for many months before by the government of the Netherlands East Indies. They were delivered not to the Netherlands East Indies, but to Australia, three weeks after the Indies had fallen.

MacArthur, pacing in his headquarters in Melbourne, was the same MacArthur who had paced the dusty road outside of Malinta tunnel on Corregidor, ignoring the dive bombers overhead. The cards were still stacked against him. He knew the necessity for quick, powerful action to hold the Philippines and to prevent the Jap from building a solid circle around his Asiatic conquests. He knew that the one way to defeat Japan was to kill Japs. Now he had no way to get at them.

When he reached Australia he had said, "I was sent here, as I understand it, for the purpose of organizing an offensive against Japan."

We soon discovered that MacArthur not only did not have sufficient forces to start a counterattack against the Philippines or to hit the Japs in the Dutch East Indies, but perhaps not even enough to defend Australia. A high-ranking Australian officer told me, "Australia, like the Philippines, is expendable in terms of global strategy."

In Australia there were some planes, but only a relative handful. It took me several weeks to reach the point where I could hear the sound of a high-flying airplane without a shiver of apprehension. For such a long time, all the planes I had heard had been hostile. On the ground our planes looked wonderful, even if they were usually lined up in straight rows on the airfields. There were some P-40's and P-39's, and some of the fast attack planes we had heard about, some B-17E's, with twin machine guns in the tail, and some medium bombers. It is fortunate that the Japs did not know how few there were.

There were American troops, too, in the streets of all the big cities and in camps scattered around the country. These Americans looked the way American soldiers should, well fed, well equipped, healthy—not starved and sick and wounded like the Americans and Filipinos in Bataan. There were trucks and tanks, jeeps and bulldozers, all of them evidence that America was on the move and starting to mobilize her mighty strength.

Supplies were coming in. We went to the soldiers' canteens and bought cigarettes and candy and all the things that, in the Philippines, had seemed part of another world. There was plenty of bustle and movement.

But in the Philippines we had learned not to be deceived by appearances. Manila's defenses had looked strong, but the Japs had knocked them out in a hurry. It looked like Australia might be another case of too little, too late.

Even in organizing the defenses of Australia, MacArthur had difficult problems. The first was the shortage of men and supplies, especially airplanes.

That was to be remedied in time. Another was that although Australia had agreed to MacArthur as supreme commander he could not get any official orders from Washington and had no official authority. Newspapermen in Australia sat on the story for nearly a month after MacArthur's arrival. Finally they cabled it home. Washington stories inspired by the reports from Australia quoted government leaders as saying there were no complications or troubles. In about a week after the Australia stories, MacArthur's directive came through. The reason for the delay was never explained.

MacArthur's command was designated as the southwest Pacific area which was bounded by a line running between New Zealand and Australia and through the eastern Solomon Islands. East of that line the American Navy was to command. No explanation was given of this division of command, but one of the reasons obviously was that the job of safeguarding the supply lines to Australia and New Zealand was up to the U.S. Navy. If that was the sole reason the division of command was justified. Within his own area MacArthur had command of all land, air, and sea forces, the latter consisting of a few American and Australian cruisers and lighter ships.

MacArthur's relatively small forces were being strengthened by the return home of Australian veterans who had served in Africa, Greece, Crete, and the Middle East. Every man made a difference, for Australia had nearly stripped herself of fighting manpower to answer the call for defense of the British Empire against Hitler. Now, with Japan looming over the horizon and their own country threatened with invasion for the first time in its short history, the Australians had been forced to call on the United States to assist in its defense. The Empire system had failed Australia in its hour of need and that was an eye-opener to the people of Australia.

To all Australia's protests against inequalities in the Imperial economic system the English answer had invariably been: Where would Australia be without the British Navy to guard you?" Now, in April of 1942, Australia knew where it was: on the spot. The few ships that England had been able to spare for the Pacific were at the bottom off the coast of Malaya, victims of Japanese bombers.

The Aussies and "Yanks" got along well. There was an especially close affinity between the healthy, unpretentious Australian girls and the good-looking, well-dressed American youngsters. This naturally caused some ill feeling between Australian and American soldiers, but all of it was of a decidedly minor nature and to be expected when vigorous young men from two countries are thrown together. There were occasional fisticuffs. One sure way for a Yank to pick a scrap was to say to an Australian, "Fine guys you are. We have to come here to defend your country for you." To which the answer was, "Oh yair! Defend yourself, mate," followed by a swinging right. The Aussies could always start a fight by remarking to a Yank, "Oh, a refugee from Pearl 'Arbor, eh?"

But on the whole relations were friendly. Every taxi driver assured you, "Yair. You Yanks and we Aussies are just the same kind of people."

The Aussies used to say, "Mac Arthur is the man for this job." "Old Mac will tell them, all right!" "Mac will get it done!"

The Americans, well-mannered and well behaved, liked the Australians too. The Australians were outspoken, forthright, and demonstrative. Every Australian was as good as the next one. They were democratic in speech and manner, much more so, perhaps, than Americans. There were no extremes of wealth and poverty. Australia, under a Labour government, was unquestionably a middle-class country. There could never be a Cinderella story in Australia, because the girl shopworker was accustomed to going to the best hotel in town for dinner and dancing once or twice a week.

In mid-April we got news of the American bombing attack on Tokyo. It was electrifying; almost too good to be true after we had been waiting so many long, bitter weeks for the United States to get started. MacArthur's staff was cheered, knowing that every blow struck at Tokyo would shorten the war.

General Royce came safely back from the Philippines, his planes loaded from nose to tail with Army and Navy men, those who were not "expendable." I met the first plane back at the Melbourne airport and was amazed when three old friends stepped out: Colonel Chiwang, with whom I had intended to accompany Bulkeley to China in the PT boats; Captain Villamor, hero of the Philippine Air Force; and Nat Floyd of the New York Times, my companion on many trips in Bataan.

A few days later Frank Hewlett arrived and then Dean Schedler, the last reporter to leave the Philippines. General Wainwright had arranged for them both to fly from Corregidor after the fall of Bataan, and Dean's plane cracked up twice on its way to Mindanao. Later the PT officers arrived, Bulkeley, Cox, Akers, and finally Kelly. Their fellow officer, Lieutenant DeLong, had missed connections with the plane at Del Monte and remained in the Philippines.

All the people who had come from the Philippines had one idea: to get back there as fast as possible with a real army, a real fleet and air force and drive out the Japs. All of them were disconsolate when they found out the truth about our forces in Australia. Those of us who had come from the P.I. were keyed to a high pitch. I had to curb a tendency to hit for cover when trolley car wheels screeched down the tracks. Night after night I dreamed of how the end must have been in Bataan, seeing our worn-out troops like hunted animals. Awakening from those dreams I felt that I wanted very much to go on living and did not want any more violence. But I overcame that feeling by telling myself over and over that if we all felt that way we could not win.

The spectacle of life as usual, or nearly usual, was a shock. We who had come from the Philippines realized that life nearly-as-usual was going on in the United States. That couldn't last long, we thought.

Fighting our feeling of despair and futility, we relaxed for a while to pre-war life. I went to the Australia Hotel in Melbourne, which was crowded with Army and Navy officers and correspondents. Colonel Lloyd Lehrbas, the AP correspondent who was now attached to MacArthur's headquarters staff, tipped some of the reporters that the Japs might attack New Caledonia, where the United States had amassed a strong force. He arranged for me and Jonathan Rice, NEA photographer, to go there by way of New Zealand.

Mel Jacoby and I had been together constantly since December 29, and I consulted him before starting on my trip. Jacoby decided to stay in Australia for a while. Brigadier General Hal George, who had commanded our fighter planes in Bataan, had invited him to inspect our air bases in Australia.

The night before they took off, Mel and Annalee came over to my room to talk things over. They promised to come to New Zealand and New Caledonia as soon as possible. Jonathan Rice, who had gone to Stanford with both of them, took a number of pictures and I kidded them about "goop-nipping," a term which we had applied on Corregidor to their exchange of honeymooners' endearments. They were still goop-nipping.

"When you get to New Zealand, Clark," Mel said, half seriously and half joking, "don't forget to look around for a line of retreat. From here we can always get to Tasmania and then to the South Pole if the Japs come. It looks like the only way out of New Zealand is to Easter Island and then to Chile. That's quite a long jump in a banca."

"You two are always talking about ways out of places," Annalee commented. "I am glad to see that for a change you are both starting to go north, in the direction of the Japs. Let's start a counteroffensive of our own."

We agreed that would be a grand idea, and long overdue. We were sick of being pushed around by the Japs.

Mel took off with General George next day and I left for Sydney. The following noon a telephone call came from Larry Lehrbas. "I think you should know," he said, "that Mel was killed yesterday." Mel and General George had reached northern Australia without incident and were standing by their parked plane on an airfield near Darwin when a P-40 got out of control in a take-off. It swerved crazily across the field and crashed into George's parked plane. Mel was killed instantly and George died within a few hours.

Before leaving Melbourne I said goodbye to General MacArthur and thanked him for his help. MacArthur was busy, working as best possible with the materials he had been given. He had pledged, "I left the Philippines and I shall return." The day of his return seemed a long time in the future. Nothing could crush his unconquerable spirit, but he bridled against the delay. Now Bataan was gone; Corregidor was about to go. The entire Orient and most of the western Pacific was overrun and subjected. Japan had taken everything she had set out to take, from Manila to Rangoon. MacArthur wanted to hit before the enemy had time to solidify his conquered areas.

On May 1, I took off from beautiful Sydney harbor in a big, four-engined British flying boat of Qantas Airways. We roared off the water in the wake of an American Navy PB2Y2, a four-engined patrol bomber which was headed for San Francisco. Shortly after dawn we flew across the white surf breaking against Manly Beach and headed out over the Tasman Sea. All the way across the Tasman to New Zealand I kept thinking of MacArthur as I had seen him since December 8; MacArthur with his intense sincerity, his flashing brain, his devotion to the soldier's code, his ability to inspire men.

I saw MacArthur not as I had seen him when I last shook hands, a man with a bitter ache in his heart, but as I had seen him first in Manila—shoulders back, cap tilted at a jaunty angle, with four stars gleaming from the shoulder of his neatly pressed shirt. I saw the man who couldn't lose.

35

LATE IN THE AFTERNOON WE FLEW ACROSS THE NARROW WAIST of the north-ernmost of New Zealand's two big islands and sat down smoothly in Auckland Harbor. On shore I immediately started looking for the American troops that we had heard were in New Zealand.

I finally found them—all four of them, five counting Brigadier General Patrick J. Hurley, the American minister.

The four officers of the Quartermaster Corps had been sent to make preparations for future troop arrivals. There was also one Marine officer and several of the United States Navy. That was important and encouraging, since it was obvious by then that if Japan's swift-moving advance was to be halted it was up to the American Navy to do it. With the exception of the hit-run raids on Japan's Mandated Islands and Marcus Island, we had not heard many reports of naval activities and we were afraid that most of our fleet had been sunk or smashed in the attack on Pearl Harbor.

The naval officers were arranging headquarters for Admiral Ghormley, who was to command the "South Pacific" area, which included New Zealand and New Caledonia and other islands east of the line beyond which MacAr-thur was supreme commander. Ghormley's command was likewise limited on the north and east, but to the south it extended all the way to the South Pole. The New Zealanders had requested to be included in the areas under MacAr-thur, but when the division was made they accepted it and pitched in to co-operate with Ghormley. Commander Mike Cheek who had escaped from Corregidor by submarine, was one of the Navy's advance guard.

Two days after my arrival in New Zealand, I received exciting, confiden-tial news. A mighty Japanese invasion force was moving into the Coral Sea. Its objective might be New Caledonia and New Zealand, or it might swing west to attack Australia and New Guinea. There was no transportation available to New Caledonia, so I started checking up on New Zealand's defenses, and almost immediately ran into the startling fact that the country was wide open to attack. If New Zealand went, Australia would go too, since we could not maintain our supply lines without New Zealand.

Five months after Pearl Harbor there were still no American troops in New Zealand. New Zealand had sent almost all of its own troops—some sixty thousand of them—overseas to fight in defense of the British Empire. They had distinguished themselves in the ghastly battle of Crete and in Libya. Now that their own country was threatened they were thousands of miles away. The sixty thousand represented the cream of the nation's manhood. New Zea-land's entire population was only one and a half million, less than that of any one of a dozen of the world's great cities.

Yet when the war came the government of New Zealand had unhesitatingly given its consent for its troops to go abroad, believing, as Prime Minister Peter Fraser told me, "This war against the Axis is the war of all Free Peoples. All of us must do our share. New Zealand has no great wealth in industry or resources to give to the common cause, so we must give our flesh and blood."

New Zealand was awaiting the arrival of American troops, who were reported on the way. They were due in a matter of weeks, while the Japanese could strike within a few days if they kept coming south. News of the Japanese approach was kept from the people, but the authorities were preparing for a death struggle. The picture looked pretty hopeless. Major General Puttick, commander in chief of the Army, was hurriedly training his infantry divisions. Every able-bodied man up to the age of 65 was in uniform or in some vital war work.

Puttick had commanded New Zealand forces in Crete.

"We fought there with the bayonet," he said, "and we will fight with it here. The Eyetie (Italians) and the Hun couldn't stand the bayonet, and I don't think the Jap will like it any better."

That was whistling in the dark. Puttick knew very well you couldn't stop an invasion force with bayonets. You had to have ships and planes out in front of you. We didn't know if there were any ships out there, but we did know what New Zealand's Air Force was. Its combat planes numbered nine P-40's, and there were a handful of trainers and a few medium bombers being used in reconnaissance. There was no shortage of airmen.

Seeking a lift to New Caledonia, I went down to Wellington, the capital, to talk to Air Force and Navy officials. The New Zealand government gave me the keys to the country. The interior department arranged interviews with Prime Minister Fraser, the Army, Navy, and Air Force commanders, and even with the leader of the "opposition" party. The opposition party, it developed, didn't have much to oppose in the Labour government's policies. New Zealand's social legislation had been in effect for many years and was firmly implanted. Job insurance, old-age pensions, a form of socialized medicine, and other reforms had been enacted in New Zealand long before the New Deal came into power in the United States.

As in Australia there were no extremes of wealth and poverty. But there were many contrasts between the two people, and because they both were essentially farming countries producing the same agricultural goods there were no close commercial ties.

The New Zealanders were less exuberant, much more reserved—"more English," as they said—than the Australians. The English people who had come out to New Zealand a century before had deliberately set out to duplicate as nearly as possible their surroundings at home.

For several decades New Zealand's original white settlers had fought with the proud and powerful Maoris, who had themselves emigrated from overseas several centuries before and had thrived in this cold climate. The fight ended in a draw, and Polynesian and Englishman settled down to live side by side on terms of complete equality.

Now Maori and white man were fighting side by side in the sands of Libya, while their homeland faced an immediate threat of invasion of which most of New Zealand's peopleware blissfully unaware. The Japanese Fleet was steaming south toward their virtually defenseless country. On May 7, the newspapers began to carry brief reports of a battle in the Coral Sea. We knew at last where the U.S. Navy was—out in front of the Antipodes and fighting it out with the Japanese

I learned the details ten days later when I hitchhiked a ride from New Zealand up to Fiji in a U.S. Navy PB2Y2. That giant plane was loaded with news. One of the passengers was taking a message from MacArthur to Washington officials, informing them that MacArthur had no political aspirations of any kind. He asked them please to send him a few more airplanes. Several of the others, Navy officers, had been in the Coral Sea Battle. One was a staff officer attached to the admiral in command; another a dive-bomber pilot who had been wounded. Their account of the battle was fascinating. Now at last the United States was in action, hitting the enemy strongly and powerfully, not fighting a last-ditch, hopeless fight like Wake and Bataan.

The Coral Sea Battle was a turning point in the Pacific war. For the first time the onward surge of Japan was stopped. And the job was done entirely by airplanes, both land-based and carrier-based. It was the first battle in history between aircraft carriers and it proved, unequivocally, that air control is absolutely vital to the movement of a force of ships.

For reasons of security our Navy did not announce details of its part in the Coral Sea fight until after the Battle of Midway, and as a result the impression was widespread that American Army land-based bombers alone had turned back the Japanese forces. Actually, both our Army and Navy participated in widely separated actions. The Japanese came down from the Mandated Islands in two groups. One, made up of transports and escorting destroyers, amounting to twenty-five ships in all, sailed southeastward along the coast of New Guinea. MacArthur's bombers struck at it time and again, and the badly battered enemy force turned back before it reached the tip of the Papuan peninsula.

The other Japanese force, consisting of aircraft carriers and other warships, was several hundred miles out in front of the transports. Its mission was to screen the troop-carrying vessels from attack by American Navy ships. The Japs apparently had information that two American task forces were prowling around the northern part of the Coral Sea. The American forces centered around the carriers Yorktown and Lexington.

Rear Admiral Frank Jack Fletcher took the Lexington and Yorktown into the Coral Sea and waited for the enemy. On May 5 and 6 our scout planes flew far out from their carriers and returned to report that the Japanese were not yet in sight. But Fletcher knew they were coming and early on May 7 the scout planes found the Jap battle force. It included at least two carriers, several battleships, ten or more cruisers, and a number of destroyers. Planes roared off the Lexington and Yorktown to hit the Japanese ships. Thus began the first battle between aircraft carriers.

I got the story of the Coral Sea Battle from Commander Jimmy Brett, who led the Lexington's torpedo planes in the bomb and torpedo attack which sank the Jap carrier Ryukaku on May 7 and damaged another carrier the following day before the Lexington herself was mortally hit by Jap planes.

I talked to Brett and his pilots for hours in Fiji, trying to learn their emotional reactions during a battle, and was amazed to find them thinking of the most unexpected things. For instance, Jimmy Brett told me he never worried about being shot down, or being killed in the air, or being left to drift at sea in a rubber boat.

"It so happens that I am a color camera fan," he said. "I am writing a book on color photography and do most of my composing in the air. When we are going in to attack I plan my next chapter."

Jimmy was mad as hell that his notes for the book went down with the Lexington.

36

THE STORIES THAT JIMMY BRETT AND HIS PILOTS TOLD ME as we sat on the cool veranda of the Grand Pacific Hotel in Suva, and later at a U.S. Army airfield where young American fliers were taking off and landing in P-39's, made me extremely anxious to go out with our Fleet. It appealed to me as a grand way to fight the war.

To get with the Fleet I had to go to Pearl Harbor to obtain accreditation as a correspondent. Also, my wife was in Honolulu, but the inevitable cablegram came from The AP: "Please proceed to New Caledonia!" New Caledonia was in the opposite direction, westward and away from home. There was nothing to do but go.

With Jimmy Brett and his fellow pilots as co-passengers, I flew across Fiji's rugged mountains in an old De Haviland cabin monoplane powered by four small Rolls-Royce motors. Some of the Navy pilots were nervous. "To hell with this flying over the land," they said. "Where will we be if those motors quit?" Apparently they never considered where they would be in their own planes if their motors quit far out over the sea.

I waited several days for a ride to New Caledonia. One evening a Consolidated PBY5A, an amphibian flying boat, swept in from the sea and landed. Admiral John S. McCain, a hard-bitten veteran from Mississippi, climbed out. He was commander of Navy and Army aircraft in the southwest Pacific area, that part of the ocean and islands eastward of General MacArthur's command.

"May I ride back with you. Admiral?" I asked.

"Sure," he said, "first thing in the morning."

I hoped to interview the admiral on the flight over, but the twin motors made too much noise for conversation. The admiral sat on a suitcase in the rear machine-gun turret and chewed gum, and I wrapped myself around a machine gun and slept most of the way. We flew low, and the trip didn't bother me. I woke up when we were circling outside the entrance to the harbor at Noumea, the only big town in New Caledonia, and awaiting acknowledgment of our recognition signals from an American warship auxiliary in the harbor.

New Caledonia flew the banner of the Fighting French. It had originally been a penal colony of France, and its population was a mélange of Pacific island races—Javanese, Malayans, and French, the last controlling the mining industry and the others working as contract laborers. After the fall of France there had been a bloodless revolution, and General De Gaulle had sent one of his most colorful assistants, Admiral d'Argenlieu, out to the colony as governor. D'Argenlieu was later transferred.

I spent ten days in New Caledonia, interviewing soldiers from New England and Chicago and the nurses from Philadelphia who were living in the woods in conditions not unlike those on Bataan—except that there was no shooting here. Major General Patch, the American Army commander, kept his forces busy in constant training and toughening maneuvers. He was looking forward to the day when our advance to the north would begin. The training that Patch and Lieutenant Colonel Alexander George gave their men came in handy months later when they relieved the Marines on Guadalcanal. The Coral Sea Battle had taken the pressure off New Caledonia and I couldn't see any chance of an attack in the north in the near future, so I decided to move on—back to Honolulu to get attached to the Fleet. This time my office didn't know exactly where I was, so there was no cable to stop my taking off in the general direction of home.

I made connections by a narrow margin. Back at Noumea, Lieutenant Arthur Train, Jr., of the Navy, son of the American author, told me a plane was leaving the next morning for Honolulu. He would have a launch at the dock to ferry me out to the PB2Y2. I got up long before dawn and stumbled through the blacked-out streets down to the dock.

It was good to be leaving Noumea. From a distance the city was picturesque with its red roofs and green hills, but close up it was anything but glamorous, especially with its open sewers. There was no launch at the dock. Finally dawn broke and I saw a small boat leave the American seaplane tender out in the harbor and head for the PBY's anchored far off in the distance. It was obviously not coming in my direction. Some American soldiers on duty at anti-aircraft guns on the waterfront came to my rescue. They telephoned to the signal station in the hills behind the city, and a message was flashed out to the tender. Train's first message had gone astray.

A launch came speeding across to the dock and picked me up. We reached the PBY just before Lieutenant Shields gunned the motors to take off. The big plane roared faster and faster across the bay with the seas splashing on the portholes. As it climbed on the step the water fell away from the windows and we enjoyed the thrill of taxiing over the water at close to 100 miles an hour. Suddenly, Shields cut the gun and the plane settled back into the water and slowed to a stop. The wind had swung us around and we had been heading directly into the hills at the mouth of the harbor. Shields taxied back and this time we took off perfectly.

On the way to Honolulu we stopped at islands X, Y, and Z. We had some excitement finding Z. We took off early in the morning in perfect weather from a coral-encircled lagoon, but as we flew eastward and north the weather clouded over and we ran into a dark, threatening storm front that covered hundreds of square miles. We had to fly through it for two hours and in that time I learned two things: the exacting skill with which our Navy fliers navigate over tremendous ocean distances from tiny island to island; and the reason that they avoid clouds.

They will never go through a cloud if they can go over or under it. In the first place you never know what is on the other side—how far the cloud extends; and secondly, clouds mean, as the aviators told me, "turbulent" air. Turbulent is a fitting word for the air in some of those clouds. Crosscurrents tear at your wings until you think they will fall off. The plane bumps sickeningly, now plunging straight downward hundreds of feet and at other times soaring upward on a current of wind.

Island Z, to which we were flying that day and where Captain Eddie Rickenbacker was taken after his rescue some months later, was usually covered by clouds. That day was no exception. For more than three hundred miles before we readied the island we were flying on instruments, catching only occasional glimpses of the sea. Yet our navigator brought us straight to the island, hitting within a quarter mile of the point for which he was aiming. He called our arrival time to the minute. To me it was a miracle of navigation, yet it was a miracle that our Navy fliers over the Pacific perform day after day in the normal course of events. It is part of a job they have mastered perfectly.

Life for our soldiers, sailors, and Marines on the Pacific islands varies from place to place. Some of them are tropically idyllic, with colorful pleasant towns, built by American or British traders and administrators. Other islands are nothing but flat bits of sand, minus trees or other vegetation, anchored in the middle of a changeless circle of ocean and besieged by the equatorial sun.

The soldiers have movies and beer, magazines and mail from home, and those things keep them from getting overwhelmingly blue and homesick. They have a favorite gag on those islands. When somebody mentions a girl they look blank and say: "What was that word 'girl'? I don't remember hearing it before."

The crews of ships and planes ferrying newcomers to the islands always regale them with stories of the beautiful Army and Navy nurses stationed there. They are quickly disillusioned on their arrival. Anyway, they can always go swimming—if they keep a sharp lookout for sharks.

I flew from one of those islands up to Honolulu. It seemed as if the plane would never get there. For four hours I sat in the bombardier's place in the nose of the PB2Y2, watching for the Hawaiian Islands until my eyes ached. When we finally sighted Oahu I didn't recognize it until we swung over Maili beach, bounced over the Marine airfield at Ewa and settled down on the waters of Pearl Harbor. It had taken me seven months to make the trip from Shanghai to Honolulu.

I telephoned my wife and apologized for being a little late getting back and would she excuse it please? She would.

I found that she was working at an airfield; and that was only one of the many changes brought to the Islands by the Japanese attack six months before. All the civilians not in Army or Navy uniform were at work, building airfields, repairing ships, constructing docks; or serving in hospitals, acting as air raid wardens, or helping the Red Cross. Everybody carried a gas mask. The blackout was strictly and seriously enforced, and you had to have a pass to go outdoors after curfew hour.

Civilians were allowed only ten gallons of gasoline a month and one quart of liquor a week. Bars and restaurants closed several hours before sundown. There were shortages of milk, eggs, meat, and vegetables as all the Island products went to the armed forces. A military governor sat in Iolani Palace, in olden days the home of Hawaiian royalty and later the peacetime office of the civilian governor. There was no doubt that Hawaii was at war.

Pearl Harbor still showed signs of the bombing. The ancient target ship Utah was lying on the bottom on the western shore of Ford Island. The Oklahoma, on its side with part of its hull looming out of the water, lay ahead of the Arizona, which had gone straight down after a bomb exploded its magazine. The West Virginia was being gradually raised.

Another battleship was in drydock after being salvaged, and still others had already been patched up and taken to the Pacific Coast for repairs. Work crews swarmed over the Oklahoma and West Virginia, and the wreck of the Arizona was being dismantled in order to remove the reminder of that disastrous Sunday morning.

At nearby Hickam Field, there were still broken windows and chipped walls to show where a bomb had plunged through a dormitory and killed or wounded three hundred men while Japanese fighters machine-gunned and destroyed our planes on the ground.

Most of the scars of battle had been removed from the Kaneohe naval air station, across the island from Pearl Harbor. At Kaneohe Japanese bombers deliberately ignored two empty hangars and laid their bombs squarely on a third, destroying at one blow most of our Navy patrol planes and killing many men. That showed that the Japanese had excellent espionage.

But as great as the debacle at Pearl Harbor had been, as staggering the loss of life, I soon became convinced that the Japanese had lost their great chance to win the war in those three flaming, terrible hours on December 7. The mistake that they had made was almost inconceivable.

Far more than our own admirals they had realized the significance of air power. Their primary targets on December 7 were undoubtedly our aircraft carriers. Through sheer good fortune our aircraft carriers were not in Pearl Harbor at the time of the attack. If, instead of hitting the battleships, the Japs had aimed their bombs and torpedoes at the docks, shops, oil tanks and shore installations in Pearl Harbor, the entire course of the war would have been changed. They could easily have knocked out Pearl Harbor as a base, forcing our Navy back to the Pacific Coast.

The men that we lost at Pearl Harbor were martyrs to unpreparedness. The battleships that we lost there were ready for the scrap pile before they were ever hit by a Japanese bomb. They were too slow for modern war. The battleship had had its day. No battleship that escaped damage at Pearl Harbor, no battleship that was damaged there and later repaired, played any part in the Battles of the Coral Sea and Midway. No battleship fired a shot in the early days of the Solomons action. Later, we reported that battleships had participated in a fight off the Solomons—at night.

Since battleships did not play any part in the fighting in the Pacific in the first eleven months of war, the question arises of why our Navy took so long to get into action against the Japanese. Our Navy was just as strong on the afternoon of December 7 when the battleships were still exploding and sinking in Pearl Harbor as it was five months later in our first fight in the Coral Sea. Why, then, couldn't our Navy save Wake Island, only two thousand miles from Pearl Harbor? A few weeks before the war the United States had been told that its Navy was the greatest fighting force in the world, supreme in the Pacific. That made it difficult to understand why a tremendous American task force was ordered to turn back when within one hundred and fifty miles of Wake Island. The fighting rank and file aboard those ships, and many of the officers, cursed and wept when they received those orders.

Later, as some of them told me, they were hopping mad when they learned that our ships had been called back because of the reported presence of Jap ships near Wake and were even more angry when they learned the Jap "force" consisted of only four destroyers going in to shell our hard-pressed Marines, fighting desperately for their lives, waiting minute by minute for help, and wirelessing back to Pearl Harbor, "Get off your fat backsides and send us more ammunition and more Japs."

The answer, apparently, is that the Pearl Harbor attack was a psychological blow to many of our admirals. They had put their faith in those "elephants" the battleships. Stripped of their battleships they were as lost as a man suddenly deprived of his trousers in the middle of Fifth Avenue. Their instinct was to cover up, to assume the defensive rather than to seek out the enemy for a finish fight. Nearly everyone who saw the Pearl Harbor attack told me that if the Japs had followed up and landed troops they could have taken Honolulu easily. Our aerial defenses had been smashed and there was a great deal of confusion and disorganization.

I was interested in the reactions of persons who had seen the Pearl Harbor attack. Almost none of them could believe their eyes. Even officers who stood on the decks of nearby ships at Pearl Harbor and watched the Japanese dive bombers and torpedo planes blow up the Arizona, thought that there must be some mistake.

Even while they were shooting at the planes they couldn't believe it. One officer who was on duty in the engine room of an undamaged ship came up on deck an hour after the attack and remarked, "Hey, these maneuvers are getting pretty rough!"

Arthur G. Hodgins, a doctor who lives at Pearl City, adjacent to the harbor, drove into Honolulu past the flaming wreckage. He told a meeting of fellow doctors that hell had broken loose. They laughed at him and went on with their business—until a call suddenly came in for all doctors to rush to Tripler General Hospital. The civilians said to one another, incredulously, "The Japs can't do this to us." But the Japs could—and did—and got away with the loss of only a few planes.

The day that I landed at Pearl Harbor was nearly six months after the attack. When I got out of the plane at Ford Island, Lieutenant Tom Quinn greeted me as an old friend. He had given me many stories when he was a member of the Honolulu police force and he gave me one now.

"The Japs have attacked the Aleutian Islands," he said. "A flash just came in."

He went on, "And something big seems to be about to happen in this area," Tom wasn't exaggerating. What happened was the Battle of Midway.

37

NEXT MORNING, THE BATTLE OF MIDWAY WAS RAGING in full fury. Nothing had been published in the newspapers, but everybody in Honolulu knew a fight was going on. Walking downtown, I met many old friends whom I was delighted to see. But they looked at me accusingly.

"Don't you think you'd like to go back to Australia, or to California, or the South Pole? Trouble follows you around and we've already had our share of it here."

I decided to stay, regardless. Honolulu was my adopted home, and besides it was only seventeen hours by plane from California. It was the farthest east I had been since 1936.

I was too late to witness the Battle of Midway, but I was in time to help cover it from Honolulu, getting the stories from the youngsters who returned flushed with the excitement and thrills of the greatest experiences in their lives.

Midway was our most important victory of the first year of war against Japan. It was won entirely by airplanes, and in turning back the Japanese our forces saved the Hawaiian Islands from invasion. Our Army, Navy, and Marine Corps functioned perfectly. Our soldiers, sailors, and Marines fought gallantly. The planning was perfect and the trap well laid.

Somehow, our Navy knew that the Japs were coming to Midway, and by knowing that they changed the course of the war. If our carriers had been plowing around the Coral Sea, waiting for the Japanese to come back there for a second drive to the south, we would have lost Midway.

I got the story in snatches. The Army pilots were first to return from Midway and they gave their accounts first. The Navy could not tell all of its story until its ships returned to port. The Marines' stories were held up for many days by the Navy censors. Admiral Nimitz, in a commendable effort to end the Army-Navy rivalry that still existed even a half year after Pearl Harbor, allowed the Army stories to go out to the mainland before the Navy accounts were written. His efforts, however, backfired into a terrific battle between Army and Navy over which should get "credit" for winning the battle.

This feeling continued to exist for many weeks. It became an angry bone of contention between Army and Navy officers, especially those of lower rank. Its repercussions were still echoing six months later. In Honolulu the bad feeling took the form of numerous fist fights between Army and Navy officers.

The big question was, "Who sank the Jap carriers?" The Army pilots, at first, claimed to have hit several carriers. The Marines reported they got several hits. The Navy carrier pilots, who attacked after the Army and Marines, said the enemy carriers were undamaged when they bombed them. Not only the lower officers participated in the squabbling. A three-star admiral said to me contemptuously, "You can't hit anything from twenty thousand feet." That reference to high-altitude bombing became a pet expression of Navy pilots. Actually, there was credit enough for everybody in the Midway Battle.

The Japanese moved on Midway in two vast armadas. The first steamed straight in from the west and included twenty or more transports and a number of escort vessels. The other force approached from the northwest and centered around four big aircraft carriers, the Kaga, Akagi, Hiryu and Soryu, flanked by cruisers, destroyers, and possibly battleships. The enemy plan called for airplanes from these carriers to hit Midway at dawn on June 4 and knock out our airplanes and land defenses. The transports were to have landed their troops and supplies the following morning. Then, with Midway consolidated, the Japanese intended to move against Oahu and fight it out for Pearl Harbor. Their plans went wrong, apparently, because they did not know the location of our own aircraft carriers. Our Army long-distance bombers found and attacked the Japanese first, on the afternoon of June 3. B-17's, led by Colonel Walter C. Sweeney, Jr., hit and damaged one cruiser or battleship which was left in flames, and also one transport and one destroyer. There were no carriers with that enemy force, and the only opposition to our planes was from anti-aircraft.

During the night of June 3, Navy patrol planes located the main Japanese battle force and the following morning all of our planes at Midway took off to attack. Midway had been quickly and effectively reinforced with planes only a few days before the battle, some of them flying from San Francisco to Honolulu, pausing to refuel, and then speeding out to Midway to pick up bombs.

Midway was ready. No planes were caught on the ground there. All of them got aloft shortly after dawn, led by the Marine fighters. Four Army B-26's, twin-engined Martin bombers, commanded by Captain Collins, took off carrying torpedoes. It was the first Army torpedo plane attack in history. Two of the B-26's got back. Six new Navy Grumman TBF (Avenger) torpedo planes also took off. One of them got back. The others were shot down by swarms of Japanese fighters and by anti-aircraft. Marine dive bombers also took off from Midway and hit at the Japanese battle fleet, and heavy Army bombers followed up the attack. The Marines reported bomb hits on two enemy carriers and two heavy surface ships. Army pilots saw their bombs blanket a carrier and they got one possible hit on the bow.

Meanwhile, the Japanese carriers had steamed within two hundred miles of Midway during the night and launched their planes at dawn. Dive bombers and high-level bombers, protected by Zero fighters and Messerschmitts, roared in to attack. They were met by Marine fighters.

The work of the Marine fighter pilots that morning has never been sufficiently praised. Six months after the start of the war they were still flying a fighter plane which the Navy had long since discarded as obsolete. The Marine fliers knew before they took off that their chances of getting back were slim. Only a few of them did. But before they were shot down they whipped into the approaching enemy planes and blasted at least forty-three dive bombers and three or four enemy fighters out of the sky.

Not more than eighteen enemy dive bombers reached Midway and only fourteen bombs hit the island, killing some of the Marine anti-aircraft men and shore defenders but not damaging the airfield. The Japs deliberately avoided bombing the runways, confidently expecting to take Midway and use the field themselves.

The surviving Japanese planes returned to their carriers to refuel and re-load for a second attack at Midway. Before it could be delivered our own Navy struck. Two American taskforces had been plowing through the calm seas two hundred miles north of Midway and now their planes pitched into the battle.

One American task force centered around two aircraft carriers; the Hornet under Admiral Fitch and another under Admiral Spruance. Nearby steamed the carrier Yorktown with Admiral Frank Jack Fletcher, who was in command of the entire operation.

Planes from our carriers flew to the west, searching for the enemy. I got the story from pilots of Bombing Squadron Three, Gordon Sherwood, Syd Bottomley, Roy Isaman, and others, all Naval Reserve lieutenants who were flying Douglas dive-bombers. Their story should be entitled "The Miracle of Midway: or The Tale, of a Puff of Smoke."

They had already flown past the Jap carriers, which were partially hidden by clouds and had failed to sight them. Then, far down in the engine room of one of the enemy ships, a fireman accidentally pulled the wrong lever. A burst of black smoke poured out of the carrier's funnel. It lasted only a few seconds but those few seconds had been enough. Out of the corner of their eyes the pilots of Bombing Three had seen the smoke. They swarmed in to attack and caught the giant Akagi with its planes on deck. They left the Akagi wrecked and burning.

Then the dive-bombing squadrons from our other two carriers, who had also flown past the Jap force, sighted the smoke of the burning Akagi and came back and attacked the other two carriers. A fourth Jap carrier was sunk later in the day, and the Japs turned and fled, pursued by our planes. Except for that puff of smoke, our planes might have missed the Jap carriers and our own carriers might have been put out of action.

Meanwhile the Yorktown had been bombed and torpedoed by Jap planes. While being towed to Pearl Harbor a day later it ran into a nest of enemy subs and was sent to the bottom.

Airplanes, courage, brilliant staff work—and a lucky puff of smoke—had saved Midway.

38

NOT ALL OF OUR PILOTS LIVED TO EXULT OVER THE DESTRUCTION of the Jap carriers at Midway.

Out of more than forty torpedo planes, only four pilots came back alive.

And there were, for instance, two Marine pilots. Major Lofton R. Henderson and Captain Richard E. Fleming. Both of their planes were hit and set afire by anti-aircraft as they dived on Japanese ships. They made no attempt to pull out or save themselves, but kept on going down and dropped their bombs and crashed—Henderson on the deck of a Japanese battleship and Fleming in the sea.

When I heard the story of what they had done my mind skipped back many months to a scene in a Shanghai restaurant where an American Marine officer had said to a Japanese naval captain "... and if your ships come into our waters our pilots will go just as low and just as close as necessary to get home their bombs and torpedoes. And if it is necessary to crash-dive on your ships, they will do that too."

And there were Navy pilots, like John Quincy Roberts, Ensign USNR, and Carl Pfeiffer, same rank and same Navy. Roberts and Pfeiffer were the most talkative members of their bombing squadron. They were always talking about what they would do to the Japs. Roberts, Pfeiffer, and a lot of other ensigns in their squadron all got their wings at the same time. Most of them were Southerners.

Roberts and Pfeiffer were pals. They roomed together and they learned to fly dive bombers together. They were always cooking up jokes together. In the air they flew wingtip to wingtip.

J.Q. Roberts played football for Alabama in the Rose Bowl and he looked it. The first thing you noticed were his sloping shoulders and his strong, powerful neck. He was only a little above middle height but he looked as strong as a bull.

His reddish-brown hair was cropped short when he joined the Navy and he grew a little mustache, like the rest of the boys in his squadron. When you looked into his eyes they made you suddenly remember Captain Arthur Wermuth, out on Bataan, and Lieutenant John Bulkeley at the helm of the PT boat roaring up toward Subic Bay. He had the same look in his eyes.

Pfeiffer was tall and good-looking with deep-set eyes and deep lines in his face from smiling a lot. His chin was square and he wore his flier's cap at a jaunty angle.

J.Q. was always kidding the "No'theners" in his squadron. He would say, "Fine crowd you damn Yankees turned out to be, havin' to get us Dixie boys to fight yoh war for you-all."

Then the Northern boys would kid J.Q. and ask him how come he was named after a damn Yankee from Boston and didn't he know the Mason-Dixon Line wasn't on the maps anymore.

J. Q. wasn't a red-hot pilot. He just didn't care about details. All he worried about was getting into action. Most of the boys would worry about getting their planes down onto the carrier deck just so, but it never bothered J.Q. Any old way so long as he got her down. The boys used to tell him, "J.Q., your right wing was too high on that landing. You came in pretty fast." And J.Q. would say, "I got her down, didn't I?"

After December 7, J.Q. used to read about those Jap pilots doing suicide dives into our ships out in the Far East, or, as the Jap accounts always said, "The heroic pilot dived his crippled plane into an enemy ship, blowing it to destruction." Those stories made J.Q. mad as hell.

"Do those damn' Japs think they are trying to teach Americans what it is to be heroic?" J.Q. would ask the boys. "They're not going to teach me anything. When we get our first crack at them I'm going to dive down and lay my egg right on the middle of the deck of their biggest carrier. And if I miss I'm going to keep right on diving down into the funnel and set that ship on fire."

And Pfeiffer would say, "I'll be right behind you, J.Q."

The skipper of their squadron didn't like the way J.Q. and Pfeiffer looked when they said that. He told them, "Look, boys, you don't have to do that. If you miss, why, hell, come back for another bomb and go back and don't miss the second time."

But J.Q. would say, "Captain, I've only got one life to live and one death to die. If I live I've got a girl I want to marry. If I die I've made up my mind to die for my country and nobody can talk me out of it."

And Pfeiffer would say, "I'll be right behind you, J.Q."

Ensign Johnny Butler was another one like J.Q. and Pfeiffer. Butler should have been a fighter pilot. He was just crazy about fighting in the air. He knew his dive bomber wasn't built for fighting but it didn't make any difference. He swore he would tackle the first Zero he saw and shoot it down. The boys told him that Zeros could climb pretty fast and turnaround a lot quicker than his dive bomber, but Butler said that didn't matter, he was going to get him a Zero anyway.

Their squadron went aboard the Hornet about the end of May and the ship headed out from Pearl Harbor as if it had important business to perform. The admiral told the boys aboard that they were going out to tangle with Yamamoto's big fleet that was heading for Midway.

Their skipper took the squadron off on the morning of June 4 and they headed out to tangle with Yamamoto's fleet. The Akagi was already burning when they found the Jap ships. They pushed over at twenty thousand feet to hit the Kaga. They fixed their sights on the big carrier squirming and turning down there on the water. They held their sticks forward and grabbed their bomb releases firmly in their left hands. They counted a slow "O-N-E" for each thousand feet of altitude they were losing.

The first pilots to dive got hits, and flames shot up from the Kaga's deck. Then J.Q. Roberts dived and his bomb missed the deck and struck the water right alongside the carrier. Pfeiffer was right behind J.Q. and his bomb hit in the same place.

The other pilots were just above them in their dive and they saw it all.

J.Q. never tried to pull out of his dive. He kept right on going down and he dived his plane right into the Kaga's funnel. Pfeiffer was right behind him. There was a big sheet of flame and two big explosions that tossed the other plane around in the sky.

The other boys pulled out and away and joined up on their squadron leader. The last they saw of Butler he was dog-fighting a Zero. The Jap did a quick climb and a loop and came down on Butler's tail and the other boys could see his 20-mm. cannon biting big pieces out of Johnny's plane.

The boys who used to fly with J.Q. and Pfeiffer and Butler often talk about those three. They miss them a lot. But they reckon that when the Japs hear about J.Q. and his buddies they won't try to teach Americans any more lessons in how to be heroic.

39

WHEN WE CLEANED UP THE STORY OF MIDWAY in the AP office I began to think again about going home for a few weeks. My mother was ill and I wanted to see her. But the usual telegram came. This time Alan Gould wired, "Desire Lee join Honolulu staff." I did not protest my assignment. I wanted to go out with the Fleet, which was the only American fighting force that could still do any fighting in the Pacific. There were no more land fronts and if any offensive was to be undertaken the Navy had to carry the burden.

I did not know at the time that "global strategy" called for us to fight a delaying action in the Pacific. I believed we were ready for an all-out attack and I wanted to see our first offensive. The Navy granted my request for assignment to an aircraft carrier. Carriers had been in the heart of the action at Coral Sea and Midway, and would undoubtedly be in the middle of whatever we were going into. The crews of the carriers were proud of their exposed duties. They were the chief targets for enemy attacks, and an average of 10 per cent of them wouldn't ever come home again if Japanese dive bombers and torpedo planes got through to hit their ship. But they were also, through their planes, our chief weapon for doing damage to the enemy. My great ambition was to witness a carrier battle and to fly over the Japs and drop bombs on them. That would be my personal revenge for hours of cowering in foxholes on Corregidor and Bataan while Jap planes circled lazily in the air above us.

Shortly after July 4, I got orders to go aboard the carrier. I was glad that it was one of the biggest ships afloat. I had ridden on the smallest of the Navy's ships, the PT's in the Philippines, and now I hoped to see action on one of the largest. This carrier had arrived too late for the Battle of Midway and its fliers and crew were impatiently waiting to mix it with the Japs.

We boarded a launch at Pearl Harbor and rode out to the ship. In the month since I had arrived from Australia a great deal of salvage work had been done. One of the battleships that had been on the bottom a month before was in dry dock now; another was afloat, and the Arizona was being dismantled. Only the Oklahoma looked the same. There was constant activity at Pearl Harbor; ships being loaded and their ammunition supplies replenished; sailors going aboard their carriers, cruisers, and destroyers after their last shore leave; a tangible air of excitement which told, unmistakably, that something big was cooking.

Jack Singer of the INS, and Al Brick, Fox movie cameraman who had filmed the Jap attack on Pearl Harbor as well as the Battle of Midway, were assigned to the carrier with me. Joe Custer of the UP, went to the Astoria; Foster Hailey of the New York Times to another cruiser. Singer and I thought we were sitting pretty for observing operations—we could fly; we could also get our fliers' stories, and if our task force were attacked our ship would be the target.

As things worked out, Joe Custer also had a box seat. He was wounded and narrowly missed losing an eye when the Astoria was sunk in the Savo Island Battle on August 9.

For a few nights we slept on the carrier in "Pearl"—which is what our Navy calls Pearl Harbor. Aboard ship it was sweltering. When they are anchored or tied up, warships get heated through and through and it takes a couple of weeks at sea for them to cool off. Except for the heat, life aboard the carrier was comfortable, almost luxurious, with mess attendants to wait on us in the officers' wardroom, make our beds, and shine shoes.

This war at sea wasn't anything like war in Bataan. There the pressure was never off. Here it came only in brief flashes at long intervals. Up until the time of our attack in the Solomons not a single ship of our Pacific Fleet had fired a shot at any enemy surface vessel except in the brief raids on Japan's Mandated Islands. Most of our ships had been at sea nearly continuously since Pearl Harbor, but there had been only short, sharp action in the Coral Sea and at Midway where our ships were attacked by Japanese dive bombers and torpedo planes and fought off the attacks with their anti-aircraft guns. The rest of the time was spent cruising around.

Cruising around day after day and week after week was highly monotonous, and the thousands of men aboard the ships in our task forces dreamed day and night of once more getting back to port—any port on the mainland. Many of them would rather remain at sea than put into Pearl Harbor, where the intense heat in their ships and the lack of any amusing diversions only added to their loneliness.

Life with the Fleet in wartime is a lot better than life in the trenches, but there are many other more pleasant ways of passing a lifetime. Even on a carrier, where the crew eats well and can have an ice-cream sundae in the afternoons, and there is an occasional movie and plenty of room for handball, touch football, and games of catch on the flight deck, the days are monotonous.

Our carrier sailed out of Pearl Harbor early on July 7. We twisted down the channel, picking up speed, and headed out into the open sea and to the southwest. The cruisers and destroyers in our task force took up their positions flanking us, alert for lurking submarines. There were more than fourteen ships in our force, but after a few days the other ships became just a part of the scenery and we never noticed them except when they were hunting submarines or practice firing their anti-aircraft guns.

With Captain "Duke" Ramsey, who was bound for his first fight in the Pacific, we stood on the bridge overlooking the huge flight deck, as long as three football fields. It was bare of planes, but the plane handlers, wearing purple, red, or yellow jerseys and cloth helmets to make their assignments more easily distinguishable, were busy about the deck. Singer and I didn't know exactly where we were going, and Captain Ramsey couldn't tell us just yet. But he promised action.

"We are not going out on a joy ride," he said. He pointed to a great rainbow rising out of the mists and clouds hanging over the green mountains of Oahu. "Let's see what we find at the other end of that rainbow."

He introduced us to Admiral Frank Jack Fletcher, who was in command of operations with the carrier as his flagship, and to Colonel Melvin J. Maas, a member both of Congress and of the U.S. Marine Corps.

We were out of sight of land by lunchtime, and afterward I went down below for a siesta. I had been assigned a room in the "Officers' Country" with Lieutenant Gordon Sherwood. The room resembled a cabin on a liner, with a bed, swinging bunk, desk, drawers, clothes closet, and wash basin. I had just gone to sleep when there was a terrific burst of noise. It sounded as if hundreds of guns were firing, right over my head.

I ran up to the flight deck. All the guns along the port side of the deck—5-inchers, 20-millimeters, and 1.1-inch pom-poms were firing at a plane that was coming straight in at us low over the water. Bright lines of tracer bullets streamed out of the ship and black shells from the five-inchers burst all around the plane. It still kept coming, so close that it looked as if it was going to hit us. Then it zoomed up and circled our stern and headed for a nearby cruiser. Finally, it wobbled and crashed into the sea. The plane was a "drone," not flown by a pilot but radio-controlled from another plane high above it.

"The aviators on board kidded the life out of our gunners. 'You guys can't even shoot down a drone,' they said.

"How can anti-aircraft guns alone stop a torpedo plane attack or keep dive bombers off our heads? Even the most modern gun-aiming devices cannot follow the maneuvers of a dive-bomber."

The anti-aircraft men tried to convince the fliers that anti-aircraft was the answer to airplanes, but the pilots contended that ships can be protected from aerial attack only by fighter planes, and the fighters must intercept the enemy formations far enough away to give them time to shoot down all the attackers. If even four or five planes get through, the chances are that they will get enough hits with bombs and torpedoes and cause enough damage to force the ships to return to dry dock for repairs—if they remain afloat.

Late that afternoon our own planes came aboard from land bases in the Hawaiian Islands. The dive bombers plunged out of the sun and dropped miniature water bombs at a target "sled" towed behind our ship, fighters roared low and strafed it, and the torpedo planes made practice runs at us.

Then the planes got into the "landing circle" and one by one came in to sit down on the deck.

The fliers never tired of watching their fellow pilots land. They were kindly but severely critical of each other, and a landing had to be exceptionally good to win praise. I found that the pilots flew much more smoothly under stress. When we were in action they all came aboard quickly and perfectly. At other times they had good days and bad ones. Bad landings seemed to be contagious. If one pilot got a wave-off, four or five behind him might also make bad approaches. Sometimes a pilot would have to make two or three approaches before getting into good landing position.

Our pilots were a grand bunch, healthy and uninhibited. Most of them were officers, with only a few enlisted pilots. They did their work in a matter-of-fact, unconcerned manner. Occasionally, a pilot found that the strain of day-after-day flying over water, with only a single motor between him and death in the sea, was too much. He would report his condition to the squadron doctor and would be quietly transferred to other duties. Our pilots joked about being "expendable." They didn't mind being expended in action. It was their job, and they said, "What the hell! You have to die sometime." They did protest when lives were expended unnecessarily, as the time when one dive bomber crash-landed in the sea only twenty-eight miles from our ships and nothing was done—until it was far too late—to send out a destroyer to pick the crew up; or when they were ordered out in weather so bad that their chances of getting back aboard were almost nil; or when, due to delays, they were kept in the air so long that they ran out of gasoline and were forced to sit down in the water.

The second day out of Honolulu I flew in the rear seat of a dive bomber. I wanted to know what it was like so as to be able to write about it more authoritatively. Jack Singer flew too, on a practice mission that was a rehearsal for the operations we were to carry out in the Solomons. Jack hated airplanes. He even hated roller coasters, but he thought it his duty to go.

Dive bombing was a little rougher than roller coasting. In a dive bomber you go up above fifteen thousand feet, lift the plane's nose to slow its speed while you crack open your diving flaps, then nose over and head straight down at your target. The plane is straight up and down in relation to the ground—a go-degree angle—but because of forward motion the approach to the target is at about 70 degrees.

The Japs glide-bomb, rather than dive-bomb, coming in at a 45-degree angle. In our dive bombers you release your bomb at somewhere under 2,500 feet and then pull back your control stick and level out. Unless you are used to it, the pull-out almost snaps your neck off. Sometimes you miss with a dive-bomber, but usually you come close enough at least to damage your target. Dive bombers have been one of the most damaging weapons in the Pacific war.

Jack Singer and I flew in the dive bombers in order to accustom the officers of our carrier to the idea that correspondents habitually flew in Navy planes. Since the carrier had not previously been in action and had not had reporters aboard, the officers didn't know of any regulations to the contrary and very generously permitted us to fly whenever we wished.

One day I was flying in a dive bomber with Lieutenant Fred Schroeder on patrol over our task force. Our job was to look for submarines. I had told Freddie of my few flying lessons years before and he let me handle the controls.

Visibility was bad from the rear seat of the SBD and I had some trouble at first keeping the plane in level flight. Then I got the hang of it. Finally I got tired and called to Fred over the microphone: "You take over now, Fred."

About fifteen minutes later Fred called me, "Hey, you're letting the left wing get too far down. Hold her a little straighter."

I gasped. haven't touched the controls for fifteen minutes. I thought you had the stick."

"And I thought you had it," Fred answered, unruffled. "Just goes to show you that these SBD's are so well built that they'll fly themselves."

To kill time on the carrier, we did a lot of arguing. For several hours a day I was writing about the losing battle in Bataan and reliving intensely the anxiety and horror of those days. I asked some of the officers the questions that had been asked me so often in Bataan.

"Where the hell was our Navy while the Japs were taking the Philippines, Singapore, Malaya, and Burma?"

"Why didn't we relieve Wake?"

One of the younger officers on Admiral Fletcher's staff argued with me at the dinner table every night.

"If we had gone there we might have lost our ships," he said. "We couldn't afford to do that."

"What if we did lose some ships as long as we were hitting the enemy? The Marines on Wake were losing their lives. So were the people on Bataan. What is to be saved in this war, and what expended?"

"You don't understand naval strategy. You have no right to discuss it."

"How about this present mission, whatever it is?" I asked "Are we going to risk this carrier?"

"Not if we can help it."

It seemed to me that some of our officers thought only of NOT losing more ships, and it was in that mood that we undertook our early operations in the Solomons.

On the way to the attack, I argued that audacity would pay us dividends, as it had paid the Japs dividends and won them a mighty empire. I thought we should sail in, smack-smack-smack, and let the devil and Davy Jones pick up the pieces. If the Japs sank our ships, why, we still had airplanes to defend the West Coast and our Islands. Some of the officers resented what they probably considered my telling them how to run the Navy.

There were other points of dispute. I thought the crew of the ship, the enlisted men, should be informed as fully as possible of what was ahead of them when a fight was looming. It would be good for morale and efficiency. It seemed to me, also, that there was a clear-cut division between the reserve officers and those from Annapolis. The reservists got longer terms of sea duty, less leave, and slower promotion. Not wearing the Annapolis class ring, they were "outsiders." Moreover the Annapolis officers tended to think of the ships of the Navy as their own private property, instead of the property of the American people. They rejected all suggestions that this was a people's war and, within reason, the people should be kept fully informed of how it was progressing.

Besides discussing those points we spent several hours every night fighting the Army-Navy war. As neutrals. Jack Singer and I took the part of the Army, but only to the extent of urging that the hatchet be buried and the two services get together. Jack was a valuable ally. Only 27 and slight, he possessed a quick wit and a flashing sense of humor. This was his first experience with war—"all these people riding around in ships, flying airplanes, shooting off guns"—and he thought it was all highly nonsensical. But he was deeply concerned by the feeling between Army and Navy.

The dispute centered around flying. The Navy officers would say, "Those Army guys can't fly."

"Well. They sure are trying. They've had to rush their pilot training program along faster than yours. They flew their hearts out at Midway," we would reply.

"They can't navigate and they can't shoot."

"Well, why in hell don't you teach them?"

"They can't hit anything from twenty thousand feet."

"Do you expect them to use Flying Fortresses as dive bombers? Do you mean they are afraid of coming below twenty thousand?"

"No, not afraid. But they didn't hit half as much as they claimed at Midway. Our dive bombers did the work and they got the credit."

"We'll admit that the Army high command was over anxious to claim undeserved results at Midway. But—, you aren't going to win the war in headlines. Maybe the Fortresses can't hit moving ships from high altitudes, but there is no reason why they can't hit land targets from any height. Can't you guys realize you are all Americans—Army and Navy—and all fighting the same war?" And so on...

It may sound incredible, but when on occasion our pilots from our carrier landed at South Pacific island bases operated by the Army, they were amazed to find that "those Army fliers aren't such bad guys after all." The nearer the front the two services got, the more they forgot their differences.

The Navy men had been so thoroughly impregnated with the idea that the Army was composed only of "glory grabbers" and "headline hunters" that it took some time for them to realize that the youngsters flying the Army planes were their fellow Americans. My analysis of this attitude was definitely not over-exaggerated. The situation was so bad that many of our officers were seriously worried about it. Some were even reported to have found it necessary to suggest that unless differences between Army, Navy, and Marines were wiped out, it might be advisable to put all the forces in identical uniforms with the words "U.S. Pacific Forces" printed on the shirts.

I became convinced that the Navy's traditional feeling about the Army—and possibly vice versa—would have to be drastically modified before real cooperation would be possible. The "Franklin Field mentality," a holdover from football rivalry, would have to disappear. The feeling was much less intense among the reserve officers in both branches and practically nonexistent among the enlisted men.

I concluded that a single, unified command was absolutely essential if we were going to win the war with the smallest possible expenditure of lives; and that possibly it would eventually become necessary to put all our services into one common uniform, with the same ranks and the same pay. By the end of the year, almost all of them were in the same uniform-khaki shirts and pants in tropical climates.

The ideal solution, I believe, would be a single fighting force organized along the lines of the U.S. Marines, with the Marines' pride and devotion in their service to their country, and with their efficiency and lack of pretense, red tape, and snobbery.

About three weeks out of Honolulu on the carrier, we rendezvoused one sunshiny Sunday afternoon with a tremendous force of ships. I counted nearly ninety vessels stretched to the horizon on all sides; two carriers beside our own, cruisers, destroyers, a modern battleship, transports, tankers, and fleet auxiliaries. It was the biggest thrill of the war! Everybody on board was excited. When we saw the transports we knew that it was to be a landing operation. Most of the crew guessed that we were going to make a headlong, all-out attack on Truk, Japan's biggest base in the Mandated Islands; or at least try to capture Rabaul, the key to Australia, New Guinea, and the neighboring islands.

A few days later, we found out that our objective was the southeastern part of the Solomon Islands. Looking at the map of the Solomons and the Jap positions there, many of the younger officers decided that our plan of attack was limited by over conservatism. Hitting that limited area, we would leave Jap bases all around us.

"It seems like sending ten men on a football team around the left end, and the ball carrier around the right," one aviator said.

Anyway, there it was. And at least it was an offensive.

40

THE TRANSPORTS WITH US WERE CARRYING MARINE RAIDERS who had undergone months of special trainings They were to occupy and hold part of the north shore of Guadalcanal Island, where the Japs were completing an airfield, and the small islands of Tulagi, Gavutu, and Tanambogo, which lay twenty miles north of Guadalcanal across sheltered waters.

The Japs had other bases in the Solomons, the nearest only 125 miles from Guadalcanal, but we were not going to attack them immediately.

Our offensive had been well timed, as the airfield was almost ready for operation and the area was not yet strongly defended. But, except for photographs furnished by Army bombers operating from the New Hebrides—an outstanding example of the importance of Army-Navy co-operation—we did not have an abundance of advance information about the Japanese defenses in the Solomons or the islands themselves. The only reference work aboard our carrier had been written in 1911, but the Navy had some modern charts.

We began our run-in to the Solomons on the night of August 6. That afternoon was the crucial period, just as the afternoon before the Pearl Harbor attack had been crucial for the Japanese. At Pearl Harbor they had escaped detection, but going into Midway they were sighted and sunk. As far as we knew, no enemy plane or submarine had yet seen our force.

The weather was highly favorable for our run-in. The skies were overcast until after four in the afternoon, when we knew that the last Jap patrol plane would have to turn back to its base. Then the skies began to clear and the setting sun shone brightly on our tremendous armada—the greatest ever assembled in the Pacific—as the ships plowed steadily along through a smooth sea.

Once during the afternoon there was an alarm of an approaching plane and we went to general quarters, with the crews manning their guns.

I walked along the flight deck at sundown. The anticipation of battle seemed to have heightened perceptions. The evening star gleamed brighter than it had during the long monotonous days since we left Pearl Harbor; the air seemed cleaner and fresher; the deck crews were working faster as they gassed and armed the planes and loaded torpedoes and bombs.

I went down for a shower after a serve-yourself supper of a sandwich and a cup of chocolate. Gordon Sherwood, Syd Bottomley, Red McNair, Freddie Schroeder, and several other pilots were crowded into our room, chatting with far more animation than usual, and from Robbie Robinson's room across the passageway a phonograph was alternately playing two pieces: "I Don't Want to Set the World on Fire," and then "Las Golondrinas," the stirring Mexican song of farewell. Down the passageway, Al Wright, Bill Henry, and some of the younger pilots were listening to an impromptu performance by a swing band of Filipino mess attendants.

The pilots gathered in the wardroom for a brief, final study of the already familiar maps of the Tulagi-Guadalcanal area. Night after night they had attended "skull sessions" at which they had learned their assignments for the attack. Our planes were to knock out the Jap Air Force in the Guadalcanal-Tulagi area and cover the Marine landings.

After the pilots had turned in, Jack Singer and I sat up and pounded our typewriters a while and then walked and talked on the dark flight deck until 2 A.M. Our transports and their escorting cruisers had already left us, to begin their speedy approach to the landing areas, but we could see in faint outline the other carriers and escort vessels in our task forces.

Jack and I had wanted to fly in dive bombers on the first attack, and we had practiced shooting the SBD machine guns at towed targets. But it was decided that inasmuch as we were supposedly "non-belligerents"—and also because the dive-bomber pilots valued their necks—the regular machine gunner-radiomen should fly in the SBD's and Jack and I would go in the extra observer's seat in Grumman Avengers in the second wave of attack planes. By the time of the second attack it would be light enough to see what was going on.

No reporters had yet flown in combat in the Pacific, but Jack and I felt sure we would come through the operations. "It's just one of those things that you know," Jack said. "I'm absolutely certain I'm not going to get killed out here. I can see myself eating a big steak at Toots Shor's back in New York."

The deck crews were still working when we finally turned in. It was only a couple of hours later when general quarters sounded. Jack and I had been accustomed to sleeping through the usual morning alerts despite the noise of planes taking off above our heads, but this morning our roommates shook us out of a groggy sleep.

The planes were already warming up when I reached the flight deck, the blue flashes of their exhausts punctuating the roar of many motors. A fresh, strong breeze blew in our faces, and a quarter-moon cast a warm glow along the broad deck.

Swiftly the minutes sped by, and soon the horn on the flight bridge bellowed the take-off signal. I climbed to a 5-inch gun gallery overlooking the deck. Commander LeRoy Simpler, commander of the fighter squadron, squared his Wildcat away in the take-off position and sped down the deck between the twin rows of runway lights. As soon as he was in the air he switched on his wingtip lights. Quickly the other planes climbed aloft after him and soon the air was filled with circling lights as the fighter, dive-bomber, and torpedo planes felt their way into position behind their squadron leaders.

One dive bomber crashed into the sea alongside of us; another accidentally dropped his bombs a few hundred yards ahead of the ship and bright orange flashes flew up as it hit the water. Dawn was breaking when the last plane took off.

It was fully light when I climbed into the seat of a torpedo plane behind Lieutenant Bruce Harwood, a big, easygoing pilot who was itching for his first action of the war.

"Hope they leave us something to hit," he said over the interplane microphone. Over the radio we could hear the pilots of our advance attack group talking as they circled over Guadalcanal and Tulagi, searching out targets. The fighters strafed the field and supplies along the beach; and the SBD's were diving on anti-aircraft gun emplacements. A number of float Zeros and patrol planes had been caught on the water and destroyed by machine-gun fire. Not a single Jap plane got into the air.

Our first dive bombers were already coming back when we took off. Bruce climbed fast and circled while our machine gunners test-fired their guns and the other planes in our squadron got into position on our wingtips. Overhead the sky was clear, and in the distance we could see the mountains of Guadalcanal through a thick layer of white clouds.

Flying over the sharply sloping mountains we heard our group commander giving orders to the planes attack Tulagi and Guadalcanal. We circled down through the clouds and came out over the north shore of Guadalcanal. Beneath the overcast we saw our invasion force of transports, cruisers, and destroyers bunched off Guadalcanal and off Tulagi, dimly discernible in the distance.

Guadalcanal looked almost as familiar as Honolulu. We quickly located the Jap runway, stretching from behind the coconut groves lining the channel shore back to the foothills of the jungle-covered mountains. The brown landing strip ran from northeast to southwest, with three thousand feet already surfaced and steel hangars partly completed.

Two miles west of the runway the island jutted sharply at Lunga Point, and there and at nearby Kukoom, Japanese huts and stores were blazing from fires set by our dive bombers. East of the airfield open stretches of flat grassy plane divided the jungle areas which extended from the coconut trees to the foothills.

We circled the airfield and watched one of our cruisers firing, its guns spitting blue flame. The shells hit in trenches near the landing field, throwing up sharp clouds of black dirt.

Out near the transports hundreds of Marine landing boats circled and then headed shoreward. We saw the first one hit the beach at Tenaru plantation at exactly 9:10 A.M., and the first Marines jump out with rifles at the ready. But there was no opposition. Most of the Japanese on Guadalcanal were labor troops and they took to the hills when our planes attacked. Our Marines came ashore quickly and their tanks were soon pushing cautiously inland through a clearing leading to the Tenaru River and the airfield.

Bruce circled low over the airfield, followed by our other planes and waiting for orders from the group commander flying overhead in his dive bomber.

Finally, the order came, "Bruce, go over and get a bunch of Japs hiding in the woods down there off the runway."

I got a tremendous thrill out of watching the bright blue flash of our bombs bursting in the woods. There was no way for me to express my emotion except to write in my notebook. When we got back to the carrier that day, I found I had scribbled over and over again: "Hit 'em. Hit the bastards. Kill the lousy Japs."

Meanwhile we kept circling the field, looking for new targets, flying so low that when our bombs landed the plane jumped from the concussion. Throughout the morning, as our planes circled triumphant and powerful over their heads, the Marines kept coming ashore. I spotted two targets for Bruce: one an anti-aircraft gun firing from a corner of the woods behind the airfield; and the other a pile of stores on the beach near Kukoom with a Japanese flag flying from a tower above them.

I passed Bruce a note around the corner of his seat, and after our last bombs had been dropped he took me back over the Marine landing beach, where the Higgins boats were putting ashore more troops and supplies. We were just above their heads, but the Marines never looked up at us. I realized how reassuring it must be for them to know that all the planes in the sky were friendly.

That afternoon, however, they got their first taste of enemy planes. We had gone back to our carrier to refuel and while we were there an alarm came that Jap dive bombers had left Rabaul and were speeding in our direction. I decided to remain on the carrier to see if we were attacked.

The Japs flew straight for our transports in the channel between Tulagi and Guadalcanal. The dive bombers came in at nine thousand feet. Our patrolling fighters were flying at ten thousand and they jumped the dive bombers. Then some escorting Zeros dived on our Wildcats. Our planes shot down fourteen of the Japs, and we lost nine fighters. Only two of our ships were damaged.

Next morning I flew into Tulagi with Lieutenant Harold Larsen in his torpedo plane. The marines were meeting bitter, last-ditch resistance on Tulagi and on the nearby island of Tanambogo. It was the same kind of fighting we had faced on Bataan and later faced in New Guinea.

As on the previous day our planes were carrying bombs instead of torpedoes. Clouds hung low over Tulagi and the mists were brightened by rainbows of unusual shapes and sizes. I recalled Captain Ramsey's remark when we had left Pearl Harbor under a similar tropical rainbow. Here was the end of that rainbow; and at the end of it we bombed the Japs on Tanambogo and Tulagi to give support to the Marines.

The Marine shock troops—the "Raiders"—were more than a match for the Japs. Armed with tommy guns, grenades, bayonets, knives, and bravery, the Marines calmly and coolly fought their way across the mile-long, quarter-mile-wide island of Tulagi. Supported by shelling from our ships, the Marines wiped out the last Jap after two days of fighting and firmly consolidated their hold on Tulagi and the nearby islands.

On Guadalcanal they reached the airport and seized it within two days. One day later it was ready for our planes.

Everything went well those first two days of the landing. The Japs came back on the afternoon of August 8 with torpedo planes, but twenty-one out of twenty-four of them were blasted out of the air by our fighters and the anti-aircraft guns of ships in the channel. The Japs never located our carriers.

The afternoon of August 8, aboard the carrier, I heard that a small Jap warship force was coming down toward Guadalcanal. Army and Navy reconnaissance planes reported that it consisted of two or three cruisers and a couple of destroyers.

One of the torpedo plane pilots came to me. "Get your lifejacket and helmet," he said. "Maybe we'll be taking off soon to hit those babies. They seem to be well within range. Here we are with three-quarters of the striking power of the U.S. Fleet and those guys have the nerve to come down with a handful of ships. It hasn't been decided yet whether we'll send in surface ships or planes, but whichever it is we'll hand them a licking. Better be ready to take off with us if you want to see the fun."

But the planes never took off. When all the planes were back aboard that evening our carriers and their screening ships turned around and headed south. The following morning they were still heading south. The planes were launched and flew as far as the south shore of Guadalcanal Island, but by that time the Japanese had attacked and their ships were safely speeding back to Rabaul, undamaged, after striking one of the most devastating blows in the Pacific war.

41

IN MANY WAYS, THE BATTLE OF SAVO ISLAND on the morning of August 9 was as disastrous for the United States as the Pearl Harbor attack eight months and two days before. It delayed our whole schedule for further attacks in the Solomons, took the initiative out of our hands, and put us in a defensive position which we were still maintaining at the end of the first year of war. At Savo Island we lost permanently sunk the cruisers Astoria, Quincy, and Vincennes plus the Australian cruiser Canberra. The loss of life was never announced but both directly, in ships' crews killed, and indirectly, in Marines who lost their lives as a result of failure to land their supplies, it was very large.

From aerial reconnaissance reports on the afternoon of August 8, it had been decided that the approaching Japanese ships could not reach the vicinity of our vessels until daylight the following morning. Our cruisers which had gone in the Tulagi-Guadalcanal area to cover the Marine landings were deployed across the entrance to the harbor. The Canberra and an American cruiser steamed back and forth between Savo Island, at the mouth of the harbor area and Guadalcanal, while the Quincy, Astoria, and Vincennes patrolled the northern channel between Savo and Florida Island. Several destroyers were out in front of the cruisers, but their radio equipment failed to detect the Japanese ships.

The enemy vessels slipped in among our cruisers at 1:55 A.M., made a circle of Savo Island from south to north, and sped out again. As they had done in the Java Sea Battle, the Japanese used cruiser planes to drop flares which silhouetted our ships for their gunners.

Our crews were not at general quarters, and the first they knew of the presence of the Japanese was when torpedoes and shells crashed into their ships. The Quincy and Vincennes were blown up and sank within a few minutes; the Astoria and Canberra were so badly damaged that they went down the next morning. The crews never had a chance to fight for their lives.

The news of these losses was, quite justifiably, withheld from the American public for some time, for there was no way that the Japanese could be absolutely certain of how amazingly successful they had been. It is true that during the battle some of our ships opened up with their radios and described in uncoded English exactly what was going on, but there was always a possibility that the Jap ships had not intercepted these reports.

However, once the losses had been announced there was no justification for attempting to lighten the disaster by claiming that it was a partial victory. Three months after the battle, high officials in Washington were still asserting that the Japs had not achieved their objectives because they had not continued on into the Guadalcanal-Tulagi area and attacked our transports.

The truth was that the Japs accomplished their objectives without sinking the transports, for the transports never were fully unloaded.

The transports stayed in the harbor all day Sunday, August 9, unloading supplies. All their troops were already ashore. But that night all the transports upped anchor and scattered from the Solomons to various parts of the South Pacific. Some of them were still almost fully loaded. Only approximately one-fifth of the supplies for the Marines was put ashore, and consequently the landing forces were short of gasoline, bombs, bullets, airplane parts, food, and medicine for many weeks. During those weeks the Japs succeeded in landing reinforcements on Guadalcanal and it was not until sometime later – almost too late – that our own transports returned again and put ashore supplies and infantry reinforcements for our battle-weary Marines.

Despite the fact that air power had won every victory in the Pacific up to that time, our Marines were put ashore at Guadalcanal without any provision for air protection after the afternoon of August 8, when our carriers withdrew to the south. The Guadalcanal airfield, which was renamed Henderson Field, was put into shape for airplane operations within three days after the Marines landed, but it was not until August 20 that the first planes—eighteen fighters and eleven dive bombers ferried from Honolulu—were put ashore.

While the American public was being fed reports of our growing airplane construction and accepting those reports as accurate, the startling fact was that eight months after the start of the war our Navy in the Pacific could get only twenty-nine planes to send into Guadalcanal, and those arrived nearly two weeks after the landing!

Also, there were no torpedo boats sent into Guadalcanal until many weeks after the occupation, although those hard-hitting craft had proved their value in the Philippines and the waters around the Solomons were ideal for torpedo boat operation.

The Japs took immediate advantage of this situation. Unopposed, they landed about one thousand troops on the north shore of Guadalcanal on August 18 and advanced to within two miles of Henderson Field before they were wiped out by Marine machine guns and tanks.

Meanwhile, our vast task force was too far away to give air or sea support to the Marines, but when the small carrier with the Marine planes arrived from Honolulu we moved back up to the vicinity of Guadalcanal and waited for the Japs to make a major attempt to retake the islands we had captured. Reconnaissance planes spotted the Japanese coming southward in three strong forces on August 23. With two carriers we steamed out to meet and fight them about 150 miles north of Malaita Island in the southeastern Solomons.

At last! Our long-awaited carrier battle was just over the horizon.

42

SHORTLY AFTER LUNCH ON AUGUST 23 ALL PILOTS of the scouting, bombing and torpedo squadrons were summoned to the wardroom. I put on my yellow lifejacket, grabbed my helmet, and after unsuccessfully searching for Jack Singer (it turned out later that he was sitting in one of the gun galleries) went down to join the pilots. Lieutenant Harold (Swede) Larsen, skipper of the torpedo squadron, signaled me to come sit with his pilots at their long dining table, covered now with a green cloth.

Commander Don Felt, the group commander who controlled the airplanes in flight and flew a dive bomber himself, pointed to the blackboard; "PBY's have sighted an enemy force of eight ships, cruisers and destroyers, within striking range of our planes and headed for Guadalcanal." The pilots wrote on their charts the disposition, location, and course of the Jap ships.

Felt, who was older than most of his pilots—slim, dark, and a fighter—went on: "The PBY's are looking for the Jap carriers that must be somewhere nearby. There is no doubt that the Japs are about to make a major effort to recapture Guadalcanal and the other islands. I hope that we will be ordered to attack them today. The weather is very bad but we will try to find them.

"Both scouts and bombers will carry one-thousand-pound bombs. Torpedo planes have been loaded with one-ton torpedoes. Let's make every bomb and torpedo count!"

The waiting seemed interminable. It was nearly two hours later when the telephone on the wall rang. Felt turned away from it with a satisfied grin. "Let's go, boys! No carriers have been found. We will attack the cruisers."

At the last minute I decided to change the short-sleeved Australian army shirt I was wearing. If we should be forced down and have to drift around in the ocean, it would be wise to be protected against the sun. By the time I got back up on deck the first scout bomber was already in the air and other planes were taxiing one by one to the take-off position. I slipped and crawled past the murderously whirling props, clinging to the wings of planes, back to the rear of the deck where the big Grumman torpedo planes were warming up. Somebody gave me a hand up onto the wing of "Number 10." Swede Larsen cut his throttle a little while I climbed into the seat behind him.

Our motor revved up faster now. I fastened my parachute, plugged in my earphones, and struggled with the safety belt. Up to this time I had never been able to get a safety belt fastened properly before a take-off and Swede warned me to adjust it right.

Otherwise, if we hit the water in our take-off, I would almost certainly be knocked out and unable to get out of the plane. A hundred times, both in the torpedo planes and in my imagination, I practiced what to do if we hit the water. The directions were printed on the handle which released the glass cockpit, and every time I got in one of the planes I rehearsed the motions.

Over the radio Swede called the radio man, who was in the gun turret behind me, and the tunnel gunner down in the rear of the plane.

"All set, Johnson?"

"Yes, Mr. Larsen."

"Okay, Conrad?"

"Aye-aye, sir."

"You okay, Clark?"

"Except for this damn safety belt; okay, I got it. All set. Swede."

"Okay."

Swede maneuvered skillfully down the deck to the take-off position. A horn blew in our ears as he pushed the lever which swings the folding wings out into position. He stepped hard on the brakes and squared the plane around. Over the wing, I saw the "Fly" officer. Lieutenant Commander Wagner, with his black and white checkered flag and yellow helmet. Beside him was a member of the deck crew, standing in the position of an umpire calling a baseball runner "out" on a close play at first. His upturned thumb meant that our flaps were lowered to give us more lift in the take-off; tires okay, tail hook up and locked. Everything set.

Wagner shook his flag faster and faster, as if trying to keep pace with our speeding motor. Swede took a last quick look at his instruments and nodded at Wagner. "Fly" swung his arm down in a decisive sweep—the signal to go. Swede stepped off the brakes and we rolled down the deck, quickly gathering speed. Our tail came up within a few yards. As we passed the flight bridge I waved to Robinson and Burke, Flynn and McMahon, Doc Bowers and Bill Godwin. Before we reached the end of the long deck we were already airborne.

We went up in a fast climb, and the other planes lined upon us. Swede was in the center with the torpedo planes, and Don Felt flew a little above and behind us. Stretched out to the right were the planes of the scouting squadron and to the left those of Bombing Three. Both scouting and bombing squadrons flew the same planes—Douglas SBD dive bombers—the planes which, with the Grumman fighters and torpedo planes, became the front line of America's defense and offense in the Pacific after Pearl Harbor. On their strong, slender wings depended our country's destiny. They, and not battleships, saved us from invasion.

There were no fighters with us the afternoon of August 23. That didn't look so good to me. Not having any duties with controls, radio, or guns, I had time to think over what happened the last time that torpedo planes went out without fighters on a similar attack. That was at Midway, and only four out of forty-three torpedo planes ever got back.

The weather was thick and dirty. There was a heavy overcast at one thousand feet with rain squalls all around our ships—now looking small and toy-like as they scurried along down on the surface. There was not a sign of sunlight. Minute by minute, as we flew out on our designated course, the weather got nastier. In twenty minutes we plunged into a thick stormfront, and then broke through into the clear for a minute or two. Swede signaled to the torpedo planes flying at our wingtips to break formation. Frenchy, at the controls of the Grumman on our left, grinned back from under his steel helmet as he bore off a little ways. Bert Earnest pulled away from our right wing.

Now we were back in the storm. Most of the time our own wingtips were hidden. Rain pelted the glass hood over the cockpit and grayish white mist streamed past. Occasionally, we caught a brief glimpse of the ocean, rough and angry as the winds whipped it. The air was turbulent and I noticed that our plane seemed to recover normal flying altitude very slowly after hitting a bump.

Swede called me, "Clark, is your foot by any chance on the automatic pilot?"

I pulled back my left foot, quickly and guiltily. "Sorry, Swede," I answered over the mike, "I'm afraid it was." I should have known better, having flown in the observer's seat in the Grummans often enough to become familiar with them. Trying to get comfortable in the cockpit, which was built for men smaller than myself, I had stretched out my foot against the automatic controls.

We flew on—by instrument, for it was impossible to keep in fairly level flight except with the automatic pilot—for fifty, sixty, ninety minutes. Two or three times we sighted the planes nearest to us on right or left, but most of the time we were in a world of our own. It was a good thing that Swede's pilots were all experts. Even a slight variation from the designated compass course and altitude for each individual plane might have brought two of them together in the blinding storm.

Then, gradually, the air around us seemed to grow lighter and we broke out into a relatively clear area. The clouds were much higher there, at nearly five thousand feet, and although the sun was hidden the sea was visible for many miles. All our planes were in sight. All of them had flown straight and true through the storm. The dive bombers circled in one area, the scouts in another, and the torpedo planes joined up behind us.

That was where we expected to find the Japs. We scanned the sea intently, looking for the wakes of ships, but it was mirror-calm and unbroken.

Don Felt opened up on the radio. "We'll fly northward for fifteen minutes more." We flew along, and at the end of fifteen minutes reached the edge of the clear area and started to plunge into a new storm. Our gasoline was none too high.

"No use going farther," Felt said. "Head for Guadalcanal. Swede, you take the lead."

On the way back we flew through storm after storm. We lost sight of the bombers and scouts, but the torpedo planes stayed close behind us. It was fast getting dark.

"Keep a sharp lookout for land," Swede warned. We had to find land—soon, and we had to find clear weather over it or take the chance of running into a mountainside.

I strained my eyes looking for land. Finally I sighted it and called Swede, "There's a small, cone-shaped island off our port bow, through the mists. And there are a flock of those big white birds flying past the plane on our starboard."

"Nice going. Thanks," Swede answered.

A few minutes later there was more land, on our right. It was a long, low island with its low peaks hidden by clouds. It was one of the Solomons but there was no way of telling which island, nor which direction from Guadalcanal. The weather was gradually clearing and the visibility improving.

Off the island to our right we spotted two small shapes that looked like ships. Swede dipped his wings, to signal our other planes, and we went over to look at them.

Swede switched to the interplane radio.

"Prepare to launch torpedoes!" he ordered. "Gunners, test-fire your machine guns again."

The plane shook as our gunners fired a few rounds of tracers into the sea. When we were almost directly over the shapes we saw that they were not ships, but small islands. The surf breaking on their rocky shores had looked like the wakes of vessels, adding to the illusion.

It was twilight by the time we got back on course, and Swede switched on his wingtip lights. The other planes did likewise and we all sped along together through the gathering dusk, a unit of men and machines looking for home.

By this time there were islands on all sides of us, in the distance, but we didn't know which was which.

The pilot of the plane on our right pulled up alongside and signaled with his arm and hand. I told Swede, who called him on the radio.

"What's up?"

"I think that is Guadalcanal over to the right, Mr. Larsen."

"No," Swede said. "I think it is straight ahead. That must be Savo Island we are approaching." It was still raining, but the clouds were much higher.

We kept on course and in a few minutes flew over the channel off Savo Island, the graveyard of the Astoria, Vincennes, Quincy, and Canberra, and of a good many of their crews.

A few minutes later, I spotted the runway on Guadalcanal. Swede had never been to Guadalcanal—he flew over Tulagi in our landing operations on August 7 and 8—and he failed to see the field immediately.

I heard him calling the airfield and requesting radio directions from the Marines. I was about to pick up my mike and tell him where the field was when he spotted it himself and canceled his request. We circled down fast over Lunga Point, keeping clear of the path of our dive bombers going in to land. Rows of flares lined each side of the runway. As we made our last turn, a Jap machine gun opened up from the woods above the field. Swede saw its blue tracers at the same time.

"Put on your tin hats back there," he ordered.

Not having any tin hat, I sat and watched. The tracers were low and behind us, for the Japs had nothing to aim at except some speeding light in the darkness. Swede sat the Grumman down without any waste of time. A Marine climbed up on our wing and with a flashlight guided us off the runway.

The crews of most of our bombers were already on the ground, sloshing around happily in the mud after so many weeks at sea. They were congratulating each other on being alive, although they regretted not having found the Jap ships.

thought every one of us was a goner," said "Bullet Lou" Kern, skipper of the scouts. Sherwood, McNair, Elder, Cobb Bottomley, Isaman, Soupy Campbell, Fred Schroeder, Bob Elder, and the others agreed that it was the worst weather they had ever flown through. Marine ground crews began pushing and towing our planes back toward the runway to refuel them in preparation for a take-off at any time. The Marines told us Jap snipers were in the woods all around the runway, but gradually were being wiped out.

"These planes sure look good to us," one husky Marine told me. I understood his feeling perfectly.

Swede and I rode in a Marine jeep to the top of a hill at onside of the runway. The Japs had built a shelter there and the Marines took it over. As I might have expected. Commander Walter Shindler of Admiral Fletcher's staff was there too. We first met in New Zealand and later we found ourselves fellow passengers on the carrier. Shindler was conferring with a young Marine captain in command of the handful of planes stationed at the field—Grumman fighters, SBD's, and a few Army P-38's.

"There is one Navy amphibian PBY available," the Marine captain said. "We will send it out at midnight to drop flares over the eastern channel while a Marine dive bomber scouts over the west channel."

"If you sight any Jap ships," Shindler replied, "our pilots will take off and attack." He turned to Larsen. "Go back to the pilots, Swede, and pass the word. Tell them to sleep in their planes."

Commander Shindler took me in another jeep over to meet General Vandegrift, commander of the Marine forces on Guadalcanal. While we were riding across the cleared space surrounding the airfield, a bluish white flare shot up over the waterfront at Lunga Point, some two miles away. Then there was a salvo of shells bursting along the beach.

"That's a Jap sub," the Marine driver explained. "He hangs around there and comes up about this time every night and kills a few of our boys. Sure wish we had a destroyer or two hereabouts to take care of him!"

General Vandegrift's headquarters were in one of a group of tents in the woods bordering the airfield. The general told me the Marines had already beaten off one Japanese landing, killing nearly one thousand Japs who were put ashore on August 18 from a couple of destroyers and transports. The Japs were cut to pieces as they tried to cross the Tenaru River to reach Henderson Field.

"Now, it looks like they are coming down in force," the general went on. "This show isn't over yet by a long shot. Tomorrow—or maybe tonight—will tell part of the story."

The scene outside the general's tent, with his officers sitting. Around talking and smoking in the darkness, brought back vivid memories of Bataan. I hoped that the Guadalcanal Americans would never find themselves like those on Bataan. It was up to our Navy to keep them from getting into a situation like that. Our Navy had to bring in supplies for them and break up the Jap task forces and transports before they ever reached Guadalcanal.

Through the bamboo wireless Bob Miller of the UP learned that I was talking to the general. He came over and gave me a couple of bottles of captured Asahi beer and a bar of chocolate, the first of either I had tasted since leaving Honolulu.

In drenching rain Bob took me in a jeep back to the airfield headquarters, where I found Swede. Together we located our plane, which had been moved to the end of the runway, and then sat in one of the hangars that the Japs had been building and shared the beer. Swede decided to sleep in his pilot's cockpit, sitting up, while I crawled into the rear of "Number 10" and curled up around the bombsight and machine gun. I slept so soundly that I didn't even hear the Jap sub when it came up at 2 A.M. and fired a few more shells into the shore.

43

THE MORNING SUN—AND THE CRACKLE OF RIFLES—awakened me. A few yards behind our plane two Marines emerged from the jungle undergrowth, dragging a trio of badly frightened Japs. They had surrendered when the smell of the Marines' breakfast preparations, only a few feet from their hideout, got the best of their Shinto heroism.

Swede, Elder, and I followed the Marines as they took their captives over to a wire-enclosed area in the coconut grove. There were about three hundred Jap prisoners, all but seven of them in a big enclosure. The seven were locked up separately. They were soldiers, in contrast to the others who were civilian workers.

"It's a cinch to tell the soldiers," a tough-looking Marine guard explained. "They all claim to be civilians, but when we put a soldier in the big pen he can't resist ordering the others around. In a few minutes they are waiting on him, and bringing him food and cigarettes. Then out he comes—and into the soldiers' pen."

It was time for the morning rollcall, and the Japs came out of the enclosure in groups of five. The recent prisoners were told to strip off their rain-soaked, tattered clothing and were given new equipment from a pile of captured supplies. The Marines examined their purses and found a variety of currency. Some had two or three hundred Bank of Japan yen; others had American dollars, and military currency from China, the Philippines, and Malaya. The labor troops had not been in those places, but had probably obtained the money by swapping souvenirs with soldiers who served in the China campaign and fought later in the Philippines or Malaya.

I edged over to the soldiers' enclosure and started to talk to one of the prisoners in my halting Japanese.

"Tobacco, dozo," he requested. I gave him a cigarette.

"Where are you from?"

"Kobe."

"In what places have you fought?"

Just then the Marine guard came over. "Hey, you can't talk to those guys!" He looked like he meant it, so I broke off the interview. We walked back across the muddy runway to our planes and sat around on gasoline drums. We learned that we were to return to the carrier shortly. Marine ground crews were unloading the bombs from our SBD's. The bombs were to be left behind for the Marines, who were short of gasoline and ammunition also.

Swede's pilots were standing by their planes—all except Frenchy who kept wandering off to talk to Marines, inspect anti-aircraft gun emplacements, and look over the wreckage of a Grumman Wildcat which had crash-landed a few days before with its wounded Marine pilot. Swede called him back, "Frenchy, blast you! Stay within twenty-five feet of your plane." Frenchy stayed, but he was too full of spirits to be repressed. He gamboled about on the grass in imitation of a ballet dancer doing the "Spring Song." The morning air was fresh and cool, the storm had blown far away to the north, and sunlight bathed the rugged green peaks of Guadalcanal.

Don Felt taxied his plane to the end of the runway and took off. The dive bombers followed and then we got into the air, our wheels throwing up rocks from the rough runway and peppering our wings. One dive bomber was still on the ground. Elder was having trouble with his motor, which had become clogged with carbon yesterday when he flew for some time at full throttle. After we had reached the edge of Guadalcanal looked back and saw Elder take off. But his plane seemed to be faltering and after a few minutes he turned back and made an emergency landing. He sat down upwind, as several of our planes had done the night before.

Marine fighter pilots escorted us a short distance as we climbed up through scattered clouds and headed over Malaita Island, home of cannibals and of a few hardy missionaries. Far-out over the sea we spotted our task forces, speeding into the wind and in the direction of the Japs. Long swells were running but the air was clear and unclouded, with an after-the-storm freshness.

On board our carrier there was an atmosphere of quiet excitement. It was like the last few seconds before the gong rings to start a heavyweight championship fight. This was the day, and no mistake.

I went to the fighter pilot's ready room off the flight deck to find out what was going on. Little Frank Green, a good-looking, quiet boy who came from a farm just outside of St. Louis, gave me the news.

"Two Jap Kawanishi four-engined seaplanes were shot down within sight of the ship this morning," he said. "That means they radioed our positions to their own bases and ships."

"Did you get one of them, Frankie?" I asked. Frank had been having bad luck. He was a natural flier, a great pilot, but he hadn't gotten any Japs yet. Twice his machine guns had jammed just as he was going into action.

"No, doggone it," said Frank. "I was patrolling in another sector."

"Don't let it worry you, Frank," said Carleton Starkes, "there'll be plenty of chances." Starkes, who came from Memphis and whose blond hair was cropped close to his head, already had three Japs to his credit in the fighting over Guadalcanal on the afternoons of August 7 and 8. Starkes was my partner in the nightly bridge games and Jack Singer and I had nicknamed him "Acey." Singer and I were carrying on a friendly rivalry. Before the Solomons landings we had each chosen "teams" of fighter pilots, picking out those we thought most likely to shoot down the most Japs. Actually, several dark-horse pilots had won the honors on the 7th and 8th, and Jack and I had immediately claimed that they had been on our team all along. Carleton Starkes was one of the dark horses.

I went down to the wardroom and found Commander Felt. "Our scouts are out searching for the Jap carriers," he said. "When they find them we'll take off and attack. Today you'll get the action you've been clamoring for."

While we were having brunch—we had been eating mostly corned beef and rice for several weeks—another Jap patrol bomber penetrated to within three miles of our force before our fighters jumped it and literally tore its wings off with their .50-caliber machine guns. Our pilots loved to spot those Kawanishis—great lumbering whaleboats with wings on them and without as many defensive guns as our own PBY's. It was usually only about fifteen seconds from the time the pilots reported over the radio, "There he is!" and their triumphant shout, "There he goes into the drink! A flamer!" I went up to see who had brought this one down. Frank Green was sitting in the pilot's ready room, looking disconsolate.

"Doggone," he said, "I was just getting lined up to make a run on that guy when Dick Gray and Dave Richardson beat me to it."

I was in the shower, washing off some of the Guadalcanal mud, when general quarters sounded. Men ran to their battle stations, closing down hatches and locking the big iron doors in the interior of the ship. The loudspeaker blared exciting news:

"Our scout planes have located enemy carrier force about two hundred miles northwest of us. Our planes will take off to attack the enemy. Be prepared for an attack on our ships."

Before I could get dressed and up on deck most of our planes were already in the air. I saw the first torpedo plane speed away. Lieutenant Bruce Harwood was at the controls and Jack Singer was in the observer's seat behind him. Jack and I had been trying to scoop each other by witnessing a torpedo-plane attack. We had agreed that the story would be worth the slim chance of getting back alive. Yesterday I had gone out and we had failed to find the Japs. Today Jack was going and it was too late for me to get into a plane. Then I saw Swede Larsen standing on deck, watching the take-offs.

"What's up, Swede? Aren't you going?"

"No, they are holding us in reserve—the planes that went into Guadalcanal yesterday. If we get orders to go later I'll let you know."

"Okay. I'll either be here in the fighter pilots' room or upon the bridge. Please don't forget to call me."

Our torpedo planes and dive bombers rendezvoused in the air and quickly disappeared from sight. We followed them over the radio. Scouts had sighted a huge Jap force, three carriers with escort vessels and, over a few miles, a fourth carrier; and farther away two separate groups, one of transports and the other of heavy warships. The nearest Jap vessels were about 175 miles from our ships and about the same distance from Guadalcanal. Jap planes from Rabaul, twin-engined bombers, were attacking Guadalcanal where Marine pilots took their Grummans off Henderson Field and shot down twenty-four enemy ships in a few minutes of flaming action.

In the fighter pilots' ready room we listened to Don Felt giving orders to our dive bombers and torpedo planes. They had sighted one Jap carrier. Gordon Sherwood was the first to see the tell-tale white wakes of the enemy ships. He reported it in matter-of-fact tones, "There's a carrier over there. Compass bearing three-forty-five degrees. Also a couple of cruisers and destroyers."

Commander Felt directed: "Lou, you hit the carrier. Gordon, take that cruiser over there with your section. Bruce, send the first section of your torpedo planes against the carrier and the others at that cruiser. Let's go."

The radio was silent for a few minutes. Then Felt spoke:

"Nice going. Got a hit on the carrier."

"Bruce! One torpedo hit the cruiser."

"That carrier is slowing down now and burning."

"Holy smokes! A destroyer alongside the carrier has disappeared. A torpedo must have hit it."

Only half our attention was on the radio. We were waiting momentarily for the Japs to find us. There was a flurry of movement on deck. Planes were being pushed forward and two dive bombers were landing. It was Bob Elder, whom we had left behind at Guadalcanal, and his wingman, Phil Cobb. Marines had repaired Elder's engine. Then the planes were quickly pushed back again, with the fighters in the forward positions, ready to go.

A few minutes later the bullhorn on the flight bridge above us bellowed and the loudspeaker cracked, "Fighter pilots, man your planes!" We knew what that meant. The Jap attack group was on its way to hit us. The fighter pilots sprinted to their planes, and swiftly roared down the deck and into the air, one after another. They climbed sharply, grabbing for altitude, and headed out toward the approaching enemy.

Swede Larsen ran by me, followed by Frenchy and his other pilots. Only Swede had his chart with him. The others didn't have even helmets, goggles, or gloves. I grabbed my life jacket and tin helmet and started to run after Swede.

"No use coming," he gasped over his shoulder. "We are just going up to circle the ship." Swede's planes took off, followed by Elder and Cobb. A few minutes after they got in the air the radio ordered them out to search for the other Jap carriers. Once more I had missed my chance to participate in a torpedo attack. But the Japs were on their way and there might be just as good a story on board. I ran up the ladder to the topmost bridge and stood next to Commander Shindler, who had come back with us from Guadalcanal and was scanning the sky with his binoculars. He, Admiral Fletcher, and the other officers wore blue "anti-flash" suits as a protection against bomb blasts.

Our ships picked up speed. Within a few minutes our carrier was bulling through the water at close to thirty knots as the engineers poured the oil into her. Our escort vessels were keeping pace.

In the long heavy swells the destroyers were bouncing almost out of the water, lifting their bows so high that you could see the horizon under them and then plunging down so far that white spray splashed over their topmasts.

Another carrier was a few miles over, racing like ourselves—one of our best defenses was speed—to try to dodge at least some of the Jap bombs. While we were waiting for the planes to come, I had a momentary flash of the old, familiar feeling of fear. Then it disappeared. After all, if the planes hit us, the chances were ten to one against being killed. I had wanted to see action at sea, and here it was.

It came quickly and was over with incredible speed. There was an air of unreality about it. It seemed like something seen on a movie screen, with the action moving at twice normal speed.

There was a puff of smoke in the air beyond our other carrier and then a long plume of smoke trailing into the sea, where it suddenly snuffed out. Then another, and another Jap plane plunged in flames, until the air was full of those long trailers of smoke. Our fighters were doing their work.

The decks of the carrier and her escorting vessels seemed to burst into flame as the anti-aircraft guns opened up. The sky blossomed with the black and yellow bursts of their exploding shells. Planes flashed through the smoke puffs, the sunlight glinting on their wings.

Out of nearly fifty dive bombers in the attacking force, only ten reached the point where they could push over to dive on the carrier.

The first Jap dive bomber nosed over and down. Anti-air-craft bursts surrounded it, and it disintegrated with a brilliant flash. Another plunged flaming into the sea alongside the deck, its bomb exploding as it hit the water.

Then a bomb burst squarely on the carrier's flight deck. A long streamer of smoke trailed out to the rear of the still speeding ship. Another bomb hit, plunged down into the hangar deck, and exploded. Near misses splashed the crews as they ran to drag out fire hoses and fight the flames.

The lookout standing beside me on the bridge tensed suddenly. He called into his telephone, "Dive bombers overhead coming down out of sun." Then a second later, "Torpedo planes coming in from port quarter." But those planes were our own fighters coming aboard. The first crashed into the barrier, and its pilot, red-haired Lieutenant Chick Harmer, limped out with three bullet holes in his legs. Deck crews pushed his wrecked plane into the sea.

The other fighters hurried aboard in relays, refueled, and got back into the air. But there was no need for haste—the battle was over, for us.

We counted noses in the fighter pilots' room. Lieutenant Marion Dufilho was missing, and Ensign Bass. One other plane had not turned up.

I went over to Frank Green. "How many did you get, Frankie?" Frank looked sick. "As usual, nothing happened. I was assigned to combat patrol over our ship and the Japs never got this far."

Starkes had shot down three planes, Jensen three. Chief Machinist's Mate Runyon had shot down four Jap planes three dive bombers and one Zero.

Our own attack group and planes from the other carrier, came in to land. Our deck was quickly crowded with planes and others were still circling in the air. But Bill Godwin, our signal officer, was bringing the planes in so quickly and skill-fully that only a few ran out of gas and sat down in the water. Destroyers picked up the crews, hurrying to get them aboard before night fell.

Not a single one of the planes that had gone out with Don Felt was missing. Jack Singer climbed shakily out of Bruce Harwood's torpedo plane. He had scooped me and had one of the best stories of the war. I congratulated him, both for his story and on being alive. It was almost Jack's last story. A short time later he was killed when the Wasp was torpedoed and sunk.

Swede Larsen was still missing, but about three hours after dark he came aboard. Frenchy, who had been doing a gay "Spring Dance" on the Guadalcanal airfield that morning, failed to come back with him. We gave him up for dead, but a week later he was picked up from a small island where he had crash-landed after dark. Elder was missing too. He was one of my favorite pilots, a tall, handsome youngster whose father owned a hardware store in Milwaukie, Oregon.

I cornered Swede. "What did you hit?"

"We looked for the three Jap carriers but couldn't find them. About fifteen minutes before sunset we sighted a Jap battleship of the Mutsu class with an escort of six heavy cruisers, six light cruisers, and four or more destroyers. Elder saw them at the same time. He and Cobb dived on the battleship, and got at least one hit. We attacked the cruiser and put one fish [torpedo] in her. Elder saw it hit. I'm sorry he is missing."

Just then Elder walked into the wardroom with Cobb. "I got lost but the Lord was with me," Elder said. "We should have run out of gas some time ago. We made it with about the last drop in our tanks."

Doctor Lewis passed out the small bottles of brandy that are given to the aviators after they have been in combat. I rated one because of my flight the day before. There was just enough in the bottles to make the pilots relax. Bit by bit their excited chatter died down, and one by one they went off to "crawl in the sack" and sleep until time for their patrols next morning.

Next day the officers tallied results. Ninety-six planes had been shot down by our Navy pilots, the Marines over Guadalcanal, and our anti-aircraft fire. Three Navy and three Marine fighter pilots were missing; plus Frenchy and one other torpedo plane pilot from our carrier. Naval Aviation Pilot Corl—one of the three torpedo-plane pilots who survived the Midway Battle—had been shot down by Zeros. He had flown off the other carrier.

One small Jap carrier was dead in the water and burning. In addition to the carrier, which was either the Ryujo or Hosho, one Jap destroyer, a cruiser, and a transport had been sunk, and many other ships damaged.

Our attack planes had failed to establish contact with the three big Jap carriers, but their torpedo planes and dive-bombers had also failed to find us, with the exception of the small group that hit our other carrier. Our pilots reported that the Jap pilots were definitely inferior to those they had fought at Midway and in the Coral Sea.

The Japs had lost so many planes that they were forced to turn back to Truk to replenish their carrier air groups. Their first major attempt to retake the Solomons had been beaten back—but not for long. They struck back soon with characteristic vigor and viciousness, in a prolonged series of attacks that threatened to make Guadalcanal another Wake or Bataan.

During those weeks our Navy was consistently on the defensive in the Solomons. There were no ships out in front of our Marines to break up the Jap attacks. Planes fought valiantly but they were too few to prevent the Japs landing reinforcements. Part of the time they were pinned to the ground by the lack of gasoline and bombs—still an aftermath of the Savo Island Battle. Night after night Jap warships steamed with impunity into the channel off Guadalcanal and poured shells into the airfield and into our beach positions. Jap transports landed more and more troops, until the Marines were finally outnumbered. The Japs pushed so close to Henderson Field that their artillery pitched shells onto the runway and our pilots had to take off and land between shell bursts. A campaign that had started out to be a cheap, quick victory was beginning to look as if it would become a disastrous defeat.

Then, just in time, our admirals got busy. Transports successfully ran into the Solomons and landed some Army troops and, more important, gasoline for our planes. Finally, we recovered from the Savo Island disaster and began to take the initiative. I believe the change dated from the appointment of Admiral William F. Halsey as commander in chief of our South Pacific forces. The old idea of "we can't go there because the Japs are there," was replaced by Halsey's watchword, "Attack: Repeat: Attack."

Halsey was the kind of leader our sailors could understand and love. He made no secret of the fact that he—like every other courageous man—knew what it was to be afraid. He was not ashamed to show his fear when bombs crashed down on his carrier. He knew that war was brutal and tough, but that it had to be fought and that it would be won only by attack, not defense. The sailors knew that Halsey meant what he said. When he told the crew on his battered carrier, "Boys, I am so proud of you I could cry," they saw real tears trickling down his cheeks. Halsey was the man for the job.

He was all the United States Navy needed. The Navy had always had the guns and the gunners and the guts, it had the ships and it could shoot. It needed the confidence that comes with knowledge that you are attacking and not retreating; fighting aggressively instead of defensively.

Only once since Savo Island had the Navy slugged it out with the Japs, on the night of October 11-12 when the Boise fought gallantly and successfully against great odds. Then a month later, on the night of November 13, Rear Admiral Daniel J. Callaghan led a force of cruisers between two groups of Japanese surface ships and fought it out to a finish against a Jap battleship and other heavy vessels at point-blank range. Callaghan was killed and his flagship, the cruiser San Francisco, damaged and other of our ships sunk, but we won the fight and the Japs turned back.

Between those two surface battles there had been another carrier fight late in October. One of our carriers, the Hornet, was bombed and sunk, but several Jap carriers were badly damaged and possibly sunk; and that time, too, the Japs were forced to retreat.

Meanwhile, between August and early October, Guadalcanal had been held despite the lack of surface support by our naval vessels. It was held by Navy and Marine dive bombers and fighters—when they had the gasoline to fly—and it was held by exhausted, often hungry Marines, who killed Japs, and more Japs, and still more Japs until they were sick of killing. Planes, now amply supplied with gasoline, bombs and torpedoes, had provided the killing blow that smashed the big Jap attacks on November 11-15. Planes had sunk eight of twelve transports and had sent to the bottom the cruisers and battleships damaged by our ships in the night action on the 13th. Planes, and Marines, had held Guadalcanal.

That part of the action in the Solomons I followed through the newspapers back home. After our air battle on August 24, our carrier had gone back to the southeast of the Solomons to await another Jap offensive. There was a letdown aboard, and we were just counting the days until we would have to put into port to reprovision, Charles McMurtry and Jack Rice had come out from Pearl Harbor on other ships, so the AP was covered and I was free to leave. We figured that within two weeks at the most we would head for some port to pick up food, gasoline, plane parts, and ammunition. Meanwhile we were riding around waiting for something to happen. Something did shortly.

44

WHEN REPORTERS LEAVE PEARL HARBOR ON FLEET assignments they tell their friends they are "going fishing." The crew of our ship, when we were milling around apparently aimlessly, would jokingly remark that we were headed for "Torpedo Junction to keep a date with a submarine." On August 31, we arrived at Torpedo Junction and caught our fish.

Two Jap submarines crept in close to our screening force and fired four torpedoes at us. We knew subs were in the vicinity. They had been spotted early in the morning by detector devices; and again a half hour later. The ship had been speeded up briefly when planes were launched for the morning search. Then torpedo wakes were sighted. A young junior grade lieutenant was on the bridge and he did everything right: sounded general quarters, swung the ship, and called the captain.

I was asleep when the torpedo hit us, at 7:48 A.M. There was no mistaking what it was. The ship shook like a house in a severe earthquake. The chair in our room slammed over onto the floor; bottles and glasses fell out of the cabinet over the wash basin. Before they hit the deck I was out of bed and dressing. In a couple of minutes I had reached the flight deck.

The carrier was beginning to lose speed and within a few minutes the giant ship was dead in the water under a leaden, but clearing, sky. Our escort cruisers stopped with us. Every eye in the task force was watching for torpedo wakes and the cruisers were ready to intercept the torpedoes with their own hulls, if necessary, to keep them from hitting the carrier.

Destroyers raced back and forth on our starboard side a mile away, hunting the subs that had hit us. A destroyer would halt, like a race horse suddenly reined in, then seem to gather itself together and sprint for a few hundred yards like a spurred horse. Depth charges from the destroyers shook our ship, and it was beginning to list to starboard.

Jack Singer came walking along the sloping flight deck.

"It looks like we'll get in sooner than we expected," he said.

Both he and I were carrying watertight rubber packages in which, weeks before, we had enclosed copies of our stories and other papers in the event of our having to swim.

"Let's pray their bombers don't find us now," I said. And Jack looked at the sky and murmured, "Amen!"

Miraculously, no one was dead. The two fire rooms where the torpedo had exploded were empty at the time. Oil was splattered over the flight deck and the planes on the starboard side, and the crews were busy cleaning it. One man slipped and broke his leg. He was the only casualty.

A half hour before, the carrier had been one of the greatest fighting ships in the world, its massed planes on deck a symbol of tensed strength and terrible power. Now it was wounded and crippled; its strength gone; its planes a helpless target.

Men walked aimlessly about the flight deck, conversing quietly in small groups. Every few minutes somebody looked nervously at his watch and began to estimate how soon the big Jap bombers would arrive from Rabaul. Singer and I couldn't resist kidding our fliers who up to then had insisted that big bombers couldn't hit anything from high altitudes. "Oh," they explained, "this is different. We are lying here helpless and they might get a lucky hit on a target this big."

Down in the damaged control room, where huge electric cables had been short-circuited by the shock of the torpedo, trained men were working swiftly. From time to time, Commander Henry Grady, the veteran and hardy chief engineer who had been within a few months of retirement when the war started, came up from below and hurried up to the bridge to report to Admiral Fletcher. He would slip us a few words as he passed, "Doesn't look so good." And, on a subsequent trip, "Maybe we can get her going after all!"

Two hours after we had been hit, the loudspeaker boomed: "Great number of unidentified planes approaching." Men scurried for their steel helmets and ran to their battle stations. The destroyers were still racing around, dropping depth charges. A big oil slick was pouring out of the wound in our side.

A few minutes later, the loudspeaker announced, "Those planes are army B-17's." The entire ship seemed to gasp with relief.

Finally, late in the morning, Chief Grady got the engines turning over again. The ship limped ahead at three knots, so slowly that we could scarcely trace our movement through the water. The engineers trimmed the ship, and the flight deck leveled out. Then the speed gradually increased, up to eight knots, and the ship headed into the wind.

Our pilots had been told to prepare to take off and land at a shore base not far away. They were allowed one small suitcase each, and most of them put in their girls' pictures and a book or two. Their other belongings remained aboard. The ship was temporarily out of the war but they and their planes still could fight. They were needed desperately at Guadalcanal.

Now the loudspeakers ordered, "Pilots, man your planes." The planes were pushed as far to the rear of the deck as possible, to give them every possible inch of room for taking off in compensation for the ship's lack of speed. One by one they roared down the deck and got into the air; first the fighters, then dive bombers, and finally the big TBF's. Later, a few of the fighters came back to protect us on our trip to port. The other planes kept going and eventually reached Henderson Field, where for many weeks they fought under incredible conditions.

When the planes left us, their mechanical crews transferred to a destroyer which came alongside our limping ship and took aboard load after load of tools, ammunition, personal belongings, airplane propellers, and parts. Jack Singer went aboard the destroyer and the last time I saw him he was hanging limply over the bridge rail of the pitching ship, waving wanly to his friends lining the flight deck of the carrier.

All day long our destroyers circled and raced around us, keeping enemy subs from sneaking in close enough to deal the carrier a deathblow. By nightfall Chief Grady was able to push on a few more knots and next morning we were out of range of the Jap land-based bombers. There were still subs in our vicinity, apparently trailing the huge oil slick we were leaving behind us, but the destroyers maintained their protective guard and no subs got through,

A week or so later we put in to a South Sea island harbor to make temporary repairs. I flew ashore in a TBF and landed at an airfield manned by U.S. Army pilots. They told me a Pan American Airways plane was coming through next morning on a survey trip of island harbors, and in the morning I was sitting on the dock when the twin-engine Martin patrol bomber landed and the crew and passengers came ashore. The first man out of the small boat was Martin Agronsky, the NBC correspondent whom I had last seen in Australia when we discovered that we had both studied journalism at Rutgers.

"How's chances for a lift?" I asked Martin.

He pointed out a slim, young-looking man, in Navy khaki with his Pan-American cap tilted over one eye. "That's Captain Joe Chase. Better ask him."

"Any room for a hitchhiker?" I asked the captain.

"Not a chance," Joe said. "We are heavily overloaded now. The baggage is in the bomb bays. If one engine quits we'll dump the baggage. If we still lose altitude we'll throw the newspapermen overboard first and then the Navy officers. Haven't got any room for you." Then, without changing expression, he added, "Get your baggage and be here at one o'clock this afternoon."

I had taken Joe so seriously that I was going to leave my typewriter behind as a present to an American sailor on guard duty at the dock. But Joe told me to bring it along. We flew four days, stopping at islands so remote that most of them don't appear on standard maps of the Pacific. At each of them were American Army, Navy, or Marine fliers with the usual handful of planes. The trip was uneventful except for the time when one of the engines suddenly coughed and quit. Agronsky and I looked at each other silently. Then the engines picked up again.

Joe made me pay for my trip by initiating me into the Short Snorters and by beating me consistently at the dice game of Bidou, which we both had learned in South America and which we played in the officers' clubs at our overnight island stops.

Finally we landed at Pearl Harbor. Salvage work on the damaged battleships had progressed greatly in the ten weeks since I had left on the carrier.

Several of the battleships were ready for sea duty again. The shops on shore were working night and day, and installations were being extended.

This time there was no telegram to keep me from going home—only a message telling me that I was too late to see my mother. She had died the day of our sea battle north of the Solomons. I decided to go back anyway, to see what the United States looked like after six years, to learn to speak English again, and to find out if the people realized what we were up against in the Pacific. My wife was to join me in New York. The trip up to the coast on a cruiser was peaceful and the skyline of San Francisco was the most beautiful sight I had seen in my life—up to then.

There are three other scenes which I hope to live long enough to witness.

I want to be there when General Douglas MacArthur raises the American flag over Corregidor again; and then hauls it down and with his own hand raises the flag of the Republic of the Philippines, the symbol of a nation which won its right to life by learning how to suffer and how to die.

I want to be with Generalissimo Chiang Kai-shek when he marches once again into Nanking after the last Jap has been killed or driven from China.

And I want to see Jonathan Wainwright and Joe Smith and Arthur Wermuth and some Filipino Scouts and Vandergrift his Marines ride down the main street of Tokyo; and with Admiral Halsey and his sailors drive in tanks and armored cars across the moat and enter the Imperial Palace, while American airplanes fly overhead in clouds so thick that they hide the rising sun.

Made in United States
North Haven, CT
17 June 2024

53743706R00159